Digital Design Exercises for Architecture Students

Digital Design Exercises for Architecture Students teaches you the basics of digital design and fabrication tools with creative design exercises, featuring over 200 illustrations, which emphasize process and evaluation as key to designing in digital mediums. The book is software neutral, letting you choose the software with which to edit raster and vector graphics and to model digital objects. The clear, jargon-free introductions to key concepts and terms help you experiment and build your digital media skills. During the fabrication exercises you will learn strategies for laser cutting, CNC (computer-numerically controlled) milling, and 3D printing to help you focus on the processes of design thinking. Reading lists and essays from practitioners, instructors, and theorists ground the exercises in both broader and deeper contexts and encourage you to continue your investigative journey.

Jason S. Johnson is an associate professor of architecture and co-director of the Laboratory for Integrative Design at the University of Calgary in Alberta, Canada. He is an award-winning designer and the founder of Minus Architecture Studio.

Joshua Vermillion is an assistant professor and SimLab coordinator at the University of Nevada, Las Vegas, USA.

Digital Design Exercises for Architecture Students

Edited by Jason S. Johnson and Joshua Vermillion

Routledge
Taylor & Francis Group

NEW YORK AND LONDON

First published 2016
by Routledge
711 Third Avenue, New York, NY 10017

and by Routledge
2 Park Square, Milton Park, Abingdon, Oxon OX14 4RN

Routledge is an imprint of the Taylor & Francis Group, an informa business

Library of Congress Cataloguing in Publication Data
Names: Johnson, Jason S., editor. | Vermillion, Joshua, editor.
Title: Digital design exercises for architecture students / Jason S. Johnson and Joshua Vermillion, editors.
Description: New York, NY : Routledge, 2016. | Includes bibliographical references and index.
Identifiers: LCCN 2015034997| ISBN 9781138823129 (hardback : alk. paper) | ISBN 9781138823143 (pbk. : alk. paper) | ISBN 9781315742229 (ebook)
Subjects: LCSH: Architectural design--Data processing. | Architectural design--Problems, exercises, etc.
Classification: LCC NA2728 .D53 2016 | DDC 729.0285--dc23
LC record available at http://lccn.loc.gov/2015034997

ISBN: 978-1-138-82312-9 (hbk)
ISBN: 978-1-138-82314-3 (pbk)
ISBN: 978-1-315-74222-9 (ebk)

Acquisition Editor: Wendy Fuller
Editorial Assistant: Grace Harrison
Production Editor: Alanna Donaldson

Typeset in Bembo by
Servis Filmsetting Ltd, Stockport, Cheshire

Contents

Contents

Foreword

Digital natives and primitives – the emergence of technological culture

Tom Verebes

> Modern Industry had therefore itself to take in hand the machine, its characteristic instrument of production, and to construct machines by machines.[1]

> Karl Marx, *Capital*, vol. I, p.384

Karl Marx's machines, which make machines, were recapitulated over a century later in 1969, with Nicholas Negroponte's forecast of automated "machines to assist the design process."[2] Negroponte highlighted the evolutionary capacities and processes with which unique and optimal outcomes can be generated. In today's emerging technological culture, the inherent intelligence and autopoetic production of machinic-making raises questions of precisely what is the remit of the designer, the limits of his/her design thinking, and, lastly, the possible scope of material production. Also, and perhaps not so coincidentally, in 1969 the cybernetician and early adopter of complexity theory Gordon Pask noted how the role of the designer and his/her relation to the subject was turning towards "the interaction between the designer and the system he designs, rather than the interaction between the system and the people who inhabit it."[3] Pask, polemically, no longer conceived the designer as the controller, or "authoritarian apparatus" of the design outcome, but rather, the designer is now the designer of the apparatus that will design the product.[4] He asks where the target for the designer is located and the nature of its outcome. The role of design as a form of control then becomes an "odd mixture of catalyst, crutch, memory and arbiter."[5] From the early anthropology of digital experimentation, pursued sometimes blindly but most often bravely by a generation of *digital natives*, we are now witnessing the consolidation of the primitive discoveries of early adopters, to the civilization of a maturing technological culture.

Publishing a textbook in 2015 on how one learns to design computationally raises a paradox of the topic relating to rapidly evolving technologies driven by opportunistic communities of users. Despite the demonstrable cutting-edge design methods, tools, and techniques featured in this book, the longevity of instrumentality of the book's content should be called into question. The syllabi of architectural courses teaching computational design have so often been updated that there seems to be few, if any, constants in a computational curriculum over the last two decades. This raises the question of how quickly a book focusing on digital design pedagogy will become a history book soon after its publication. Quickly shifting paradigms and the corresponding rapidity of technological innovations render a textbook simultaneously potentially *just so last year*, and so quickly, possibly, another important book on the history, or the later archeology of digital practices. This book may not be about teaching computational design. Perhaps this book is more about the establishment of the culture surrounding these technologies than it is an explicit handbook of how to learn and apply the tools themselves.

Educating natives: learning not teaching

The digital natives represented in this book are evidence of the emergence of an autodidact generation in which teaching has become less effective than learning. Peer-to-peer learning from others, through haptic opportunity, accident, and serendipity, has all but rendered obsolete the traditional authoritative role of the teacher to the student absorbing knowledge passively. For years I have been asserting, within the context of designing and amending university curricula, how architecture schools will soon no longer need to "teach" computation. This is not to say that computational design and production will be out of fashion, although there remains no shortage of people in architecture who would wish this to be the case. This implies how digital natives no longer require the basics to be taught. If natives do not know the basics already, they will quickly teach themselves. As a personal anecdote, my son was born definitively in the digital age, in 1999. At the age of 11, in 2010, he phoned me at work to tell me he had downloaded a free software application called Sketch-Up and had modeled our house and had also made an animation fly-through. The authors and designers included in this book, not its younger readers, should tremble at the facility, fluency, and latent power of the next generation, the true *digital natives*.

Collaborative models and the opening of sources

In the 1980s, when greed, individuality, and the early days of *starchitecture* flourished, information was under-valued and rarified, and the conduits of networks were limited to one-to-one. In a world of digital communication, where we can all quickly access vast flows of information, sent from one to the many, a context of open source sharing is firmly a more powerful resource than any university library can provide the digital learner.

Fundamental changes in theories of corporate and managerial organization in the 1990s were brought about by digitization – or the inception of information and communication technologies into the office (any kind of office), which had effects upon the patterns and tendencies of work. Noteworthy to this Foreword is the shared background of several of the contributors and editors of having completed their Masters' degree at the Architectural Association (AA) in London. In the series of multiple-year research agendas of the pre-eminent Design Research Lab (DRL) at the AA, at which I had taught and later co-directed the program, the initial research agenda we had pursued was titled *Corporate Fields*. It was by no accident that this first research agenda focused on the architectural and organizational repercussions of computers, or information and communication technologies, in the workplace. We queried the architectural repercussions of hot-desking, collaboration, informality, and responsiveness. Curiously, and counter to some predictions, by the end of the 1990s, few of us ended up working in our underwear in huts in remote forests, communicating only through screen interfaces and telephones. Despite the benefits of having a good Wi-Fi connection to be able to "work" remotely with anyone, and the crisis of the converse, we need, more than ever, each other, to share our knowledge and expertise, in physically proximate platforms, to learn from each other.

Lewis Mumford, in *The Myth of the Machine* (1944), heralds a "shift from an empirical, tradition-bound technics to an experimental mode" which had opened new technological realms, such as "nuclear energy, supersonic transportation, cybernetic intelligence, and instantaneous distant communication."[6] According to Steven Johnson, the city, both practically and metaphorically, is an environment which "squelches new ideas … effortlessly" and persists as an environment which is "powerfully suited for the creation, diffusion and adoption of good ideas."[7] He claims innovations are most often made when relying upon platforms of collaboration, and the recognition of serendipity, error, or misappropriation, as credible bases on which most innovations occur.[8] This book consolidates an immense intensity of flow of vast quantities of information, in what Jason Johnson, co-editor of this book, calls "ubiquitous simultaneity." This book, in his terms, challenges "certainty, authorship, authority, and autonomy." This generation of *digital natives* is one of specialists not generalists.

The emergence of network modes of architectural practice wikis and online open source vehicles are just some of the indications of a cultural shift in the digital age towards cooperation, collective knowledge databases, collective action, civic hacking, and complex interdependency. From the formation of encyclopedia and eventually dictionaries, and in our time, the advent of wikis and shared platforms for emerging technological culture, seemingly everyone can have access to knowledge. Data Mapping, modeling complexity, and experience of the immersive qualities of information today are highlighted by Simon Kim in his essay which sketches a world which makes increasingly ambiguous the distinctions between the body, perception, and interaction with digital environments.

Disruptive innovations are often incremental, cumulative, and are not ultimately applied for their intended uses, and thus accidental. Marc Fornes aptly theorizes how "failure" is increasingly a fundamental part of today's technological culture of innovation and experimentation. Fornes represents a generation of designers who are seemingly no longer dogged by the increasingly litigious culture of professional architecture, but rather fascinated, committed to, and even obsessed by the "blue sky" researching of novel design arenas through explorations of technology. Digital natives embrace accidents. They make discoveries through serendipity. Digital natives find liberating experiences in haptic play. Architecture, in an age of complexity, migrates across various disciplines: the natural sciences, computation, mathematics, and other fields of knowledge. The theoretical background and community of this vastly expanding cultural practice of technology is fundamentally interdisciplinary. Yochai Benkler, in *The Wealth of Networks* (2006), claims our increasingly information-dependent world promises greater individual freedom and democratic participation, and a culture which is more critical and reflexive, all with the aim of human betterment.[9]

Profound changes in how we work are turning users into producers, and through the multiplication of the advancement of knowledge, hence also turning producers to innovators. Amidst the Post-Fordism and the many post-modernities of which digital culture has been just one of the many emergent new cultural avenues, architecture is still seeking a clear means of escape away from Modernism. In this book, Benjamin Bratton's interview with Joshua Taron lends timely insights to the changes in the political and social context of today's information-saturated world. Andrew Kudless exposes his cutting teaching methods and outcomes in an article which sheds insight into what Jason Johnson locates as an architecture in formation, yet beyond human subjectivity, and fundamentally anesthetic.

Ongoing histories and new paradigms

In 1957, Luigi Moretti established the Institute for Mathematical and Operational Research in Urbanism (IRMOU), in which he announced a newly named *parametric architecture*, "its ineluctable geometric character, its rigorous concatenation of forms, the absolute freedom of fantasy that will spring up in places where equations cannot fix their own roots, will give it a crystal splendor."[10] Today's architecture, then, seems less innovative but rather following a trajectory that is, in fact, pre-digital. Increasingly vast extents of computational power through planetary-scale computation, as Bratton calls "the stack," or the proliferation of cloud computing, smart cities, and next-generation interfaces, are the basis of twenty-first-century engagement as computational designers. Today, we simulate, not as truth, but as a mode of approximating control systems. Prediction is increasingly sought as a mechanism with which to engage and control indeterminacy. Amidst the urge to know the future, it holds surprises, still, thankfully.

Given the current industrial production paradigm shift, architects are working increasingly promiscuously at multiple scales, from furniture to urban master plans, with greater prevalence, sophistication, and elegance. Tools that were once cutting edge are quickly being embedded into conventional practices, normalizing the paradigm shift we've been migrating through. This book, only a decade ago, would have been focused strictly on computation. Today, this book is structured as a migration of information and methods between ordering complexity through modeling, coding, and simulation interfaces, towards performance-driven material prototyping, fabrication, and construction manufacturing and assembly. The digital has never been so material. Craft has been reawakened in the digital age. Prototyping, remains, in any design arena, a set of methods by which to aim for "progressive updating and optimization via feedback from demonstrations of performance" and through iteration and recursion. The material model thus becomes "a design instrument, different from the notion of a model as an ultimate representation of a final design proposal."[11] The prototype is always wrong, as in it is always testing the value of a design resolution.

Change no longer emanates from the top downwards, from corporations to consumers, but also increasingly, from users of technology, who are hungry for the expansion of their knowledge, skills, and the incentive and time (to waste or spend). Technological revolutions flow from users of technology, who are often ahead of the producers of technology, toward the ongoing innovations of practitioners. In the absence of definitive turning points and universal "theories of transition" in industrial paradigms, transitions which are rather evolutions feature a "mixture of continuity and change" from one dominant phase to the next.[12] The people and the forms of practice included in this book represent both the indication of a change in paradigm, as well as the forefront of driving this shift to new ways of thinking about and designing architecture. This book is, in fact, not a textbook in the traditional sense. I suspect there will be several volumes, editions (or "releases" in digital software parlance) of this book, so that it will indeed, over time, become a piece of valuable history with which to uncover further knowledge of the formative technological culture of the early twenty-first century.

Notes

1 Karl Marx, *Capital*, vol. I, 1848, p. 384.
2 Nicholas Negroponte, "Towards a Humanism Through Machines," *Architectural Design*, 7/6, 511.
3 Gordon Pask, "The Architectural Relevance of Cybernetics," first published in 1967; republished in *Cyber_Reader: Critical Writings for the Digital Era*, Neil Spiller ed. (London: Phaidon, 2002), 82.
4 Tom Verebes, *Masterplanning the Adaptive City: Computational Urbanism in the Twenty-First Century* (New York: Routledge, 2013) 93–94.
5 Pask, "The Architectural Relevance of Cybernetics."
6 Lewis Mumford, *The Lewis Mumford Reader*, D.L., Miller ed. (New York: Pantheon Books, 1986), 304.
7 Steven Johnson, *Where Good Ideas Come From: The Natural History of Innovation* (New York: Penguin, 2010), 16.

8 Verebes, *Masterplanning the Adaptive City*, 272.

9 Yochai Benkler, *The Wealth of Networks* (New Haven and London: Yale University Press, 2006), 2.

10 Luigi Moretti, "Form as Structure," 1957. Quoted in Federico Bucci and Mario Mulazzani (eds.), *Luigi Moretti Works and Writings* (New York: Princeton Architectural Press, 2002), 183–184.

11 Verebes, *Masterplanning the Adaptive City*, 224.

12 Ash Amin, "Post-Fordism: Models, Fantasies and Phantoms of Transition," in *Post-Fordism: A Reader*, ed. Ash Amin (Oxford and Cambridge, MA: Blackwell Publishers, 1994), 3.

Acknowledgments

First and foremost, we would like to thank all of the students, teaching colleagues, and professionals who have contributed work for this book. The photographs, drawings, and writings contained in this text are only a snapshot of the countless hours of work performed to generate them. Also, we give our heartfelt gratitude to the writers who graciously took the time to author the foreword and essays, especially Tom Verebes for his continued support. It was exciting and humbling to work with these well-respected educators and designers.

We have both worked with many talented colleagues who have helped us grow intellectually and professionally. Specifically, we would like to acknowledge fellow faculty members who helped develop some of these exercises in courses we co-taught, especially (in alphabetical order) Jonathon Anderson, Antonieta Angulo, Mahesh Daas, Michael Gibson, Dustin Headley, Jodi James, Kevin Klinger, Matt Knapic, Branko Kolarevic, Dave Rowe, Josh Taron, and Shai Yeshayahu. We would also be remiss not to thank Wendy Fuller and Grace Harrison at Routledge for helping us throughout this process with their generous assistance and patience.

We are deeply grateful to the students who assisted us, especially Christina James who helped push this project across the finish line. Matt Parker assisted in graphic production, as did Ludwing Vaca and Ella Vernon. Many thanks to all of the students over the last ten years who asked good questions and produced good work while serving as guinea pigs for testing these and other exercises.

Finally, of course, we thank our families and especially our spouses – Nicola Johnson and Stacia Vermillion – for their support and encouragement throughout this process, which is actually a continuation of their unwavering support and patience over the years. This book is dedicated to them.

Jason S. Johnson and Joshua Vermillion, Calgary and Las Vegas, July 2015

Introduction

This book is intended to introduce digital design to architecture students. So why differentiate "digital" design from other ways of designing? A digital design process leverages computational platforms (both hardware and software platforms) to negotiate, generate, and then manage design information. But in order to successfully wield these platforms in the pursuit of design goals, one must understand some of the unique aspects they provide to the design process. It's easy to recognize differences between computers and traditional, analog tools such as a pencil. Certainly the pencil is (still) great at assisting humans with certain tasks, but computers are great at other sorts of tasks. They execute and re-execute procedures, crunch numbers at incredible speeds, and store and recall rules, associations, geometric information, metadata, and procedural histories. With these specific abilities, computational tools allow us to design complex systems that simply aren't practical to generate and manage with a pencil and paper.[1]

These abilities also bring about a different kind of interaction between the designer and the computer as a tool – one in which the designer might relinquish some control on the direct shaping of form and order, and instead orchestrate strategic relationships, rules, and parameters to govern a generative design system[2] – sometimes guiding, and sometimes discovering design propositions by shaping the tools that create them.[3] This process is still reliant on a feedback loop of generation–evaluation–regeneration; in other words, digital design processes should be iterative investigations and as digital skill fluencies are developed, more iterative investigations are possible within a decreasing amount of time.

Digital media should help create rich, generative design environments with multivalent results. We think that we share this value with most designers and educators and it deeply informed the careful crafting of this book.

We have tried to balance between algorithmic and intuitive approaches to learning basic design and graphic skills – an approach that allows students to learn basic literacy of digital design and fabrication tools by deploying them in an experimental but thoughtful way. It is our hope that this book presents the feedback-loop-informed process of iteration as both a design instrument and a design ethos.

This book is a response to a glaring lack of texts focused on computational technique for the beginning design student. In some ways this is understandable as digital design thinking has for many years been closely tied to the tools that enable it. Teaching texts in technique have been replaced with software manuals and tutorials focused on specific tools. This book will not attempt to replicate those materials, but rather acknowledges the widespread integration of these varied tools in the design practice of academia and the profession. This book proposes a series of creative design exercises that take advantage of this digital design environment as a place for design experimentation.

We (the authors) have taught courses dealing with digital design and media and are well aware of all the many great texts, essays, and tutorials about these topics; however, we have yet to find a suitable combination of these for someone who is new to the topic of digital design, much less someone who is fairly new to architectural design and graphics. This book is our best effort to strike a balanced combination of textbook, essays, and exercises for newcomers who wish to learn about digital design and media.

Each set of exercises starts with introductions to key computational concepts and terms. Framed on these concepts, the exercises that follow ask the participant to build digital media skills by practicing generative graphic and modeling techniques. There are no tutorials for making diagrids, voronoi patterns, or widgets (with hidden internal code) – there are no shortcuts. In fact, none of the exercises are prescriptive of final results; rather, they are open-ended provocations that emphasize process and evaluation. Our ambiguity is intended to allow instructors or students to custom-tailor exercises to situational projects. We have also strived for software neutrality – we all have our favorite tools, but this book is not about particular buttons in particular software. One only needs to search YouTube or an online tutorial service such as Lynda in order to find resources specific to software toolbars. To perform most of the exercises you will need software (of your choosing) to edit raster and vector graphics, to draw, to model, and to render.

The exercises are arranged and written in a modular fashion, and, while we carefully arranged them in a particular sequence, they can also be reconfigured or used non-sequentially (in fact, this is encouraged). We also understand that the exercises themselves might not be of the highest value to everyone. However, each exercise introduces key concepts for computational design for the beginner and shows relevant examples of student and professional work. Additionally, this book provides reading lists along with invited essays from respected practitioners, educators, and theoreticians to ground the exercises in both broader and deeper contexts. If the exercises are useful in creating a solid foundation of skills and understanding, then we hope the readings suggest future paths for students to continue this journey. But, regardless of how you use this book, it is our goal that students engage in a rigorous exploration of the opportunities presented by the integration of digital tools with their design education.

Notes

1 Of course, the logical next question is why we would advocate designing "impractical" complex systems. We hope that the remainder of the book sheds light on why we would advocate such a position and why complex systems aren't necessarily impractical.

2 Cristiano Ceccato, associate director at Zaha Hadid Architects, wrote about this relationship between the digital-savvy designer and the computer: "Computers become interlocutors, designer and computer form a partnership of complements, each contributing specific abilities and knowledge to the overall task of architecture." Quoted from "Integration: Master, Planner, Programmer, Builder", in *The Proceedings of the 4th Conference and Exhibition on Generative Art 2001*, Celestino Soddu *et al*. ed., Politechnico di Milano University, Italy, 2001.

Bernard Cache reinforced this necessity of shaping digital design systems when he wrote: "we hope that our explanations here will go some way towards the argument that digital technologies really put at stake the architecture of information lying behind the buildings, and that this architecture with digits also has to be designed." Quoted from "Philibert De L'Orme Pavilion: Towards an Associative Architecture," in Mark Taylor, ed. *Surface Consciousness* (London: Academy Editions 2003), 25.

3 Branko Kolarevic discusses this shift from "the making of form to the finding of form" in the chapter "Digital Morphogenesis" in *Architecture in the Digital Age: Design and Manufacturing* (New York: Taylor & Francis, 2003), 13.

A DIGITAL CRAFT FRAMEWORK

Andrew Kudless

The tools available to an architect today can be overwhelming in their depth and complexity. While only a generation ago an architect's tools consisted of tracing paper, a few lead holders and pens, and a drafting table, architects today are expected to use a plethora of digital modeling applications to design, visualize, analyze, and document their projects. Furthermore, architects need to be familiar with a range of automated workflows that manage the intricacies of translating one form of data into another. Finally, digital fabrication has radically decreased the gap between design and fabrication, enabling architects with greater control and expanded formal opportunities. The artful mediation of these complexities requires a new sense of craftsmanship that extends across the physical and digital. Over the last ten years I have focused on developing strategies for this new digital craft of architecture and will describe below a framework for students to manage the complexity of contemporary architectural design and production. Using examples from my own teaching as well as from my colleagues in the Digital Craft Lab at the California College of the Arts, I hope to convey a range of simple strategies that empower students to find their way through the chaos of contemporary digital practice.

Sketch

Paradoxically, my first suggestion is to sketch in whatever medium you are most fluid throughout the entire design process. Two of the most vexing problems of contemporary digital design tools are their quantity and their mutability. That is, in comparison to a pencil or cutting blade, which have remained relatively consistent in their functionality for decades if not centuries, the tools available within any particular design application are both so numerous as to become overwhelming and so inconsistent between one application and another (or even one version to the next of the same application) as to become frustrating. Learning digital design takes time, focus, and patience, and these qualities are not often conducive to simply getting a rough idea out before it vanishes from the mind's eye. In the rush to teach students how to use digital design tools, I feel we sometimes forget the value of imprecision, illogic, and the handmade as these serve as a counter-balance to the rigor required when engaging the digital. Too often I see students struggle to digitally model a bad idea when a simple sketch of the idea would have shown the idea's deficiencies in only a few minutes. Or, even worse, I have seen students with a good idea give up on it because they did not know how to digitally model it yet. I suggest students find ways to quickly produce rough versions of ideas in a medium that resists the tyranny of syntax or the impotence of inexperience. Draw in a notebook, build physical sketch models, and do whatever you can to quickly flesh ideas out without the overhead imposed by most digital tools.

Parameterize

As your ideas take form through sketches, begin the process of parameterizing them. Parameters and their interrelationships are the core of contemporary digital design techniques so it is essential that students are able to translate their vague and sketchy ideas into a network of logical relationships and parametric values. Surprisingly, this process of thinking parametrically isn't actually all that new within the discipline. For generations architects have been trained to think analytically and to find relationships between things; however, only recently have architects had the digital tools to make this way of thinking much more productive and generative. The introduction of parametric modeling tools into the design process has enabled architects to build flexible models that are able to respond to a variety of design criteria. The parametric space of these models can be explored, expanded, and modified with great speed. Furthermore, once a relationship has been parametrically modeled, it can be reused in countless other projects that share the same fundamental logical relationships, despite differences in their parameters.

Unfortunately, due to a mistaken conflation of the concept of parametric design with a certain style of architecture (i.e., Parametricism) exemplified by organic and curvilinear forms, I have seen some students reject the concept and tools entirely due to their lack of interest in the style. This is throwing the baby out with the bathwater in that, although Parametricism takes advantage of parametric thinking, the core concept is far more powerful, useful, and extensible to any architectural style and should not be seen as the domain of a specific style.

In order to avoid this conflation of the concept of parametric design with a specific architectural style, I have introduced parametric concepts in my own courses by looking at the history of procedural art. Using painting and drawing examples from artists such as Ellsworth Kelly, Eva Hesse, and Sol Lewitt, I am able to discuss topics such as randomness, recursion, and conditional logics without having to immediately jump to architectural

break down functions to create something bigger

case studies. This gap between concept and specific architectural application allows students to more freely grasp the essential concepts.

This pedagogy was developed further in a recent course I taught in the CCA Digital Craft Lab, called Kinematic Code, where students were not only responsible for developing a parametric process for the digital generation of a drawing, but they had to extend this to the physical creation of a drawing or painting using computer-numerically controlled (CNC) equipment such as laser cutters, CNC routers, and industrial robots. Within this context, students were required to innovate in three areas: *methods, mediums, and machines.* The methods were essentially the digital processes that were used to construct an algorithmically produced drawing, such as the use of a recursive procedure. The mediums were the physical implements used to draw or paint and the material surfaces on which they were placed. Finally, the machines referred to an exploration into the parameters of the specific equipment being used such that the drawing exploited the nature of the

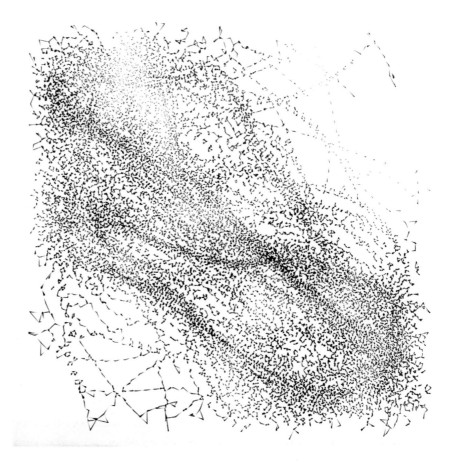

Figure 1.1 Drawing made with Sharpie and CNC router by Alan Cation and Evan Kuester in Andrew Kudless's Kinematic Code seminar, spring 2015.

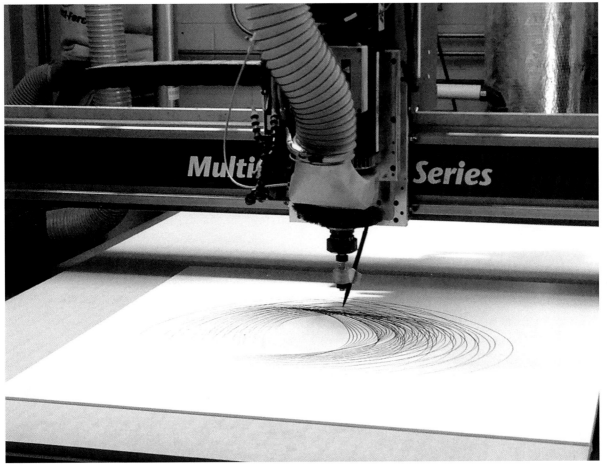

Figure 1.2 Drawing made on CNC router by Jared Clifton in Andrew Kudless's Kinematic Code seminar, spring 2015.

machine to produce an effect only possible on that machine. The combination of these three focus areas enabled students to explore the interrelationships between digital, physical, and machine parameters to produce a family of related, yet different artifacts.

Materialize

As stated earlier, architecture has a long history of using analysis to understand the parametric relationships between certain design criteria. For example, nearly every project begins with an analysis of a project's site and program whereby parameters such as sun angle, view directions, programmatic adjacencies, and areas are calculated. Typically from this analysis a certain abstract formal solution is proposed which is eventually developed into a specific

Figure 1.3 Robotic painting by Carlos Sabogal and Jared Clifton in Andrew Kudless's Kinematic Code seminar, spring 2015.

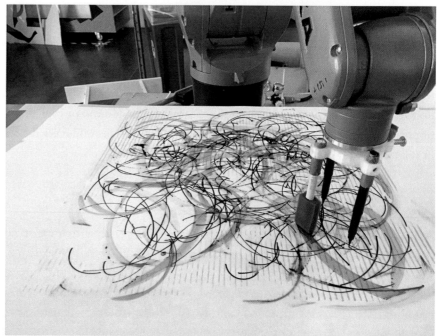

Figure 1.4 Robotic painting by Carlos Sabogal and Jared Clifton in Andrew Kudless's Kinematic Code seminar, spring 2015.

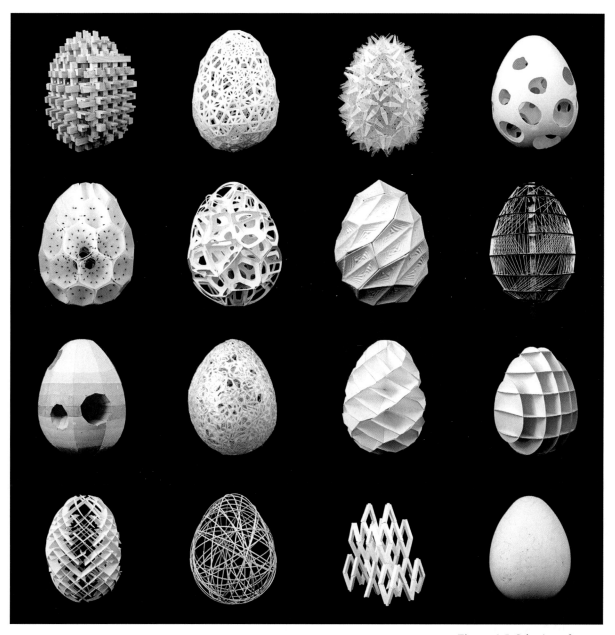

Figure 1.5 Selection of egg prototypes made by various students in Andrew Kudless's SEAcraft studio, spring 2013.

material system; i.e., an integration of form, material, and performance such as a certain spacing, sizing, and material for a structural grid. However, this design process has become so ingrained in architectural education and practice as to almost completely preclude any other possible process. The parameters of site and program are typically so primary that we often forget the power and potential of material to suggest design opportunities.

11

Figure 1.6 Selection of Egg prototypes made by Bryan Loza in Andrew Kudless's Wild & Domestic studio, Spring 2014.

Creating eggs through removable string (no adhesion, Just tension) led to the same idea in a large project involving a floating floor illusion

As an experiment over the last two years, I have conducted three advanced studios that placed material parameters as the primary design drivers. Rather than start the studios with a specific site and program, students were asked to choose a material and a way of making that interested them and to produce five egg-shaped artifacts over the first four weeks of the studio. These artifacts were not scaled representations but were full-scale material prototypes. Students were asked to iterate quickly and to learn from the successes and failures of each iteration. At the end of the four weeks, most students had become highly skilled in a particular way of making and deeply understood the parameters of that material system. Only at that point were students given a specific site and program and were then asked to parametrically modify their material system to address the needs of the program in relation to the site. This inversion, placing material as primary and site and program as secondary, enabled students to develop much more innovative designs that more fully integrated form, material, and performance (programmatic, climatic, structural, etc.).

For example, one of my students, Bryan Loza, chose the weaving of rope as his initial material system and during the first four weeks he developed a sophisticated system of removable forms and composite fibers to make the abstract eggs. This was then parametrically modified into a super-lightweight structural system for a house and maker space in his final design using carbon

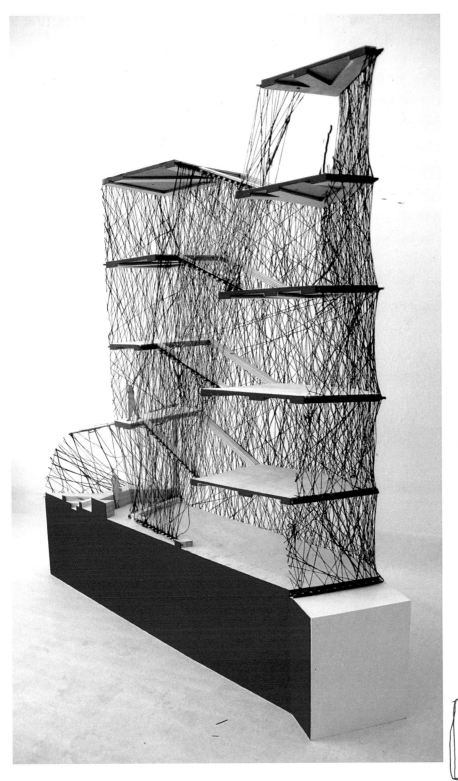

Strings giving the illusion of floating floor

Figure 1.7 Final house prototypes made by Bryan Loza in Andrew Kudless's Wild & Domestic studio, spring 2014.

fiber composites that make the house's floors appear to magically float in the air. The model that was produced was not just a scaled representation of the house design but a physical prototype demonstrating the structural capacity of the carbon fiber system. Essential to the emerging digital craft of architecture is thinking beyond models as only visual representations, but as prototypes for full-scale innovative material systems.

Prototype

The prototype has found its greatest advocate in contemporary maker culture and the architectural discipline can learn much from the DIY spirit that is integral to it. Innovation stagnates without groups of talented individuals who look beyond commodified off-the-shelf solutions. Similar to the power that parametric modeling gives designers to construct their own custom tools,

Figure 1.8 Swarmscapers final prototype by Alan Cation and Clayton Muhleman in Jason Kelly Johnson and Michael Shiloh's Creative Architecture Machines studio, fall 2014.

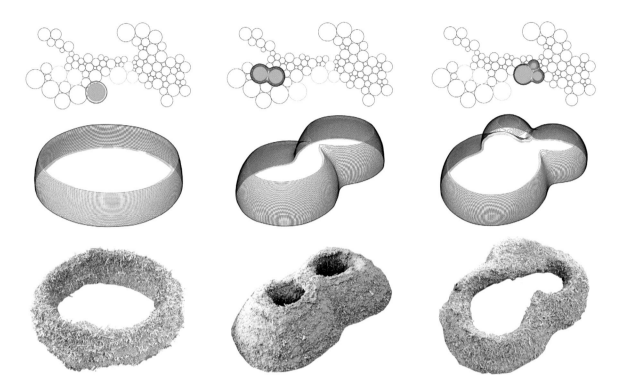

Figure 1.9 Swarmscapers diagram by Alan Cation and Clayton Muhleman in Jason Kelly Johnson and Michael Shiloh's Creative Architecture Machines studio, fall 2014.

physical prototypes allow makers to quickly test out concepts and iterate to the next level. Within the context of the CCA Digital Craft Lab, associate professors Jason Kelly Johnson and Michael Shiloh have developed a series of studios called Creative Architecture Machines that focus on the production of experimental fabrication machines that posit possible futures for the design and construction of new architectures. Groups of students work together in these studios to conceptualize, build, and test custom fabrication machines exploring the future of architectural construction.

In the latest version of the studio in the fall of 2014, a group project named "Swarmscapers" explored the potential for a swarm of tank-like drones to autonomously 3D-print large-scale structures out of sawdust. Although many people talk about large-scale 3D-printing within architecture, very few have taken this distributed approach and even fewer have actually built working prototypes.

What I find most exciting about these studios is that architectural students are given the tools and confidence to move beyond the traditional domains of the profession. Although highly speculative, the machines have to work. They bridge the fantastic with the hard reality of fabrication. Students must learn a range of tools from scripting to soldering to computer vision, and in the process learn to build connections between disparate disciplines.

Collaborate

Building connections to other disciplines may be one of the most essential aspects of the emerging digital craft within architecture. As stated earlier, the tools of the profession have increased at an explosive rate and it is nearly impossible for a singular individual to master the full range of tools needed to produce a sophisticated piece of architecture. Increasingly, diverse teams are needed that cover a wide range of disciplines. The traditional architect–engineer–contractor partnership on projects has expanded to include environmental consultants, computer programmers, interaction designers, artists, graphic designers, scientists, urban ecologists, and a whole host of highly

Figure 1.10 Adaptive Creatures project by Jill Chin-Han Chao, Hung-Yi Chou, and Sanna Lee in the Buoyant Ecologies studio by Margaret Ikeda, Evan Jones, and Adam Marcus, Fall 2014.

specialized fabricators, to name just a few. The role of the architect in this is to coordinate the collaboration and help synthesize the collective knowledge into a specific design proposal.

Another recent CCA Digital Craft Lab studio exemplifies this emerging model of design collaboration. Instructors Margaret Ikeda, Evan Jones, and Adam Marcus organized an advanced studio with Autodesk Workshop at Pier 9 as the client, Kreysler & Associates as the architectural composites fabricator and consultant, and the Moss Landing Marine Laboratories as the marine ecology consultant. Students worked in teams to design a floating extension of the Pier 9 facility that would not only serve as a public engagement space for humans, but also as habitation for marine life. The studio, titled Buoyant Ecologies, engaged students to listen, learn, and synthesize diverse bodies of knowledge from the studio partners. For example, not only did teams have to design the underside of the floating structure, but they also had to learn how to design for watertight composite fabrication while creating the surface qualities that would encourage marine life to colonize the surface.

The wealth of data available to architects during the design process will only increase in coming years and learning how to manage this flow in productive and innovative ways will be essential in forming a digital craft of architecture. We must know when to rely on simple techniques that bypass the seemingly endless rabbit holes inherent to digital design. To organize and manage complex projects, we must think parametrically and break down large, complex problems into smaller, logical relationships that are extensible and reusable. These relationships can be leveraged to create design processes that integrate form, material, and performance and allow material systems to suggest possible solutions as an initial step. We can learn to innovate by fabricating working physical prototypes that synthesize knowledge generated through productive collaborations. Digital craft is not a style but a design attitude that maximizes the power of digital computation to coordinate complexity, integrate knowledge, and fabricate advanced architectures.

working w/ other fields

2

EXERCISES FOR POINTS, LINES, AND CURVES

Jason S. Johnson and Joshua Vermillion

Introduction

Complexity is a word that seems to be repeated over and over to describe most aspects of our world, but what exactly does complexity mean? Sometimes complexity is used to describe something difficult to understand, or used interchangeably with the term complicated. To get a better understanding of the word, it's useful to see how it is used, in a more rigorous way, in other disciplines. To quote Herbert Simon:

> by a complex system I mean one made up of a large number of parts that interact in a nonsimple way. In such systems, the whole is more than the sum of the parts, not in an ultimate, metaphysical sense, but in the important pragmatic sense that, give the properties of the parts and the laws of their interaction, it is not a trivial matter to infer the properties of the whole.[1]

So one condition of having a complex system is having many parts. But how many parts are sufficient? Think of the number of parts that comprise buildings. Your home, a school building, or a hospital – all are made up of many, many parts. But quantity of parts alone is not sufficient for defining a complex system. The parts also need to be governed by a rich, interdependent set of interactions and relationships. To use Simon's words, a complex system is more than the sum of its parts and not easily reducible. With these conditions in mind, computation seems particularly well suited to help generate and manage complexity – repetition to create a large number of parts, rules to govern the interactions between these parts, and the memory and processing capacity to execute such a system. We, the authors, argue that the skills to design complex systems are not only necessary and desirable for the world in which we live, but also the logical outcome of designing and making with digital tools.

In this book we will continually ask the following question: Can we produce design systems to generate results that are complex, meaning that the results are informed by a variety of inputs along with their interactions and associations? This would also mean that the results aren't easily predicted or determined in advance. Instead, complex systems are capable of producing sophisticated orderings of parts based on bottom-up logics and rules – even when starting with very simple parts. Often, these results can have emergent properties; given enough parts and interactions, a larger behavior, order, or effect emerges that seemingly has little to do with the original parts. With all

points→line→massing

of this in mind, we will focus on designing local interactions between parts in order to create globally complex wholes.

This chapter focuses on generating geometries through a series of bottom-up processes. Using the basic building blocks of points and lines and simple operational sequences we will develop a series of assemblages, at first starting simple, and then overlaying constraints and rules to create ever more complex results. These processes will not target any specific outputs, but will instead focus on building skills in creating and adapting procedures for the production of pattern and form. At the end of these exercises you will be asked to evaluate the outputs by applying scale and context. Throughout this and the following chapters we will focus on this cyclical process of creation, evaluation, adaptation, and re-creation. To begin, we will practice two different approaches to generate drawings: algorithmic or rules-based methods, and keyframing or tweening techniques. We will start with a simple set of geometric ingredients to test our algorithms. The following list and Figure 2.1 explain some simple classifications for points, lines, and curves.

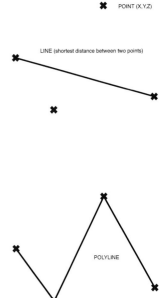

Points

Numerical ingredients: three numbers that serve as X, Y, and Z coordinates in the Cartesian coordinate space.

Line

Geometric ingredients: two points (a 'start' and an 'end').

To begin, we will draw a line as the shortest distance between a start point and an end point.

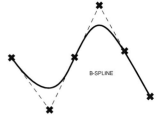

Polyline

Geometric ingredients: three or more points.

As the name suggests, polylines are composed by drawing multiple lines between multiple points in a continuous fashion (this is an intuitive definition, rather than the more complicated mathematical definition).

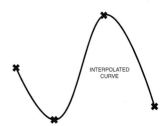

Figure 2.1 Points, lines, and curves: the geometric ingredients for the first set of exercises.

B-spline

Geometric ingredients: three or more points.

B-splines are freeform curves defined by start and end points, as well as any number of points in between that act as weights to inflect the curve.

Interpolated curve

Geometric ingredients: three or more points.

Interpolated curves are freeform curves that are fitted through all of the ingredient points (rather than acting as weights, the points are knots along the curve).

Points along curves

Ingredients: a given curve, and a given number of points.

In addition to plotting points in Cartesian space, we can place points relative to line and curve geometries. For instance, when finding a mid-point along a curve, Cartesian coordinates are of little use. Rather, we examine a curve and measure along its length to find the location of a mid-point. Similarly, if we wanted to populate a curve with equally spaced points, we would need a curve and the number of times to divide the curve as ingredients to generate the points.

Recommended reading

Mitchell, William. *The Logic of Architecture*. MIT Press, 1990.

- Chapter 3: Design Worlds, pp. 37–57.

Pottmann, Helmut, Andreas Asperl, Michael Hofer, and Axel Kilian. *Architectural Geometry*. Bentley Institute Press, 2007.

- Chapter 7: Curves and Surfaces, pp. 211–252.
- Chapter 8: Freeform Curves, pp. 253–284.

Simon, Herbert. "The Architecture of Complexity". *Proceedings of the American Philosophical Society*, 106, no. 6. (1962), pp. 467–482.
Weinstock, Michael. *The Architecture of Emergence*. Wiley, 2010.

Exercise set 1: line drivers

Algorithms are step-by-step instructions for producing or accomplishing something. Like a recipe that transforms basic ingredients into a cake, an algorithm is a rules-based system that receives inputs, performs steps, and produces outputs. We learn and use certain algorithms all the time – for instance, the method for performing long division. However, instead of performing arithmetic, we will develop our own simple algorithms that input, transform, and output geometric information such as points and curves.

To demonstrate, let's start with a very simple algorithm:

1. Create a box
2. Copy, rotate, and scale
3. Repeat…

In Figure 2.2 we can see the variations produced through the manipulation of the values for scaling and rotation. Repeating these actions while adjusting these values or parameters allows us to create increasingly complex collections of objects related to the first object. Going further, by changing other parameters such as the number of times to repeat and the axis of rotation, the algorithm can begin to produce an enormous amount of information from one simple polyline, as shown in Figure 2.3. Parameters are the changeable and malleable drivers of an algorithmic design system – changes to the parameters of a system can yield a variety of design results (sometimes dramatically different results from one to the next).

Figure 2.2 Variations from a simple algorithm using the operations of copy, rotate, and scale. Left parameters: rotate 30 degrees, scale 110%; center parameters: rotate 15 degrees, scale 90%; right parameters: rotate 10 degrees, scale 120%.

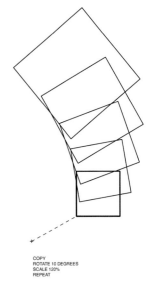

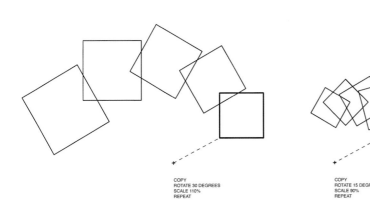

COPY
ROTATE 30 DEGREES
SCALE 110%
REPEAT

COPY
ROTATE 15 DEGREES
SCALE 90%
REPEAT

COPY
ROTATE 10 DEGREES
SCALE 120%
REPEAT

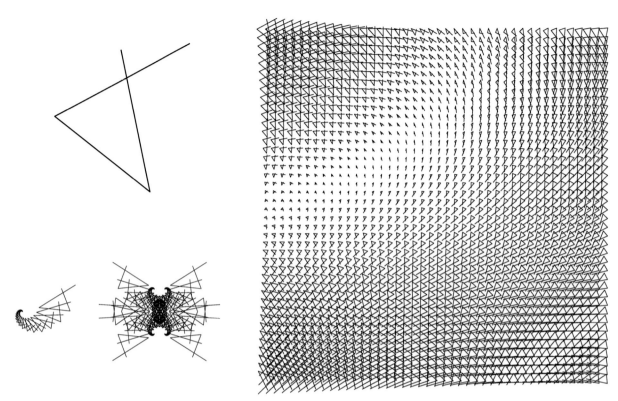

Figure 2.3 The different results generated from one simple ingredient by slightly modifying the sequence and quantity of operations in the algorithm.

Deploying an algorithm of this nature requires iterative testing in order to understand some of the possible causal relationships between ingredients, rules, parameters, and the visual qualities of the outputs. This can be difficult once you have a sufficiently complex system. So why are we starting with algorithms? It's important, when presented with a seemingly endless set of new tools, to have rules and constraints and to be able to explicitly state and understand them. Recording your algorithmic recipes enables you to be systematic with your iterative studies and focus on rules and procedures for the interactions between ingredients, which is necessary to produce complex systems. Algorithmic thinking is a foundational thread that runs through the entire book and it's instrumental for deploying more sophisticated computational tools such as scripting and parametric modeling.

First we will use simple, mostly prescribed algorithms to create drawings from simple ingredients. "Line drivers" is designed to sharpen your abilities to control individual geometric parts while generating pattern conditions as a byproduct of these localized procedures. Precision is paramount in this instance. The degree of control deployed through the assignment has everything to do with the resultant product. Rather than worrying about how the experiment will "look" in the end, focus on the logic and precision of your technique, as it will provide you with a key to understanding the qualities generated through the assignment.

Objectives

This exercise is intended to introduce and develop understandings of:

- drawing creation with lines and simple geometric operations such as move and rotate through repetitive practice;
- algorithmic processes as related to executing rules and adjusting rules and parameters.

Outcomes

By the end of this exercise set you will have nine sets of drawings generated from various algorithmic recipes.

Recommended reading

Aranda, Benjamin, and Chris Lasch. *Pamphlet Architecture 27: Tooling.* Princeton Architectural Press, 2006.
Maeda, John. *Design by Numbers.* MIT Press, 2001.
Terzidis, Kostas. *Algorithmic Architecture.* Architectural Press, 2006.

Exercise 1A

Establish a 24" × 36" (landscape-oriented) digital sheet. Within the sheet, form three 22" high × 10" wide boxes with 1" separating each box. The array of these boxes should be centered within the digital sheet. Use light construction lines to demarcate these boundaries. Continuing to use light construction lines, vertically divide each box in 2" increments to form a series of uniform horizontal bands within each boxed boundary.

Exercise procedure

Step 1: Within each horizontal band of the first (left) box, draw 2" long vertical lines with a horizontal spacing of 1". Horizontally stagger each row by 0.5" so that there is a 0.5" offset between vertical lines in adjacent rows. Starting at the top row, assign a line weight of 4pt to the 2" vertical lines. After every two rows moving in a downward direction, reduce the line weight by one half to generate a decreasing lineweight sequence of 4, 2, 1, 0.5, 0.25, 0.125.

Step 2: Within each horizontal band of the second (center) box, draw 2" long vertical lines with a line weight of 1pt. Starting at the top row, establish a horizontal spacing between lines of 1". After every two rows moving in a downward direction, decrease the horizontal spacing by one half to generate a decreasing horizontal frequency sequence of 1", 0.5", 0.25", 0.125", 0.0625", 0.03125".

Step 3: Within each horizontal band of the last (right) box, draw vertical lines with a 0.5" horizontal spacing between each line segment's base with a line weight of 1pt. Each line should span from the lower boundary of the band to the upper boundary of the band. Starting at the top left corner, the base of this first line should form a 90-degree angle with the construction line that it anchors to. Each adjacent line segment must vary by an increment of 10 degrees from its prior iteration, using the base of the line as its point of rotation. It is acceptable for lines to cross over one another within a given horizontal band. Play out this sequence until the entire right box is filled. Figure 2.4 shows example student work for Exercise 1A.

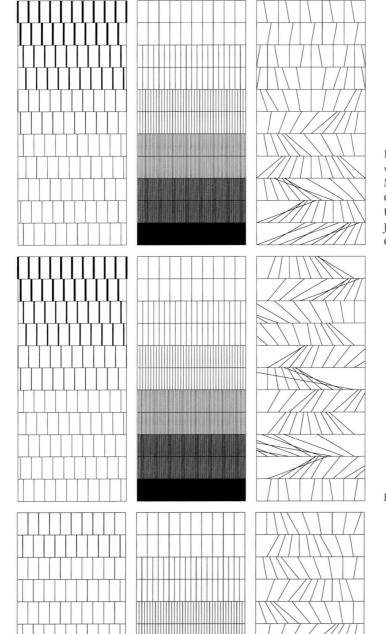

Figure 2.4a 1A student work examples. (a) Alison MacLachlan, University of Calgary; (b) Bahar Khonsari, University of Calgary; (c) Julian Wylegly, University of Calgary.

Figure 2.4b

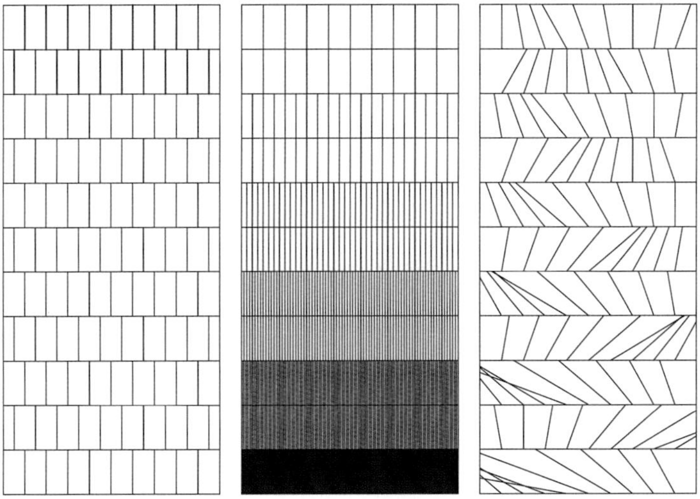

Figure 2.4c

line weights-
select

Exercise 1B

Repeat the beginning instructions for Exercise 1A with a new digital sheet for this exercise. By the end, you will develop your own algorithm to test and revise.

Exercise procedure

Step 1: Within each horizontal band in the first (left) box, draw 2" long vertical lines with a horizontal spacing of 0.5". Horizontally stagger each row by 0.25" so that there is an offset between vertical lines in adjacent rows. Starting at the top left, assign a line weight of 1pt to the first 2" vertical line. Each adjacent line must either remain the same or increase or decrease by a single increment of line weight value. Your available line weights are as follows: 4, 2, 1, 0.5, 0.25, 0.125.

Step 2: Within each horizontal band in the second (center) box, draw 2" long vertical lines with a variable horizontal spacing and line weight of 1pt. The horizontal distance between two lines and the adjacent pair must maintain a 0.25" differential increment. For example, if two vertical lines form a horizontal spacing of 0.5", the adjacent spacing must either be 0.25" or 0.75" in distance. The minimum spacing between vertical line segments is 0.25". There is no upper bound for this value. You may begin at any point within any band. You may begin with a horizontal spacing of any value divisible by 0.25" and fill the entire box.

Step 3: Using incremental line weights, variable horizontal spacing, and differential angles of incidence, create a set of rules for yourself and execute them within the entirety of the third (right) box. It is encouraged to deploy strategies of corresponding influence within this rule set – for example, angles might correspond with line weight conditions, frequency might correlate with angles, etc.

Step 4: Repeat step three, each time deploying a fresh set or variations of previous rules for each row. Figure 2.5 shows example student work for Exercise 1B.

Bonus: automate the process of executing a rules-based system. Illustrator: java script; Maya: duplicate tool; Rhino: copy-and-paste macro or use of the array tool.

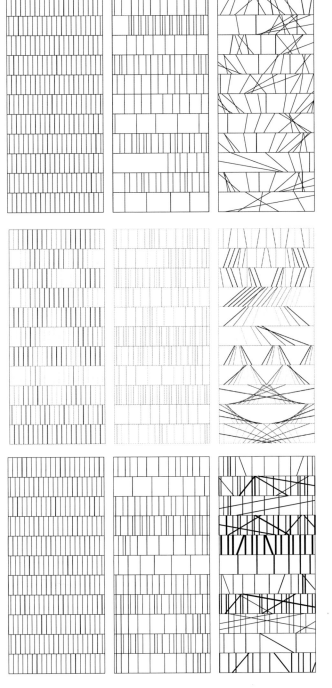

Figure 2.5a 1B Student work examples. (a) Julian Wylegly, University of Calgary; (b) Bahar Khonsari, University of Calgary; (c) Alison MacLachlan, University of Calgary.

Figure 2.5b

Figure 2.5c

Exercise 1C

Lay out a sheet in three partitions (as you did in the first two boards). For this exercise you might use tweening operations to generate your last drawing. Tweening, key-frame animation, and snapshotting are terms that are used interchangeably to describe the process of generating intermediate geometries between a starting and an ending condition (Figure 2.6). Used often in digital animation and cartoon production, tweening saves time by generating the transitions of movements and shape changes. Tweening is a useful tool for generating repetitive geometries with variation, or, in this case, to visualize the transition between drawings in this exercise.

Tween ingredients: a start curve and an end curve are needed to tween.

Key parameter: the number of steps or "tweens" to create between the start and end conditions.

Tweening generates intermediate curves, each of which morphs in a step-by-step fashion, between the start and end curves. Each new curve varies slightly from the next, creating repetition with variation.

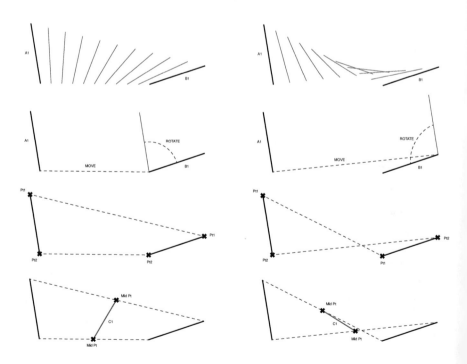

Figure 2.6 Diagram showing how a tween algorithm works.

Exercise procedure

Step 1: Place your final drawing from the last exercise in the left box. Label each line in the drawing with a specific nomenclature (e.g., A1, A2, A3). Whatever nomenclature you use, each line in the left box must carry as its syntax the letter A.

Step 2: Once all of the lines have been labeled, duplicate the drawing and place it in the right box. For the nomenclature in the right box, the syntax for each line must be changed from A to B.

Step 3: In the right box, move, shift, rotate, and scale the lines in a manner that begins to organize the sheet into a habitable/circulateable diagram. You are not allowed to add or delete any lines. Line weights must also remain constant between each drawing. For example, if line 1A has a line weight of 0.5pt, line 1B must also have a line weight of 0.5pt. The rule in this reorganization is that you should manipulate these lines to accommodate a specific scale of habitation within this diagrammatic instancing of space. You are encouraged, but not required, to achieve this by means of an iterative procedural application of rules. Be sure to keep track of each line's nomenclature.

Scale: 1" = 3' 0".

Step 4: Once you have completed one instance of this spatial reorganization, you are to create a third drawing that is exactly the "halfway" moment of transformation between the left and right boxes. This drawing is to inhabit the middle box on the sheet. In other words, in the center box, between every common pair of lines, you are to generate the precise halfway moment of its transformation between its A and B state. Lineweight is to remain constant between drawings. Figures 2.7 and 2.8 show student work examples of Exercise 1C.

Bonus: generate the "halfway" moments in a more automated way. For example, Adobe Illustrator and Rhino 3D have "blend" and "tween" tools, respectively. These allow you to generate any number of moments between the initial condition in Step 1 and the ending condition in Step 3.

J.S. Johnson and J. Vermillion

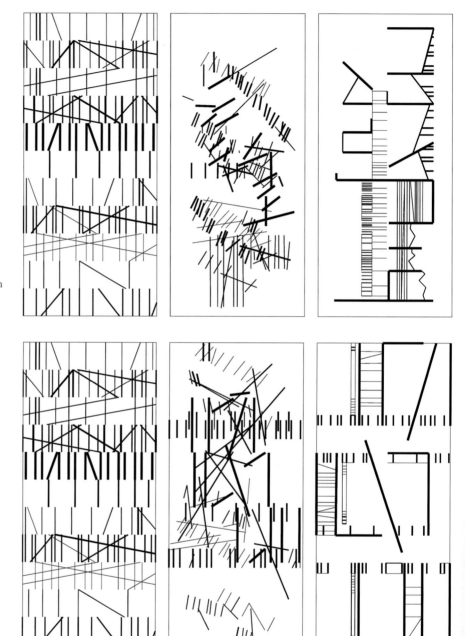

Figure 2.7a Exercise 1C student work examples. Allison MacLachlan, University of Calgary.

Figure 2.7b

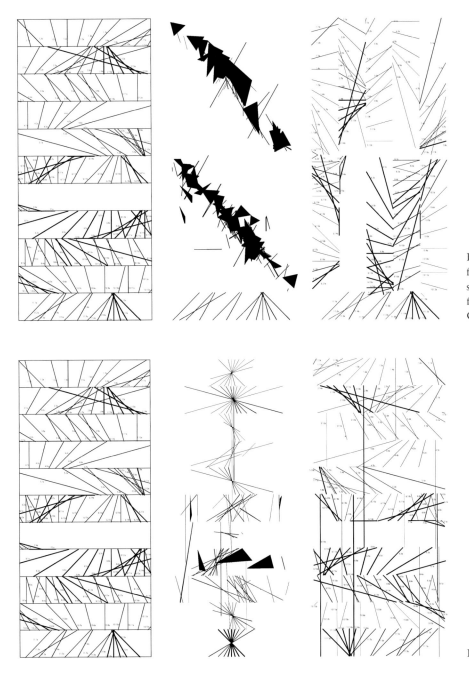

Figure 2.8a Studies generated for Exercise 1C that further study line weight and curve fills. Jodi James, University of Calgary.

Figure 2.8b

Exercise set 2: algorithmic drawings

In this exercise set, we will practice writing our own algorithmic recipes and attempt to create results with more complexity until field conditions emerge. Fields are complex organizations of parts that, through their composition, imply the presence of forces, movement, or some other phenomenon that creates an emergent visual or spatial effect. In a seminal essay, Stan Allen described fields as a matrix of diverse parts that are unified by the global behaviors brought about by all of the various internal relationships between the parts.[2] As with any complex system, fields are comprised of many parts that interact based on rules that you control. The key to evaluating your results will lie in the global behavior produced by these interactions, particularly in the visual effects that emerge.

As you produce work in this set of exercises, ask yourself if the results satisfy the criteria to be considered a field condition. Does the composition read as a visual gradient with varying densities, directions, and overlaps of line work? If not, then perhaps you need to execute your algorithm longer to generate more parts and repetition, start with different ingredients, or alter some parameters in your recipe. The key is to create a composition in which the viewer doesn't easily differentiate individual parts from the whole. This requires sufficient repetition and interactions (complexity) that leverage computation to generate something that isn't easily replicated with analog tools. While still using lines and curves as ingredients, the geometric operations for your recipe need not be too complex. You can start with simple transformations such as move, rotate, scale, and mirror. Figure 2.9 shows geometric transformations that you can use for these exercises and which are commonly found in digital design software.

Objectives

This exercise is intended to introduce and develop understandings of:

- creating algorithmic systems and executing these systems to create and assess drawings;
- complex systems and field conditions in which the inputs and rules are controlled by the designer, and the results are determined by the system;
- the repetitive use of common digital design drawing operations with points, lines, and curves, along with geometric transformations such as copy, rotate, scale, and mirror).

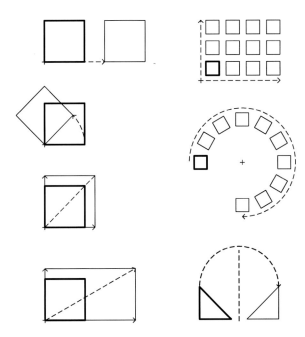

Figure 2.9 Matrix of geometric transformations for use in the following exercises. Left column, from top to bottom: copy, rotate, scale proportionally, scale non-proportionally. Right column, from top to bottom: rectangular array/duplicate/clone, radial array, mirror.

Outcomes

By the end of this exercise you will have created an algorithmic system capable of generating complex field compositions along with sample field composition drawings with varying tone, line weights, and (perhaps) color.

Recommended reading

Allen, Stan. "From Object to Field," in *Practice: Architecture, Technique and Representation*. Routledge, 2008, pp. 216–243.

Freeland, David. "Fielded Drawing," in Nathan Hume *et al.* (eds.), *Fresh Punches*. Creatspace Independent Publishing Platform, 2013, pp 225–228.

Kolarevic, Branko, and Kevin R. Klinger. *Manufacturing Material Effects: Rethinking Design and Making in Architecture*. Routledge, 2008.

Kwinter, Sanford. "La Citta Nuova: Modernity and Continuity," in *Zone 1–2*. Urzone, 1986.

Exercise 2A

Let's start by creating a simple three- or four-step algorithm. From here we can iterate – develop and execute a recipe – followed by adjusting the algorithm and re-executing.

Exercise procedure

Step 1: Draw a polyline with three or four line segments.

Step 2: Develop an algorithm with three or four rules or steps, using any of the operations shown in Figure 2.9.

Step 3: Run the algorithm ten times.

Step 4: The original algorithm might have generated some interesting results, or maybe not. This is a chance to adjust the parameters or operations. After tweaking, re-run the new algorithm from scratch 20 times.

Step 5: Run the algorithm to create three more graphic compositions from scratch. Feel free to continue to adjust the algorithms. Each time you should run through the algorithm procedures at least 30 times. Of these last two drawings, one should try to achieve compositional balance (and perhaps some symmetry), and the other drawing should be an unbalanced composition. You can strive for alternative or additional qualities to the drawings, but the key is experimenting to discover connections between changes in the parameters and the compositional qualities of the results. Figures 2.10–2.12 show student work examples for Exercise 2A.

Bonus: some design software allows you to record and run the steps of your algorithm automatically as a macro. Try creating a macro of your algorithm to automate the process.

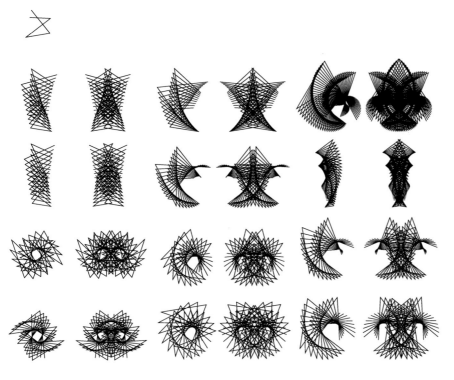

Figure 2.10 Algorithmic drawing example from Exercise 2A. The results have varying figural qualities, in spite of using the same simple polyline ingredient. Student: Andrew Martin; Faculty: Joshua Vermillion, University of Nevada Las Vegas.

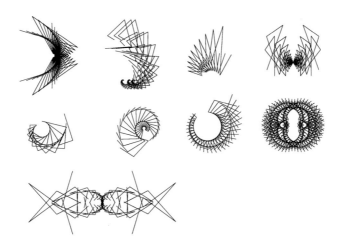

Figure 2.11 Algorithmic drawing examples with varying figural qualities. Top row: left: Christopher Marquez; right: Courtney Chin. Second and third rows: Jose Cuellar. Fourth and fifth rows: Roberto Piedra. Faculty: Joshua Vermillion, University of Nevada Las Vegas.

Figure 2.12a Further iterations of algorithmic drawing examples, trying to create results that are less figural.

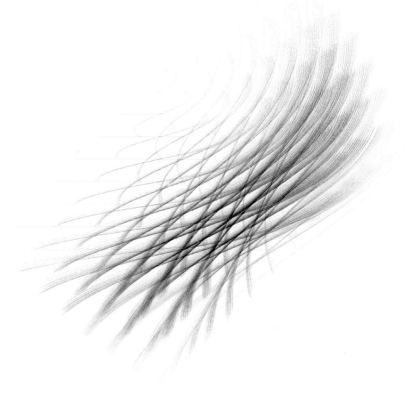

Figure 2.12b

Exercise 2B

Some of your results from Exercise 2A might have formed recognizable shapes or resembled objects, particularly if you used the mirror tool, which tends to produce symmetry. These figural results rarely read as field conditions. One way to break away from figural results is to introduce grids to an algorithm. The first part of this exercise (steps 1–5) proposes to re-execute your algorithm using a grid as an ordering device. The second part (steps 6–10) also uses a grid configuration, but reintroduces tweening or keyframing to create a field effect.

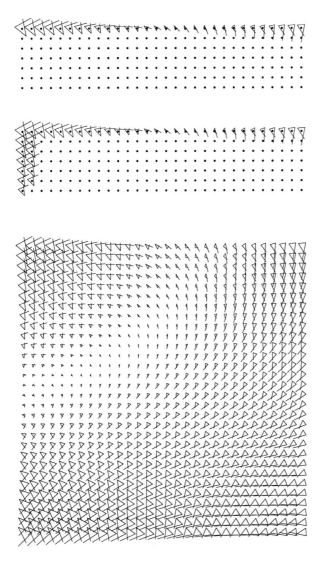

Figure 2.13 The sequence of procedures for steps 1–5.

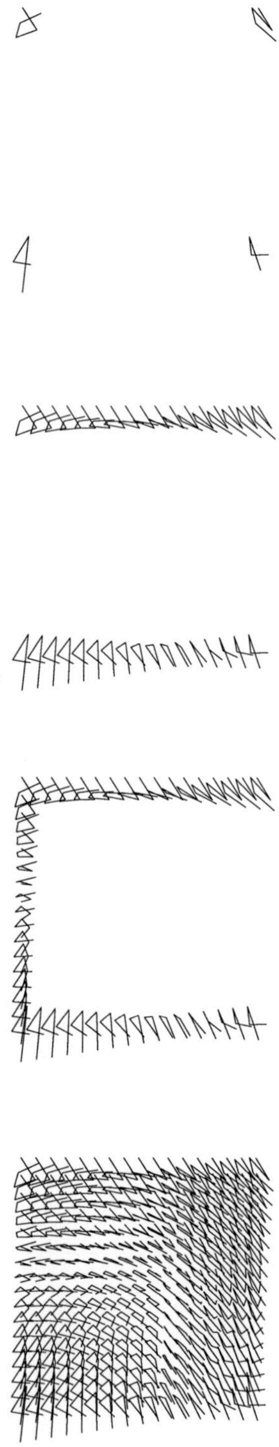

Exercise procedure

Step 1: Create a 10 × 10 point grid using the array tool. Refer to Figure 2.13 for a visual explanation of the following steps.

Step 2: Draw a polyline with three or four line segments.

Step 3: Develop an algorithm with three or four rules or steps (you can reuse a previous algorithm if desired).

Step 4: Run the algorithm iteratively across the top row of the grid, copying each new polyline from one point to the next.

Step 5: Run the algorithm iteratively down each row.

Now, lets do a similar exercise, but using tween or blend.

Step 6: Draw unique polylines or curves at each of the four corners of an implied grid. Refer to Figure 2.14 for a visual explanation of these steps.

Step 7: Tween in between the two top curves in order to create a top row of a field matrix.

Step 8: Tween in between the two bottom curves in order to create a bottom row of a field matrix.

Step 9: Tween vertically between each successive top curve and corresponding bottom curve in order to fill in the field matrix.

Step 10: Evaluate for field effect by using the criteria and questions in the exercise set introduction. In short, have the results produced an emergent visual effect? Are there enough parts and overlap of parts in the system to read as a field? Revise and re-execute the exercise as necessary. Figures 2.15 and 2.16 show student work examples for Exercise 2B.

Figure 2.14 The sequence of procedures for steps 6–10.

Figure 2.15 Initial student work from Exercise 2B. Left column (from top to bottom): Glenda Perez, Juan Carlos Castellanos, Sheryl Gordon, Patricia Gonsalves. Right column (from top to bottom): Arron Butler, Ling Lin, Shasta Percival, Roberto Piedra. Faculty: Joshua Vermillion, University of Nevada Las Vegas.

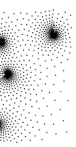
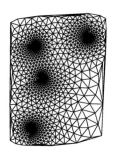
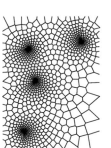
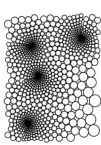

Figure 2.16 Alternative methods for creating field compositions include distorting or deforming point grids and the resulting overlaid geometries. Student authors: Brandan Siebrecht, Wayny Le, Eduardo Sanchez, Karla Arzaba, Phoebe Brown, Juan Castellanos, Curtis Wilfong, Jalania Wright. Faculty: Shai Yeshayahu and Phil Zawarus, Foundation Studio, School of Architecture, University of Nevada Las Vegas.

Exercise 2C

Thus far, the exercises in this chapter have been very prescribed, and as a result, the drawings have been fairly predictable. In this exercise you have much more latitude to revise, combine, and experiment with your recipes to create a complex field condition. Remember that repetition and a large number of parts are important keys to producing an emergent effect.

Exercise procedure

Step 1: Combine tweening and algorithmic procedures to create one drawing (as demonstrated in Figures 2.17–2.21). Based on critical in-class comments and feedback, continue to experiment with your best algorithmic recipe. The goal is to generate a complex field drawing.

Step 2: Make three copies of your final drawing and clean up in Illustrator. Below are some suggested Illustrator techniques for your drawings.

Drawing iteration 1: adjust line weights

Line weights don't have to be uniform (perhaps some lines are more or less thick). You should have complex line work (many, many curves/lines), so thinner line weights are probably best.

Drawing iteration 2: invert your drawing

Change the black line work to white, and the white background to black. Compare this drawing to the previous one. Evaluate the drawings for visual effect and clarity in communication.

Drawing iteration 3: adjust line color(s)

Select two or mores colors to apply to the line work in an ordered manner (not randomly). Of course, you should remember to always pick colors very carefully and make sure that they have a visual relationship.

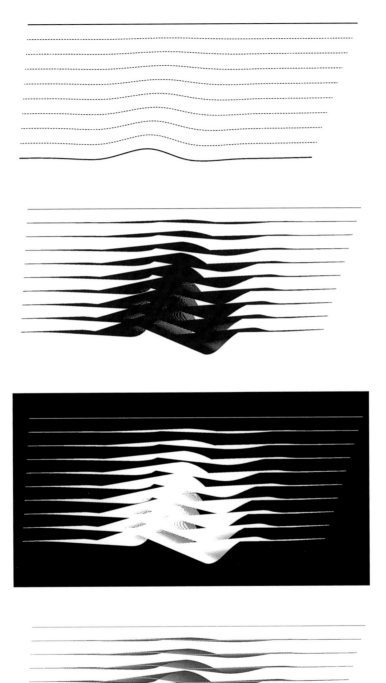

Figure 2.17 Example field compositions from Exercise 2C. Tweening operations have been added to an algorithmic recipe to generate more complex line work. Following the generation of the drawing, colors and line weights were adjusted for evaluation.

Figure 2.18 Example field compositions from Exercise 2C. Tweening operations have been added to an algorithmic recipe to generate more complex line work. Following the generation of the drawing, colors and line weights were adjusted for evaluation.

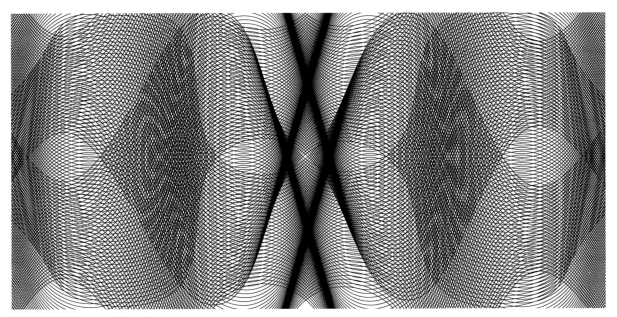

Figure 2.19 Example field composition using tweening and line weights from Exercise 2C. Student author: Xavier Zhagui, University of Nevada Las Vegas.

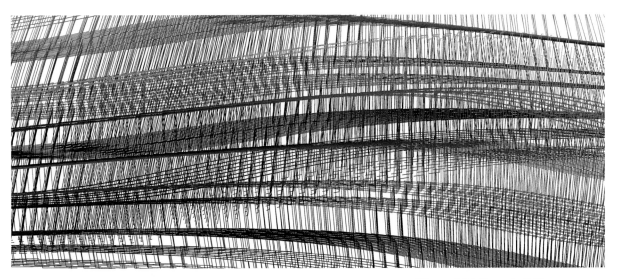

Figure 2.20 Example field compositions from Exercise 2C using tweening, and adjusting line weights and tone. Student author: Andres Diaz, University of Nevada Las Vegas.

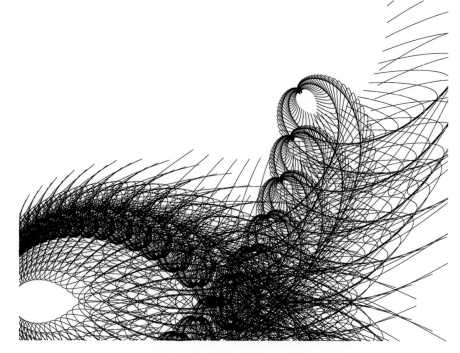

Figure 2.21a Example field compositions from Exercise 2C. Following the generation of the initial drawing, colors, line weights, and line types were adjusted for evaluation. Student author: Ludwing Vaca, University of Nevada Las Vegas.

Figure 2.21b

Figure 2.21c

Exercise set 3: bridging the gap

In this exercise set you are responsible for producing surfaces that bridge the distance between a primitive object and the boundary that surrounds it. This process will start with drawing lines and curves as the basis for surfacing based on several available surface population strategies, such as folding, packing, and bifurcating. Methods for creating surfaces often need curves and lines (and sometimes points) as ingredients. While not an exhaustive list, here are some common methods for surfacing that will be useful for this exercise (refer to Figure 2.22 for explanatory diagrams).

Figure 2.22 A diagram of some common methods for generating surfaces, for both this and later exercises.

Extrude

Ingredient: a profile curve or shape.

Parameters: an extrusion direction/axis and distance.

Extrusions start with a curve or shape that is swept along a straight path to create a surface.

Loft

Ingredients: two or more curves.

Lofting skins a surface between multiple curves, treating each curve as a sectional profile.

Sweep

Ingredients: a profile curve or shape, and a path curve (sometimes referred as a "rail").

Sweep is very similar to Extrude; however, the path of extrusion for a swept surface can be any curve (rather than limited to a straight direction).

Sweep with multiple paths

Ingredients: a profile curve or shape, and two or more path curves.

Some Sweep tools allow for multiple path curves for greater control or formal variability in the resulting surface.

Planar surfacing

Ingredients: these vary according to software, but often the ingredients needed are three or more points, a closed planar curve, or a set of curves. As the heading implies, all of these sets of ingredients need to share a common plane.

Non-planar surfacing from points or curves

Ingredients: much like their planar counterparts, these methods vary according to software and situation and use points and/or curves to define non-planar surface vertices or edges.

Objectives

This exercise is intended to introduce and develop understandings of:

- surfacing techniques from curve and point ingredients;
- the use of algorithms and drawings to generate three-dimensional constructs;
- the generation and visual communication of complex systems.

Outcomes

The deliverables generated in this exercise includes drawings, diagrams, and renderings of a proposed surface construct.

Recommended reading

Pottmann, Helmut, Andreas Asperl, Michael Hofer, and Axel Kilian. *Architectural Geometry*. Bentley Institute Press, 2007.

- Chapter 9: Traditional Surface Classes, pp. 285–330.
- Chapter 11: Freeform Surfaces, pp. 359–410.
- Chapter 12: Motions, Sweeping, and Shape Evolution, pp. 411–448.

Exercise 3A

These exercises start with an initial condition: a faceted, jewel-like object in the center of a larger rectangular boundary. In between these geometries, the space needs to be bridged, first by drawing (3A), and then by surfacing (3B). Figures 2.23–2.25 show student project examples for Exercises 3A and 3B.

Exercise procedure

Step 1: Begin experimenting with ways to bridge between the "jewel" and the boundary with lines and curves. As a provocation, the following strategies or qualities are suggested for iterative studies.

- Bifurcation: bifurcation is another way to speak of branching, forking, or splitting. As each curve splits into two, the resulting bridges grow exponentially.
- Folding: to fold, crease, break, or bend. One can start subdividing areas of the interstitial space into smaller shapes with each line or curve representing a crease edge.
- Packing: to pack, populate, or nest smaller components within the interstitial space between center and boundary. Again, one way to start is by subdividing areas into smaller shapes and packing patterns.

Step 2: Try all three strategies and compare your results before picking your favorite scheme to develop further.

Step 3: Try to develop an algorithm with steps and rules to facilitate the process and create some step-by-step diagrams of the process to demonstrate your decision-making logics.

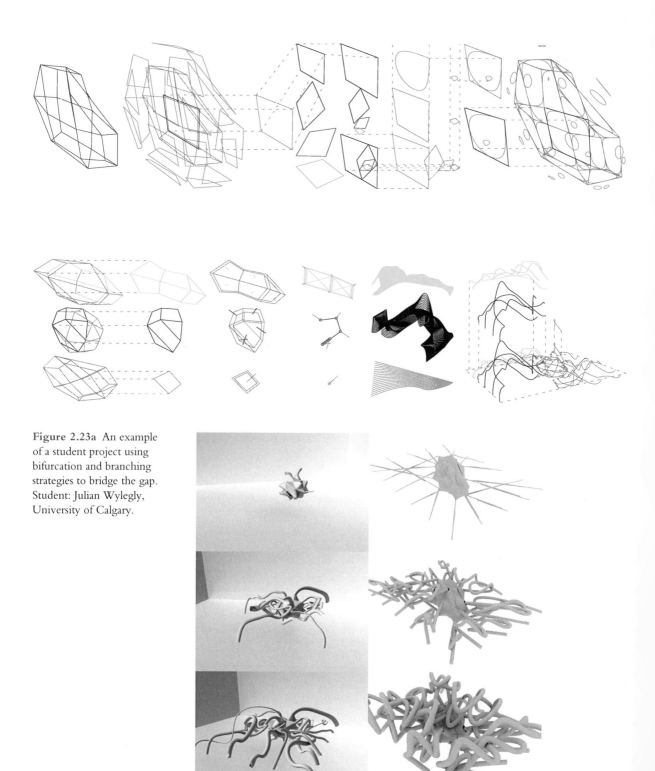

Figure 2.23a An example of a student project using bifurcation and branching strategies to bridge the gap. Student: Julian Wylegly, University of Calgary.

Figure 2.23b

Exercise 3B

This exercise will now move beyond lines and curves to utilize surface geometries to bridge between center and boundary.

Exercise procedure

Step 1: Experimenting with ways to bridge between the "jewel" and the boundary with surfaces. You can use the curves that were previously drawn (in Exercise 3A), or draw new lines and curves as scaffolds for surfacing. As in the previous exercise, try to use the following strategies for bridging with surfaces (examples of all three strategies are demonstrated in the student projects shown in Figures 2.23–2.25).

- Bifurcation
- Folding
- Packing

Step 2: Try all three strategies and compare your results before picking your favorite scheme to develop further. Do not be afraid to take some steps backward and revise (even 3A linework) in order to create multiple, iterative studies.

Step 3: Again, try to develop an algorithm with steps and rules to facilitate the process and create some step-by-step diagrams of the process to demonstrate your decision-making logics.

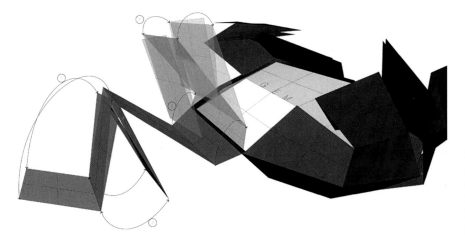

Figure 2.24a An example of a student project using folding and creasing strategies to bridge the gap. Student: Khalid Omokanye, University of Calgary.

53

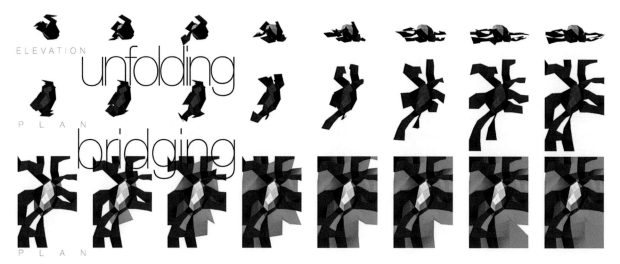

Figure 2.24b

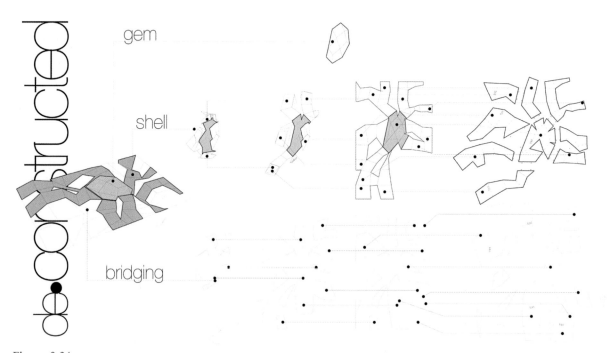

Figure 2.24c

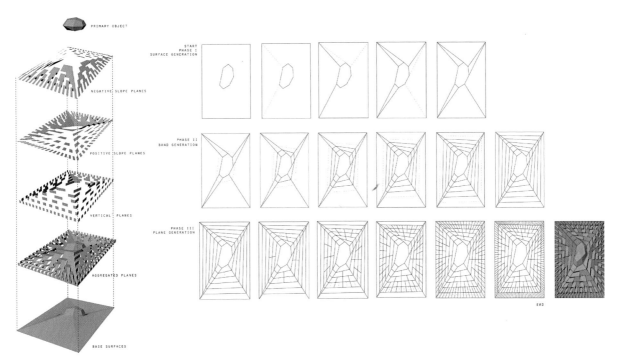

Figure 2.25a An example of a student project using packing and population strategies to bridge the gap. Student: Jodi James, University of Calgary.

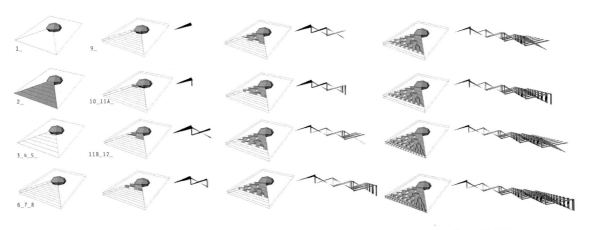

Figure 2.25b

Exercise 3C

This final exercise asks you to examine and further describe the system that you created in Exercises 3A and 3B with diagrams and renderings. Figure 2.26 shows an example of some 3C deliverables.

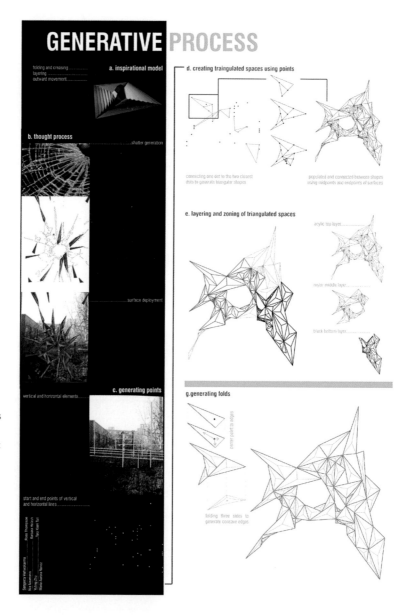

Figure 2.26a Sample diagrams and renderings for 3C. The drawings show how the project was algorithmically generated and how it might occupy space within a hypothetical site along a window edge. Students: Sangeeta Vishwakarma, Nia Neumann, Yuting Zhu, Maria Aurora Nunez, Ross Thompson, Barbara Holash, Tara Kiani Tari, University of Calgary.

Exercise procedure

Step 1: Revise and curate the diagrams produced in 3A and 3B showing the logic behind your algorithms. Also try to visually tell the story of your process along with the various trial-and-error results.

Step 2: Select a hypothetical site and produce at least one rendering showing the final construct as a full-scale spatial installation.

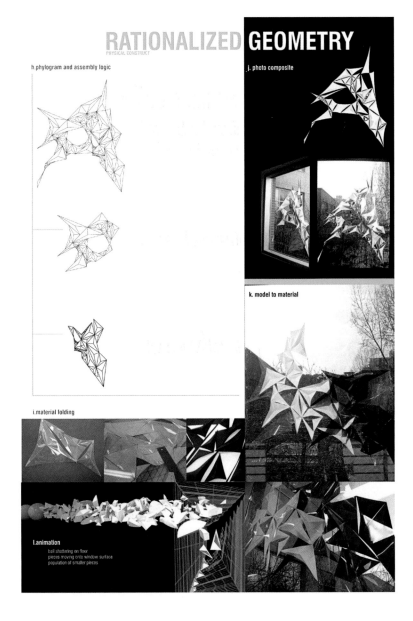

Figure 2.26b

Conclusion

This chapter provided an introduction to key concepts for computational design, such as complexity, repetition, and field conditions. Likewise, it introduced key geometric ingredients for digital design – points, lines, curves, and surfaces. Throughout the rest of the book we will build on these conceptual and geometric frameworks and deploy them repeatedly to perform more exercises. The next chapter provides a deeper investigation into surfaces and volumes, as well as repetition, recursion, and variation.

Notes

1 Herbert Simon, "The Architecture of Complexity," in *Proceedings of the American Philosophical Society*, 106, no. 6 (1962), 468.
2 Stan Allen, "From Object to Field," in *Practice: Architecture, Technique and Representation* (New York: Routledge, 2008), 217.

DISTRIBUTED ~~SENSATIONS~~

Pedagogical experimentation with anonymity in architecture

Joshua Taron

The empty space, this nothing of the jug, is what the jug is as a holding vessel…. Sides and bottom, of which the jug consists and by which it stands, are not really what does the holding. But if the holding is done by the jug's void, then the potter who forms sides and bottom on his wheel does not strictly speaking, make the jug. He only shapes the clay. No – he shapes the void. For it, in it and out of it, he forms the clay into the form. From start to finish the potter takes hold of the impalpable void and brings it forth as the container in the shape of a containing vessel.

M. Heidegger, "The Thing"[1]

Separating the architect from architecture

Let me begin by offering up a question: Can architecture be thought without the architect? At first this may sound absurd or even offensive, particularly when posed to a body of first-year architecture students (as the case may be). But is the value of a Frank Gehry, Zaha Hadid, or Rem Koolhaas project only that they were the architects of those projects? Or do the projects do something else, something more, something independent and autonomous from their authors that goes beyond any intention, aspiration, or origin?

I would also cite a (paraphrased) question raised by Graham Harmon in his 2011 lecture, *Zero Form – Zero Function*, at the University of Innsbruck,[2] where he asks: Why is it that given the infinite number of things and variables at play in any act of architecture that the human (whether architect or user) constitutes a minimum of 50 percent of the equation? His observation is revealing in that it's not a critique of having included the figure of the human in the problem, but rather the disproportional emphasis on human experience as the justification for, or rationalization of, a given design. In the context of ecological sensibilities and the basic acknowledgment of complexity, this rhetorical point seems more than reasonable. And yet there remains a deficiency of investigations in this direction in the context of mainstream architectural education (there are, of course, notable exceptions).[3]

So much of architectural culture and pedagogy is built upon an association between the architect and his/her work: firms carrying the name(s) of its principals; buildings referred to by their author as opposed to what they are or what they do; students told that their irreducible individualism is the best resource for finding the necessary and difficult solutions for the future ... as if it were just that easy. It's a cheap and effective way to motivate individuals, playing on hubris while invariably proliferating deeply engendered and often unconscious biases in the process.

Hundreds of years of architectural pedagogy has institutionally oriented architecture toward the singular figure of the liberal human subject as author or user, even despite its behavioral tendencies toward the contrary. For the Beaux Arts it was an emphasis on classical principles of order and techniques of representation modeled from the human body. For the Bauhaus it was a matter of emphasizing craft and making in order to master the production of a total work of art in the context of industrial advancement in the name of human progress. But the second half of the twentieth century created the beginnings of a schism between cultural and formal systems.[4] Late twentieth-century architectural education adopted formal experimentation with computational tools as the medium to simulate architectural conflict, once again resuscitating the great debate over architectural and political autonomy. It is precisely here, at a critique of autonomy, that we might again reformulate this pedagogical question with a continuation of computational architecture having produced the momentum to achieve an escape velocity from a perpetually anthropocentric orbit.

It is certainly the case that in the first two of these aforementioned models (Beaux Arts and Bauhaus), the subject to be trained is the architect, relying on the irreducible autonomy of the individual as the inexhaustible resource of creativity and vision that masters processes beneath their control. However, this was called into question (knowingly or not) through the modern/postmodern debate and becomes an even more complicated proposition within digital discourse where the autonomy of the individual architect is sublimated into an indeterminate set of cascading infrastructural processes – material, cultural, and computational, etc. While indeterminacy and emergence have come into the mainstream of architectural discourse, it has done so with a great deal of friction with modern conventions, such as certainty, intention, authority, authorship, and autonomy – all of which are projected upon the figure of the architect. Central to these problems has been a transition from autonomy and identity toward multiplicities and anonymity. This shift has paralleled an intensification of complexity and indeterminacy that has rendered the architect and society incapable of effectiveness without technological prosthesis. But the necessary prosthetics only further compromise the autonomy of the individual once again.

Alas, the mainstream rhetoric of architectural discourse remains insistent on the experiential, the phenomenological and the expression of anthropocentrism in one form or another. But I argue that it's this narcissism that is preventing a genuinely speculative architecture to develop – an architecture independent of many of the vices and deficiencies that we are simply incapable of escaping ourselves – the possibility of an architecture that is excepted from us, what Reza Negarestani might refer to as *inhuman*.[5] It is here that we might reconsider anonymity in a fundamental light – not just as something to be conquered and exhausted, but rather as something to be produced, sustained, and exploited for its effects precisely at the liminal edge or beyond the sensory boundaries of architectural bodies (including our own). In other words, anonymity is a means of getting ourselves out of the way when designing architecture. What is crucial to understand about an anonymous architecture is that it is not an alternative to historical modes of architectural practice and thought. Rather, it runs in parallel whereby any individual act of architecture produces an explicit form of anonymity – a form of self-subtraction manifesting as void.

But what things make deliberate use of anonymity already? And what might architecture glean from them? Nick Srnicek argues[6] that infrastructure operates precisely in this way, relying on its lack of recognition in order to exert intense degrees of force across a given territory, citing the necessity of material points of leverage when constructing the possibility of any given mode of politics. Thus anonymity is inherently political, not so much in the sense of party politics, but rather in a biopolitical sense, the infrastructure of the material and informational body that forms the polis, or rather *The Architecture of the City*.[7]

While part of this infrastructure is hidden amidst an *anesthetic* desensitization to images,[8] there are also *anesthetic* modes of infrastructural architecture that exist beyond our sensory limits. This inversion at once enables and compromises the possibility of anonymity, revealing it as a contingent effect rather than an absolute property.[9] Using Quentin Meillassoux's essay, *After Finitude*,[10] as a point of departure, I have run a graduate course titled Architecture + Anonymity for the past four years that explores a lineage of philosophical and architectural thought problematizing the material production of otherwise unknowable architectures in the context of speculative design. What has emerged is a series of investigations into the complicit relationship[11] between architecture and anonymity – using computational and material simulations to generate models of possible futures.

Starting beyond the limits of reason and sensation

What *After Finitude* provides is a proof of the possibility of detachment between thought and being – paralleling the original question separating architecture from the figure of the architect. While this may seem innocuous and even banal, Meillassoux's anhypothetical proof establishes an alternative to phenomenological and correlational models that have been incapable of mitigating the over-biased figure of the human in architectural projections. Meillassoux critiques both reason and sensation as being bound in correlationist construction. Instead, he produces a figure for absolute contingency through both the absence of human reason and human sensory perception. It is in this void that anonymity operates and it is here where a speculative architecture is in turn employed, opening up the discipline to a much needed albeit no less constrained domain than it otherwise presently enjoys.

The Architecture + Anonymity course produced a series of experimental projects that engaged a very different form of anonymity than the linear and exhaustible one subscribed to by the ancient Greeks. Rather than relying on human understanding and sensation, these projects either excise or flatten the human within the architectural project both in advance of and through its production. In simple terms, they avoid relationism by eliminating or balancing out the human constant in the relational equation – exploiting what Manuel Delanda calls "mind independent processes."[12] He states: "Any materialist philosophy must take as its point of departure the existence of a material world that is independent of our minds. But then it confronts the problem of the origin of the enduring identity of the inhabitants of that world: if the mind is not what gives identity to mountains and rivers, plants and animals, then what does?" While Delanda stresses the importance of assigning identity, we might invert his reading and accept identity as something given. By extension, a speculative approach that does away with the givenness of things also leaves identity behind and in its place remains a void of anonymity.

The question for the course's term projects lies in the possibility of exploiting radical contingency amidst this void of a flattened or universal relativism.[13] This carries with it the implication of excising of the human, best expressed in what Levi Bryant describes as the "ontic principle."[14] Beginning with the premise that to be is to make or produce difference, the ontic principle asks the question: How could difference be difference if it did not make a difference? In order to avoid the relational, Bryant notes that not all differences are important *to us*, but rather that simply because something does not make a difference *for us* does not mean that something does not or could not exist. This is effectively the challenge born of a historically anthropocentric model of architecture: can architecture address or speculate upon things that do not make a difference *for us* (i.e., absent of reason *and* sensation in its most radical form) – and if so, exactly how?

Project 1: Architecturally Augmented Curiosity

One of the paradoxes of an architecture absent the architect is that it often requires deliberate and intentional work by the architect to remove their presence from the work itself. This is perhaps most evident in the work of Hernan Diaz Alonso, whose aesthetic pursuit of the horrific produces the sensational effect of detachment of the work from its process of being made and thus from any particular origin or authorship.[15] The virtuosity necessary to achieve these effects is certainly difficult to master, but also demands a specific line of disciplinary positioning in order to properly situate the work. Emerging from the emancipatory autonomous lineage of Peter Eisenman[16] and bridging this connection to the conceptual immediacy developed in Graham Harmon's Object Oriented Ontology,[17] Ryan Cook argues in his project that "architecturally augmented curiosity (AAC) is not about how an architectural work came to be, but rather about interacting with it as a thing that exists. Not to be treated as a prototype or a miniature to be placed in a gallery, AAC is a fully scaled and absolute thing that can be architecturally queried, dissected and described through diagrams, sections, plans, elevation, perspectives, etc." Entirely removed from and unconcerned with the opinions of others, the architectural object operates relying on the incapability of any other object to totally engage, sense, or understand it when cultural conditions of form and function are levied against it. What's left is something that is undeniably seductive precisely because it sustains a condition of being withdrawn – and generates the sensation of being as such. It's not that the project is invisible – it's that it remains weird and unknown. The exercise produces a critical inversion of architectural representation, not as a means of expression or understanding but as a demonstration of resistance to any particular approach that one might take toward it.[18]

Figure 3.1 Project by Ryan Cook.

Figure 3.2 Project by Ryan Cook.

Figure 3.3 Project by Ryan Cook.

Figure 3.4 Project by Ryan Cook.

Project 2: Aging Buildings

Mehdi Einifar exploits the insistence on anatomical parallels between architectural and human bodies by subjecting building façades to facial aging software. He notes that

> comparing the face of a building to the human face has been a trend throughout the history of architecture. While both humans and architectures face the process of aging, there are some similarities and differences in the way they age. By considering the human face and a building's façade for our intervention, we can narrow down the scale of the project. Effects of aging on the human face are caused by loss of skin elasticity, loss of skin collagen, loss of volume, and gravity while effects of aging on the building's façade are due to weathering and natural causes including gravity, wind, rain etc.

Einifar goes on to recursively subject five different building façades to the processes of *Agingbooth*, an app that instantly ages facial photos. Einifar describes this process as follows:

> The aging process of the software is based on identifying the positions of different facial elements. In the case of the *Agingbooth* software the preset for this detection is automated. If the software fails to identify the positions of different elements, it gives the user the option to do the detection process manually. In some cases the building façade and a human face will be blurred to enable testing the automated system as well as the manual mode…. Continuing the re-aging process repeats the effects on the photo. An interesting and unpredicted outcome is that by repeating the process several times, each image collapses at a materially specific moment.

After a series of initial investigations, Einifar omits any superimposition of human facial imagery from the simulations and reduces the types to classical, modern, and parametric while noting the number of years they were able to advance before achieving image collapse. The results yield an interesting behavior: that classical and modern buildings are younger and capable of enduring much longer periods of simulated aging while parametric buildings, often subjected to time-based simulations in advance of their being realized, are much less resistant to the effects of time, often failing after only one or two 35-year simulated periods. What Einifar's experiment reveals is

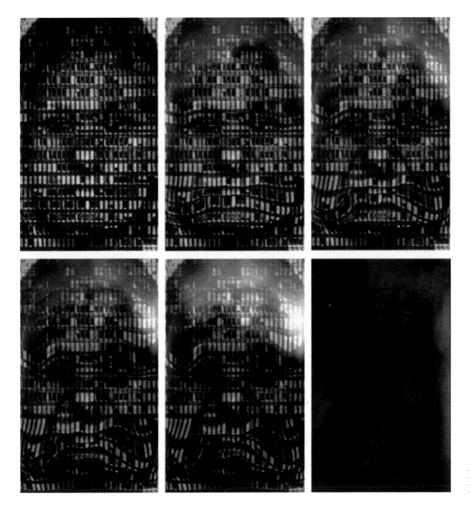

Figure 3.5 Project by Mehdi Einifar.

not an artificial simulation of a building as it ages over time, but rather a test that determines how much time has already been integrated into the form of a building. While modern and classical architectures aim at eluding time through timelessness, parametric architecture alternatively aims at literally incorporating time into its body rather than attempting to dodge it.

Project 3: Form Flux

Amber Lafontaine's *Form Flux* begins with the premise that no one can directly experience anything beyond his or her immediate sensory perception. With that in mind, Lafontaine sought out to indirectly manipulate ferrofluid as a medium through which a multitude of forces might converge.

Figure 3.6 Project by Mehdi Einifar.

Referencing the work of Perry Hall, *Form Flux* used ferrofluid to mediate the audio exchange between two individuals. The magnetic fields produced through the exchange are expressed through variations in the fluid itself, captured by a camera in real time and projected onto the wall of the space where the conversation is taking place. This creates an oversaturated environment where the information otherwise lost in the verbal exchange recursively augments the exchange itself. Audio waves becoming electromagnetic waves becoming light waves and back again. While Lafontaine's project focused primarily on the development of the infrastructure necessary for the manipulation of the ferrofluid itself, the project's larger value comes in the form of the totality of the spatial system it produces, much the same way a Jeff Koons sculpture captures the world inside of the work itself by augmenting its reflection. Only tangentially connected with the sensory experience of the space itself, each material aspect of the system (ferrofluid, speaker magnets, computational algorithms, verbal conversation, human bodies, visual projections, etc.) functions as a part greater than the whole of the design.

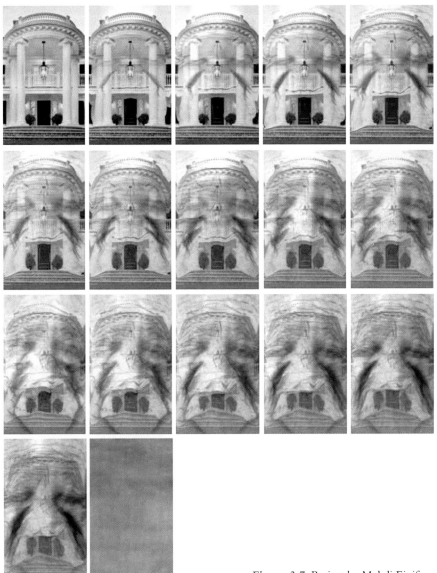

Figure 3.7 Project by Mehdi Einifar.

On the void in/of architecture

While we might be able to employ projects of anonymity to critique rather obvious limitations of givenness, authorship, and identity, the implications of work along these lines may have its greatest significance through a return to investigations that produce voids rather than objects. Denise Birkhofer's reading of Eva Hesse's work may best summarize such an endeavor. She writes:

71

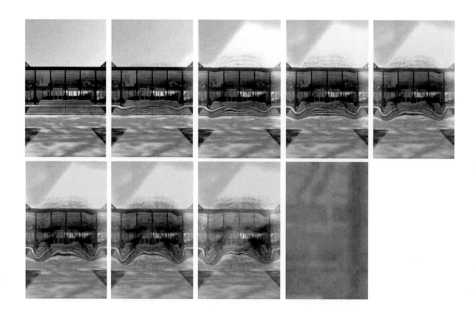

Figure 3.8 Project by Mehdi Einifar.

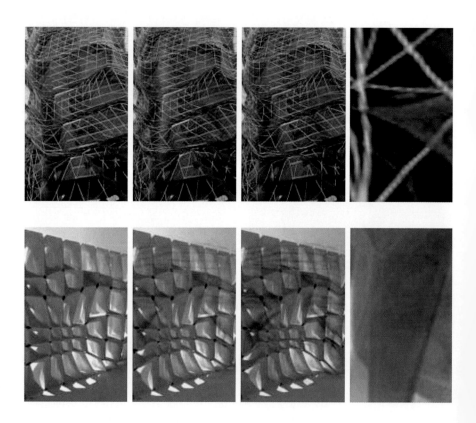

Figure 3.9 Project by Mehdi Einifar.

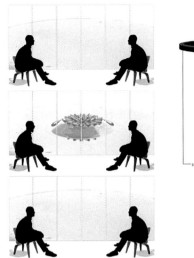

Figure 3.10 Project by Amber Lafontaine.

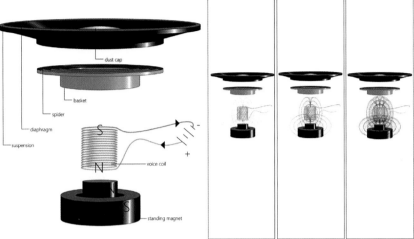

Figure 3.11 Project by Amber Lafontaine.

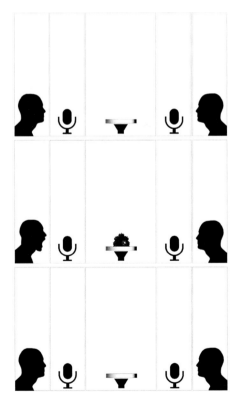

Figure 3.12 Project by Amber Lafontaine.

Figure 3.13 Project by Amber Lafontaine.

Figure 3.14 Project by Amber Lafontaine.

Even more resonant in Hesse's works than literal emptiness is the concept of nothingness subsumed under the void: nothing incarcerated into nothing. Hesse's works are reminiscent of tenuous bodilyness. The body made strange and deterritorialized into a big nothing – it is negated, rendered void – making body void once again.[19]

Figure 3.15 Project by Amber Lafontaine.

If architecture is to address a world bombarded by tactics of over- and under-mining,[20] it must become self-aware of its role in producing the anonymous void-objects that form it. In other words, architecture might benefit from investing in mastering the infrastructural production of voids – an absolute distribution of ~~sensations~~.

Notes

1 The void formed by Heidegger's jug is indicative of an anonymous space addressed in this text. Martin Heidegger, "The Thing," in Albert Hofstader (ed.), *Poetry, Language, Thought* (New York: Harper & Row, 1971).

2 The Harmon lecture can be found at: https://vimeo.com/85437398.

3 Instances of this can be found at the Laboratory for Integrative Design (LID), RPI's GeoFutures program, UCSD's Center for Design and Geopolitics (D:GP), Ed Keller's Post-Planetary Design seminar, SCI-Arc's SCI-FI program, etc.

4 K. Michael Hays, "Critical Architecture: Between Culture and Form," *Perspecta*, 21 (1984): 15–29.

5 Reza Negarestani, "Labor of the Inhuman (Parts 1 & 2)," *e-flux Journal*, 52 (2014).

6 Nick Srnicek, *The Matter of Struggle in Urban Space*, 2014: https://vimeo.com/117434029.

7 Aldo Rossi, *The Architecture of the City* (Cambridge, MA: MIT Press, 1982).

8 Neil Leach, *The Anaesthetics of Architecture* (Cambridge, MA: MIT Press, 1999).

9 Trevor Paglen, *Torture Taxi: On the Trail of the CIA's Rendition Flights* (Hoboken, NJ: Melville House, 2006).

10 Quentin Meillassoux, *After Finitude* (London: Continuum, 2009).

11 Reza Negarestani, "Contingency and Complicity," in Robin Mackay (ed.), *The Medium of Contingency* (New York: RAM Publications, 2011).

12 Manuel Delanda, *Intensive Science and Virtual Philosophy* (New York: Continuum, 2002).

13 An equally speculative approach is also possible by understanding the verticality of platforms amidst a flattened milieu. This is explored in depth in Benjamin Bratton's forthcoming book *The Stack: On Software and Sovereignty* (2015).

14 Levi R. Bryant, "The Ontic Principle," in L.R. Bryant, Nick Srnicek, and Graham Harman (eds), *The Speculative Turn: Continental Materialism and Realism* (Melbourne: re.press, 2011).

15 Archinect Interview, Amelia Taylor-Hochberg, "The Deans List: Hernan Diaz Alonso of SCI-Arc", 2014. A perhaps lesser known expression of Diaz Alonso's position can be found in Icon's Manifesto #19: Notes on Mutation and the Pursuit of Horror. A link to Manifest #19 can be found at: www.iconeye.com/404/item/3014-manifesto

16 Eisenman's list of seminal publications is extensive. A short list on this subject might include "Postfunctionalism" (1976), "The End of the Classical: The End of the Beginning, the End of the End" (1984), and "The Formal Basis of Modern Architecture" (1963).

17 Graham Harmon's Object Oriented Ontology (OOO) is rooted in his dissertation, "Tool Being" (1999), and has since been developed on a number of fronts. Perhaps the most directly applicable texts as they relate to architecture can be found in *Log 33* (Winter 2015), which includes articles written by Mark Foster Gage, Todd Gannon, Graham Harmon, David Ruy and Tom Wiscombe, and Sanford Kwinter (among many others).

18 This is also particularly evident in the work of Andrew Atwood and First Office (firstoff.net), who was cited as influencing Cook's term project.

19 Denise Birkhofer, "Eva Hesse and Mira Schendel: Voiding the Body – Embodying the Void," *Woman's Art Journal*, 31 (2010): 3–11.

20 The terms overmining and undermining are employed by Graham Harmon to describe the ways in which the inaccessibility of objects are dealt with. For an additional perspective on Harmon's terms, one might refer to Levi Bryant's blog, *Larval Subjects*, on which he posted an article in 2011 titled, "The World is Enough: On Overmining and Undermining."

EXERCISES FOR VOLUMES AND AGGREGATE ASSEMBLIES

Jason S. Johnson and Joshua Vermillion

Figure 4.1 Catch & Release Part 1. Sequential modifications based on rotation were used to produce a series of sculptural pieces that were evaluated for structural performance and scaled up to form a pavilion. Minus Architecture Studio.

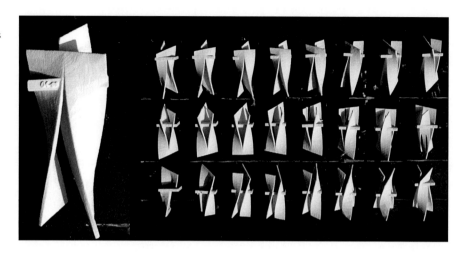

Introduction: aggregating form

The previous exercises focused on producing emergent geometries through a series of bottom-up processes. Using the basic building blocks of points and lines, you developed a series of geometries through the implementation of highly structured operational sequences. At least initially, these processes did not target any specific output, but rather focused on understanding the impact of each decision on the final set of outputs.

In other words, at the beginning of the process it is unlikely one could have predicted the results. Conversely, someone examining the final results would not likely guess the starting ingredients or the recipe that was deployed. The steps were simple, but when repeatedly applied to a number of geometric components, they produced complexity. This repetitive interaction between processes and geometries produces a vehicle for embedding complexity and variation into an assemblage.

In this chapter, the exercises again focus on generating a complex system from smaller parts through a bottom-up design process. Parts and steps, then repeat. Repetition, in fact, is a key ingredient for converting simple parts into a system with non-simple relationships. One might typically attempt to design forms that meet certain aesthetic or functional requirements based on preconceptions of what those geometries should do or what they might look like. In these exercises we will try to reject preconceptions in order to focus on formal exploration through an iterative process. The focus will be on designing and iterating the process.

Working in this way allows for a shift away from linear problem-solving toward innovation. Michael Speaks describes innovation as a more productive approach to design, as it demands adaptability to a changing set of parameters in order to understand new possibilities within the design environment.[1] Innovation is not a static process of resolving known problems, but rather an entrepreneurial approach that asks new questions of emerging processes, materials, and formal outputs.

On one hand, you have to critically examine the products that a generative algorithm creates and weigh them against your design criteria. But oftentimes, generative design is non-deterministic – not to say that it isn't goal-driven, but rather that it can provide fit results that aren't intuitive or predictable, as discussed by John Frazer and later Manuel Delanda in the recommended reading section.[2] The design process is full of many twists, turns, and directions, which can be dramatically amplified by generative techniques. Along with a critical eye, you must also be prepared to opportunistically embrace happy accidents – design results that lead you in new directions or that suggest counter-intuitive solutions.

The exercises that follow will ask you to develop an iterative process that produces a series of formal outputs. Of these outputs you might ask the question: What is this and what is it good for? Just as importantly, you will be asked to understand the process of creating these design outputs in such a way that you could ask and answer the question: What can be intensified in order to improve the result?

Recommended reading

Delanda, Manuel. "Deleuze and the Use of the Genetic Algorithm in Architecture," in *Contemporary Techniques in Architecture*, ed. Ali Rahim. Wiley, 2012, 9–12.

Frazer, John. *An Evolutionary Architecture*. Architectural Association, 1995.

Speaks, Michael. "Intelligence After Theory," in *Perspecta 38: Architecture After All*. MIT Press, 2006.

Exercise set 4: flat to fat

In these exercises you are asked to generate form by performing transformations on raster images and vector graphics. While the starting point might sound arbitrary, this will focus your attention away from form-making and, instead, focus on procedure-making for form discovery.

Objectives

- Practice image manipulation skills such as layering, adjusting color settings, and image transformations.
- Deploying basic compositional principles (symmetry, asymmetry, figure/ground, balance, visual hierarchy, color, contrast, solid/void).
- Develop and refine generative design processes, while discovering and practicing techniques.
- Understand relationships between two-dimensional and three-dimensional geometries.
- Deploy variation and iteration as a strategy for innovation.

Outcomes

- Image and form sequences.
- A repertoire of form-making strategies.
- Sequence visualizations.
- Process-embedded diagrams.

Recommended reading

Gage, Mark Foster. "Project Mayhem: Architecture in the Age of Dissensus," *Fulcrum: The AA's Weekly Free Sheet*, 18 (2011).
Goulthorpe, Mark/dECOi. "Precise Indeterminacy," *Praxis: Journal of Writing + Building*, 6 (2004), pp. 28–45.
PALLALINK. www.pallalink.net (accessed July 20, 2015).

Figure 4.2 Image Manipulation Sequence. This project captures a revolve, scale, and transparency loop that transforms a simple image into a complex mesh of overlapping lines and tones. Student: Tafadzwa Bwititi, Ball State University.

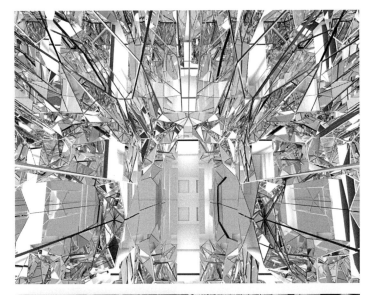

Figure 4.3a Nicola Formichetti Pop-Up Store. A physical environment based largely on faceted geometry and mirroring. Mark Foster Gage.

Figure 4.3b

Exercise 4A: image manipulation sequence

Distortion is the alteration of a predetermined order or system. In this exercise you will create volumetric objects and spaces from photography by distorting, recombining, and reinterpreting these graphics into line, curve, and surface. Using the tool palettes available to you in an image-editing software like Photoshop, you should create variations of an image of your choosing. You should select an image that has compositional qualities that you can enhance through distortion operations to eventually create spatial or volumetric constructs. Create multiple versions of the image by deploying manipulation tools that exploit the geometrical possibilities of each set of processes, such as the example shown in Figure 4.4. It may be helpful to generate a series of sketches that document your thinking about the process you have chosen and attempt to anticipate what the next steps might be.

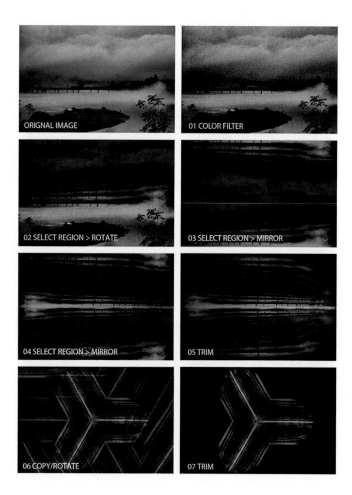

Figure 4.4 Image manipulation sequence. Annotated sequence of image manipulations that transform an implied line within the image into a "folded" assemblage. Student: Bahar Khonsari, University of Calgary.

Exercise procedure

Step 1: Select an image. The image can be relatively simple. Contrast is helpful as are geometric elements like lines, distinct color/tonal regions, or clear geometries.

Step 2: Develop distortion/manipulation strategies. This strategy should deploy simple techniques available to you in the software (see list below for examples). Stay away from overly complex filters or techniques that are not easily understood or replicable in subsequent steps. Potential manipulation techniques to experiment with include: cut, crop, copy/paste, mirror, skew, rotate, warp, and/or blur (directional or motion).

Step 3: Codify the process. Pseudo-code is a way of outlining a set of procedures in shorthand without the need to understand coding languages. A code for one such set of procedures or processes might be written as:

Select region > Crop > Mirror > Copy > Rotate > Mirror > Skew
> Mirror > Crop

Figure 4.5 Image manipulation sequence. Original image manipulated using a technique of mirroring the image. PALLALINK.

Step 4: Apply your process to the image by using image-editing software. The software need only be as complex as the tools you wish to use. Most image-editing software packages include tools for cropping, copying, pasting, and selecting regions, as well as tools for desaturation of color images. As you begin the process you should use the "save as" command at many points along the way in order to capture each step in the process. The "undo" and "redo" commands are your friend; use them often as you attempt to evaluate whether the process is moving in the right direction.

Step 5: Evaluate your results. Some questions to ask:

- Are there visible patterns or forms emerging from the project?
- Would your process benefit from focusing on more specific areas or regions of the image?
- Does your process need more steps?
- Do any of the images stand alone as compositions?
- Are you able to duplicate your results on a new image?
- What effects have emerged from the process? Can these be intensified?
- Are the results beginning to take on spatial qualities that differ from the original?
- Can the results be read as objects? Environments?

Pay attention to variations in scale, proportion, balance, and movement. Evaluate your images as you would any composition or designed artifact. If the images are not as successful as you had hoped, adjust your process and try again. For example, the mirror plane may need to change or the rotation angle may be too large or too small. The success of the image will depend on paying attention to the crafting and refining of the process.

Step 6: Revisit your process in response to your evaluation. As you change the recipe, even slightly, you are sure to see changes that generate many options, some similar, some dramatically different. Of key importance is the ability to understand any particular generative process, and how it boils down to sequence and parameters that can be altered to generate or amplify particular results or effects.

Step 7: Compose your results. There are many ways to compile the results of your process. You might choose to use a matrix or grid (Figure 4.6) of images to show the process or develop a series of diagrams that track the

Figure 4.6 Image manipulation matrix. This matrix of images shows three sequences that deploy shared techniques but result in a number of variations. Student: Michael McGie, University of Calgary.

process of specific actions and divergences or failures in the multiple attempts. Presenting your material from this exercise should be focused on understanding and communicating your process as well as the resulting images from those processes.

Bonus techniques: most image manipulation software allows for automating processes. These tools are often called "macros" or "actions," depending on the software package, but the concept is the same. This is one of the more helpful utilities of computation when applied to generative design – by automating the process you allow for massive amounts of iteration in a short period of time and produce a large set of artifacts (in this case images) that can be evaluated. Be sure to include actions in the process that export the image after each command.

Figure 4.7 Tracing difference. A volumetric ground condition is created by manipulating the heights of lines in a field, followed by a series of lofting procedures to produce a range of potential outcomes. Student: Bahar Khonsari, University of Calgary.

Exercise 4B: rasters, vectors, and form

This exercise explores the making of volumetric objects based on simple rules. As a starting point you will be using images from the prior assignment. Building on the previous project is beneficial for a number of reasons. One reason for using these images is that they enable you to engage two-dimensional and three-dimensional tools to translate a raster image into a geometric volume. This ability to develop a concept through multiple design tools is critical to developing a process that is not bound by a particular piece of software or set of techniques, but is instead capable of taking advantage of the opportunities afforded by each new set of tools you encounter.

Second, the use of this image enables you to carry forward some of the design strategies that were used in making these images. As an example, images that used mirroring techniques bring to this exercise a symmetrical organization. Symmetry or mirroring techniques are commonly used in the transformation of two-dimensional and three-dimensional spaces. This is an opportunity to practice common geometric transformations in three-dimensional space and develop a repertoire of surfacing techniques to generate volumetric constructs. By the end of this section of exercises you will have developed a catalog of versions of the same project, each influenced by the choices made in the previous iterations of the project. This recording of bias in the flow of the project will help you as a beginning design student to record and evaluate your design assumptions.

Exercise procedure

Step 1: Select an image from Exercise 4A. When selecting the image include the following fitness criteria:

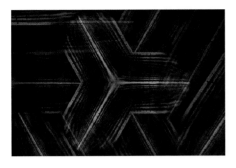

SELECT IMAGE

ISOLATE REGION > OVERLAY LINES

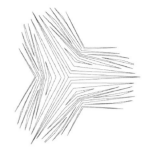

EXTRACT VECTOR INFORMATION

Figure 4.8 Extracting/ overlaying vector information. Student: Bahar Khonsari, University of Calgary.

- Implied depth in the image can be helpful in giving you clues about possible ways in which to translate two dimensions into three dimensions.
- Clear edges and boundaries can be used in subsequent steps to define points, lines, and edges which will form the basis for geometry.
- Pay special attention to the composition of the image. Is it balanced, static, or dynamic?

While each of these criteria can be useful in selecting an image, it is also important to understand that the process you develop for querying and manipulating this image toward three-dimensional geometry will be much more important to your final outcome.

Step 2: Insert the image into a vector-based image manipulation program. Vector-based software (such as Adobe Illustrator) can be used to extract vector information from raster images (in Illustrator you can use "LiveTrace" commands). If you do not have software that deals specifically with creating vector artwork you can insert the image into any number of CAD software packages and trace lines and curves over the image.

Step 3: Define edges of volumes in the image with two-dimensional lines and points. Refer to Figure 4.8 as an example of tracing an image.

Step 4: Manipulate the curves, lines, and points to create a three-dimensional assemblage. Using the base image as a reference point, design a procedure for manipulating the curves, lines and points in the assemblage. In Figure 4.9 the image is divided into regions and each region instantiates a different procedure. In Region 1, for example, the corner of each triangle closest to the center of the composition is raised one unit in the Z (up and down)

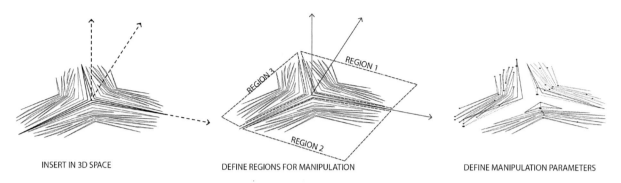

INSERT IN 3D SPACE   DEFINE REGIONS FOR MANIPULATION   DEFINE MANIPULATION PARAMETERS

Figure 4.9 Setting up the parameters for manipulating the curves in the assembly. Student: Bahar Khonsari, University of Calgary.

axis. The other two regions work with manipulating the remaining corners. This example is simplified to demonstrate that very simple moves repeated over the course of an entire series of two-dimensional geometries can lead to complex formal qualities. Potential manipulation techniques include: move, control point move, copy/paste, mirror, scale, skew, bend, project, rotate, trim, and/or explode.

Step 5: Produce volumes through surfacing tools. Using volume or surface production tools in your software package, produce a series of volumes. Lofting, extrusion, rail, and a number of other surfacing tools can be used to develop surface continuities between groups of lines (such as shown in Figures 4.10 and 4.11). Rigor and craft is as important in digital processes as it is in manual processes. It is recommended that you produce a series of manifold geometries. Manifold geometries can be described as volumes that would hold fluid within them. In other words, they don't have gaps or self-intersecting surfaces. If you are 3D printing these objects, making sure they are manifold objects is a good habit to develop. With this in mind it can be helpful in your first attempts to limit the complexity of the individual actions and allow the complexity to come from their repetition. Instead of attempting to loft surfaces between large sets of curves, focus your early efforts on minimizing the number of inputs to any one procedure. Common surfacing commands include loft, sweep, and extrude, as introduced in the previous exercise set. Additionally, you can use boolean commands (union, difference, intersection, etc.), surface offset, trim, shell, and pipe.

Step 6: Evaluate the output collection of volumes as a composition or assemblage. You might ask the questions about the functional potentials of the assembly. What is it good for? Does it communicate the processes that

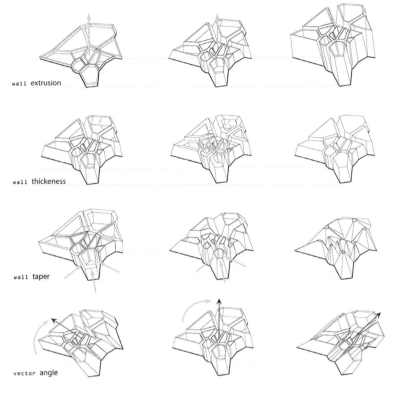

wall extrusion

wall thickeness

wall taper

vector angle

cell manipulation

Figure 4.10 Urban Garden Cell Manipulation. Voronoi cell pattern manipulations, produced by creating surface and volume from lines and curves. The sequence also shows some deformations, such as taper and skew, being applied to the composition of volumes. Minus Architecture Studio + Synthetiques.

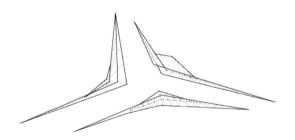

LOFT EDGES

FINAL ASSEMBLAGE

Figure 4.11 Adjacent edges are lofted to form manifold geometries. Student: Bahar Khonsari, University of Calgary.

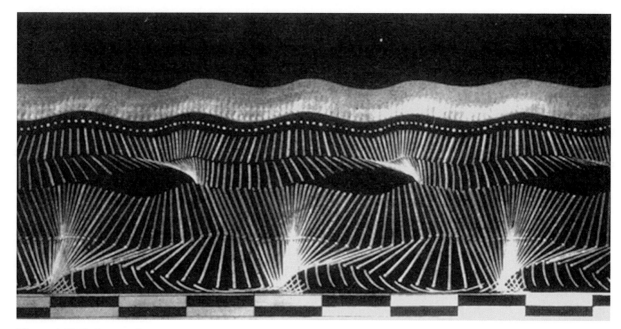

Figure 4.12 Early example of time-lapse photography. The accumulation of snapshots show the human body as a shape undergoing step-by-step series of geometric transformations. Étienne-Jules Marey.

produced it? Does it produce innovative aesthetic opportunities that could be applied to a design problem? Does it function better as an assemblage or are the individual components more compelling? Questions about the part-to-whole relationships will help you with the next exercise when we look at scale, but they might also help you to understand how certain ordering systems work. If you deployed a radial set of procedures then you might find that your final output has different functional potentials from a project that relied on linear shifting moves.

Step 7: Present your results. In presenting your work you should remember that the process by which you made this exercise has given you lots of content to work with. This content is not a representation of your project. That merely means that it is not an image created to approximate or communicate something specific about your project, but rather it is the project. The process that produced the project may have been an abstract one, but the results are not abstractions. In presenting this type of work it is important to understand the process is embedded into the project in such a way that you do not need to present all of it for someone to understand or appreciate it. An interesting process that is well understood is vitally important to your own development as a designer and to your audience, but it is not in and of itself a guarantee of a successful design. Process-based exercises are no different from any other approach in this regard.

You should see your presentation of the project as an opportunity to edit all the content you have in such a way as to demonstrate what makes your final outcome worthy of the effort. Does it have certain qualities that are an outgrowth of very specific techniques and sequencing? Is it innovative in the way it produces spatial or material organizations? Be critical with an eye towards how certain decisions within your process have produced unexpected and welcome results. In Figure 4.13 the individual components are arranged in a matrix based on their properties of rotation and branching. What was interesting in the case of this project was emergence of small variations within similar parts. These variations produce an ecology of parts that can be put to different functions depending on their scale and context.

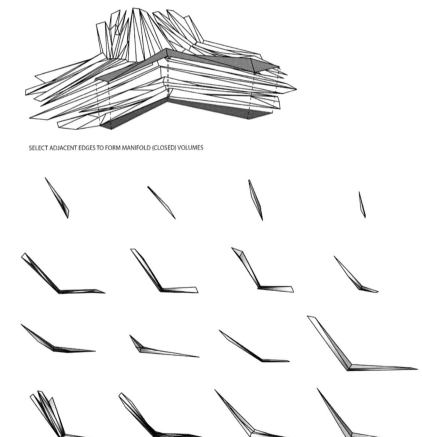

SELECT ADJACENT EDGES TO FORM MANIFOLD (CLOSED) VOLUMES

MATRIX OF RESULTANT MANIFOLD VOLUMES

Figure 4.13 Deconstructing the larger assemblage into the components. Student: Bahar Khonsari, University of Calgary.

Exercise 4C: scale

Explore the resulting geometries from Exercise 4B at a number of scales. Visualize the individual components or the larger assemblage of forms.

Exercise procedure

Produce three visualizations of the resulting project. Each image should visualize the geometry at a different scale. Suggested scales to investigate include large urban-scale intervention, a built structure, a piece of furniture, or an object. Each of these scales will demand a different level of detail and all images should include a figure or object that communicates the size of the object. Your first attempts should focus on clearly communicating the geometry of the object rather than producing a photorealistic representational image. Use lighting, materials, texture, and color, as needed, to best explain the design and its scale and context.

Figure 4.14a Folded or faceted project examples at the scale of landscape, building, and urban furniture. (a) landscape restoration of the Vall d'en Joan landfill site Garraf, Barcelona, Spain, Batlle i Roig Arquitectes. (b) Ceiling, Yokohama Ferry Terminal, Foreign Office Architects. (c) ReBarn, Institute for Digital Fabrication, Ball State University.

Figure 4.14b

Figure 4.14c

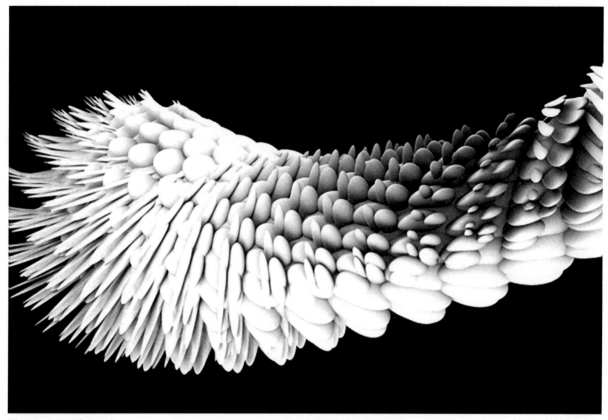

Figure 4.15 Three-dimensional array on surface. Student: Elmira Aghsaei, University of Calgary.

Exercise set 5: visual coding

For this exercise set, it is important to explicitly record the procedures you perform in sequence through words and/or graphics. You will be asked to examine, adjust, and re-execute these procedural recipes in order to generate multiple geometric candidates for further exercises.

Objectives

This exercise is intended to introduce and develop understandings of:

- pseudo-coding and other ways of recording your generative design process so it can be re-executed;
- geometric transformations that can be applied to surfaces and volumes;
- the concept of recursion;
- methods to rationalize a form into smaller parts such as subdividing.

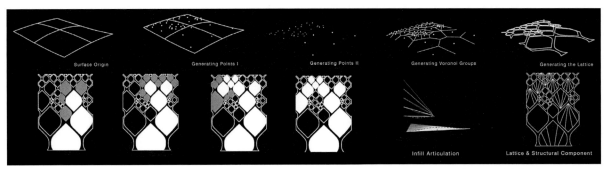

Figure 4.16 Surface articulation pseudo-code diagrams. Students: Wylegly, Ketis-Bendena, Wowk, Lawson, University of Calgary.

Outcomes

At the end of this exercise you will have your own generative sequences of operations, the resultant geometries, and three visualizations of the geometry in a hypothetical context.

Recommended reading

Foreign Office Architects. *Phylogenesis: FOA's Ark*. Actar, 2004.

Kolarevic, Branko. "Digital Morphogenesis," in *Architecture in the Digital Age: Design and Manufacturing*, Branko Kolarevic ed. Taylor & Francis, 2003.

Rocker, Ingeborg. "Evolving Architectures: Dissolving Identities – Nothing is as Persistent as Change," in *Versioning: Evolutionary Techniques in Architecture*, Sharples Holden Pasquarelli ed. Wiley, 2002, 10–17.

Sharples Holden Pasquarelli. "Introduction," *in Versioning: Evolutionary Techniques in Architecture*, Sharples Holden Pasquarelli ed. Wiley, 2002, 7–9.

Exercise 5A: pseudo-coded manipulation

So far, we have focused on process, and the importance of a step-by-step recording and editing of your process. This set of exercises begins with designing a process of simple geometric operations that are then explored and adjusted iteratively. Often, in computer programming, a developer will plan an algorithm by informally writing out each step in the order to be performed. This "pseudo-coding" is a useful exercise for us to outline a design methodology. Whereas in computer programming the desired end result is usually a known goal, we will deploy our geometric algorithms as open-ended exercises. The results of this process should not be aiming for a pre-determined design outcome, and in fact we hope you will have some happy accidents along the way.

As you execute your pseudo-coded recipes, it will be important to record and examine the results. The key is to test several variations of your algorithms, and perhaps to vary the beginning geometry to be manipulated. By the end of these exercises, you will want to have many candidates with potential for further development from which to choose from.

Figure 4.17 Component transformations. Primary component development. Students: Dekens, Coslovich, Erens, Gerlach, Wong, University of Calgary.

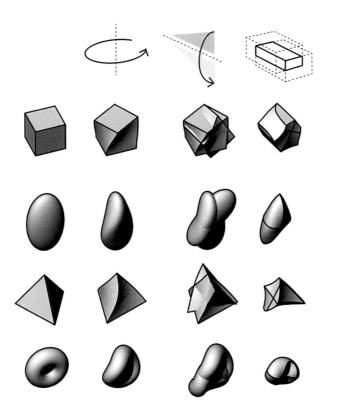

Figure 4.18 Example matrix showing a set of operations (twist, copy, mirror, and boolean intersection) performed on geometric primitives.

Figure 4.19 Component transformations. Transformation process uses scale and twist modifiers to produce a series of potential components. Students: Dekens, Coslovich, Erens, Gerlach, Wong, University of Calgary.

Exercise procedure

Step 1: Select one of the objects produced in Exercise 4B. Your selection should be guided by fitness criteria. The object should be manifold (in other words, closed with no open edges). An object with a limited number of surfaces is suggested in order to allow for more efficient computer performance.

Step 2: Develop a process for manipulating the object using simple functions in three-dimensional digital space. Write out the "pseudo-code" in simple terms using any of the following geometric transform and deform functions: scale, rotate, duplicate, move, boolean commands (union, difference, intersection, etc.), cage edit or lattice, join, and/or twist.

Step 3: Execute your pseudo-code with your object. It is important to "snapshot" the process by capturing, saving, or copying the result from each step. Each of the snapshots can be considered a candidate for further development, or a new start point as you edit the pseudo-code.

Step 4: Produce an annotated matrix of forms that indicate the procedures by which the snapshots were produced. Annotate the matrix with the pseudo-code to describe each step. A matrix is a helpful way of tracking variations and their relationships from step to step. The matrix could be in the form of a grid, a tree, a graph, or some other graphic device that shows the resulting forms in the order that they are produced.

Step 5: Edit the pseudo-code and repeat to produce variations.

Bonus technique: many CAD or modeling softwares allow users to create macros (as discussed in Exercise 4A). Executing your pseudo-code as a macro can allow you to create more variations in the same amount of time by automating the process.

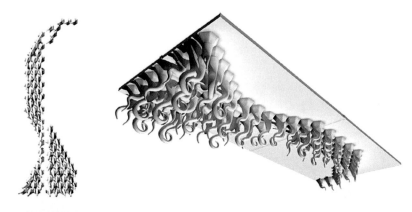

Figure 4.20 Component transformations. Series of formal transformations deployed over a surface. Students: Dekens, Coslovich, Erens, Gerlach, Wong, University of Calgary.

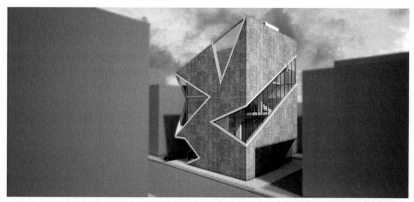

Figure 4.21a Radix Design Studio. Geometric manipulations of stretching, projecting, and subtracting based on daylighting and viewing angles. Sujit Nair Design Group.

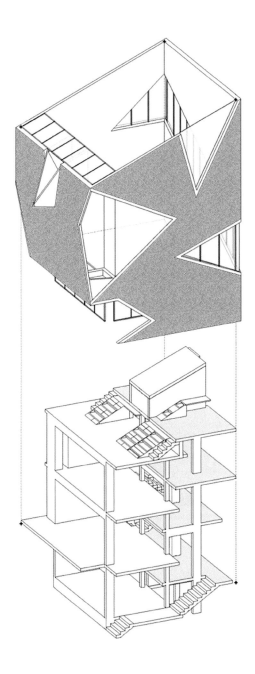

Figure 4.21b

Figure 4.21c

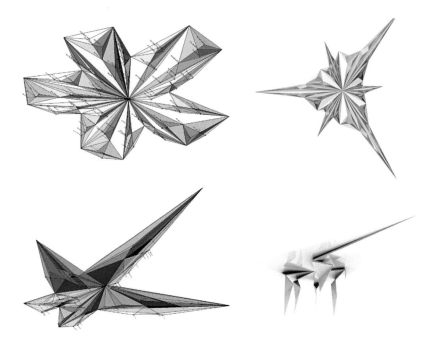

Figure 4.22 Shape subdividing studies and table prototype. An example of a recursive recipe that splits a large shape into smaller and smaller shapes. Each new smaller shape is further subdivided. Marc Fornes & THEVERYMANY.

Exercise 5B: recursion and subdivision

This next assignment relies on a special type of repetition called recursion. Recursion refers to a process "in which objects are defined in terms of other objects of the same type."[3] For example, in the following exercise we ask you to populate your selected form with similar, but scaled down, versions of itself. Upon completion, we see that the form is repeated at different scales. Given enough computing power and memory, we could perform this recursive process over and over, each time zooming in on a smaller component, only to find it is made from a set of smaller, similarly patterned and shaped parts. Recursion is a very useful tool in computer programming, mathematics, and other branches of science. For our purposes, the value of recursion is its ability to produce a large number of variations with self-similar objects. These variations can be evaluated in a number of ways in order to determine which best meet the criteria of a given problem.

Figure 4.23 Generative branching system. Each new branch splits into further curved branches. Marc Fornes & THEVERYMANY.

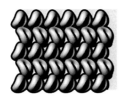

Figure 4.24 Subdivision and population example. From left to right: the original form; a basic grid arrangement of scaled parts based on the original; subdividing the form according to UV coordinates; each UV cell populated with the scaled parts. Each part was deformed according to the size, shape, and orientation of the corresponding UV cell.

Exercise procedure

Step 1: Select an object in your matrix from Exercise 5A. For fitness criteria, again make sure that the object you select is manifold. Also, surfaces should not be self-intersecting. If you do want to choose self-intersecting surfaces then you should clean up the geometry using trim or boolean operations.

Step 2: Subdivide each surface into a number of smaller surfaces using UV grids, projected geometry, or other subdivision tools. By subdividing we mean breaking down a surface into smaller parts or regions, hopefully in an ordered way, such as a grid or radial pattern. You are encouraged to try different subdivision strategies – points, surface patches, etc.

Step 3: Populate each of these subdivisions with a scaled-down version of the object.

Figure 4.25 In-situ rendering. The composite images situate this assembly as a ceiling for a lounge. Students: Dekens, Coslovich, Erens, Gerlach, Wong, University of Calgary.

Exercise 5C: scale

Explore the resulting geometries from Exercise 5B at a number of scales. What is the relationship of geometry to the body? Is it something that is worn, held, inhabited or embedded into other assemblies? In Figure 4.25 students embedded their geometry into an existing drop panel ceiling using the scale of the panels that were replaced.

Exercise procedure

Produce three visualizations, each demonstrating the resulting geometries at a different scale. Suggested scales: clothing, prosthetics, surfaces, furniture, and landscape.

Figure 4.26 Water Cathedral.
GUN Arquitectos.

Exercise set 6: accumulations

In this exercise set you will apply geometric deformations to the forms generated in the prior exercises in order to produce variation within your geometric constructs. Once these variations have been produced you are asked to study how they can accumulate into larger systems to create a field condition. As in previous exercise steps, at the end of this exercise you will need to provide a spatial and performative context for deploying your system.

Objectives

This exercise is intended to introduce and develop an understanding of:

- geometric deforming operations;
- how to produce larger accumulations of variable, yet similar, geometric volumes and forms;
- developing your own set of performance criteria for the results based on visual and spatial effect.

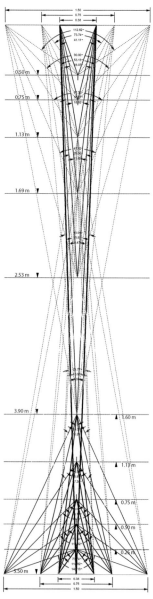

Figure 4.27 Water Cathedral. GUN Arquitectos.

Outcomes

By the end of this exercise set, you should have a system of accumulated geometric variants along with visualizations of this system within a hypothetical context.

Recommended reading

Hensel, Michael, Achim Menges, and Michael Weinstock. *Emergent Technologies and Design: Towards a Biological Paradigm for Architecture.* Routledge, 2010.

Lynn, Greg. *Animate Form.* Princeton Architectural Press, 1999.

Reiser, Jesse, and Nanako Umemoto. "Geometry," in *Atlas of Novel Tectonics.* Princeton Architectural Press, 2006.

Thompson, D'Arcy Wentworth. *On Growth and Form.* Cambridge University Press, 1917.

Wolfram, Stephen. *A New Kind of Science.* Wolfram Media, 2002.

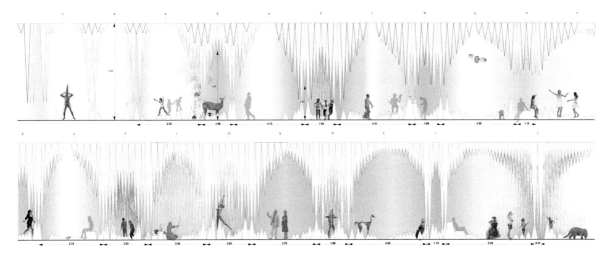

Figure 4.28 Water Cathedral. These drawings describe the range of differentiation for the component units used in the Water Cathedral. The variation in size was deployed in such a way as to produce a variety in both the spatial constraints and experiential aspects of the space. In addition to variations in size the components varied in material transparency (Figure 4.34). GUN Arquitectos.

Exercise 6A: topological transformations

The first part of this exercise will focus on small, incremental changes to produce formal variations. Only use one or two geometric transform functions to deform your shape. Avoid cutting, joining, or introducing any holes, as this process should produce a family of topologically similar shapes. Common transform commands available for use include: scale (one-, two-, three-dimensional), rotate, cage edit, twist, bend, skew, and stretch.

Exercise procedure

Step 1: Select one or two deformation tools from above to deploy. Examples could include twisting, scaling, or rotating. Remember to be selective with these tools. The focus is on incremental (rather than dramatic) change at each step. These step-by-step systemic changes are sometimes referred to as "modulations."

Step 2: Use your identified deformations to develop slight variations of your form in a precise manner. Each set should have a limited number of manipulations to very specific parameters (i.e., the axis of scaling, twisting, or rotating related to the overall object). Each snapshot in the sequence should differ minimally from the preceding step to create a gradual accumulation of morphological change. If you are using animation software, this process can be sped up by keyframing an initial shape and an ending shape

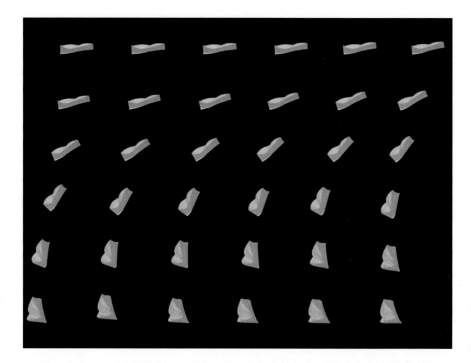

Figure 4.29 Example of a keyframed morphing sequence arranged in a grid. Student: Tafadzwa Bwititi, Ball State University.

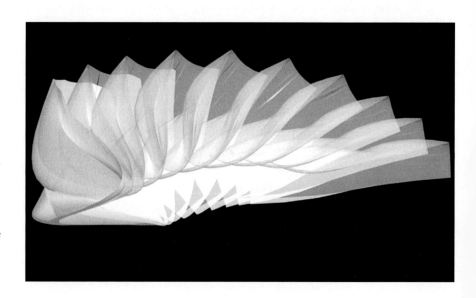

Figure 4.30 Examples of keyframed morphing arranged in an overlapping linear sequence. This sequence is produced using the same set of parameters used by the designer in the previous figure (see Figure 4.29). Student: Tafadzwa Bwititi, Ball State University.

on the animation timeline. As the animation is produced, each frame on the timeline produces the modulated forms. Refer to Greg Lynn's *Animate Form* in the recommended reading list for examples of form finding using deformation techniques.

Step 3: Produce a matrix of the resulting forms. To produce this matrix, graph, or sequence, capture the steps of the process as though you filmed the deformation and then sampled the video stills, as shown in Figures 4.29–4.30.

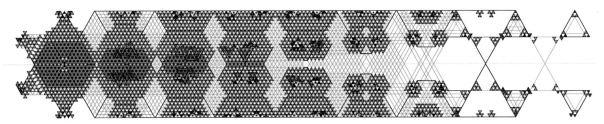

Figure 4.31 Water Cathedral. This drawing shows the plan layout for the overhead and ground elements of the pavilion. In each case programmatic variation is achieved through variation in the density of the components. GUN Arquitectos.

Figure 4.32 Water Cathedral. GUN Arquitectos.

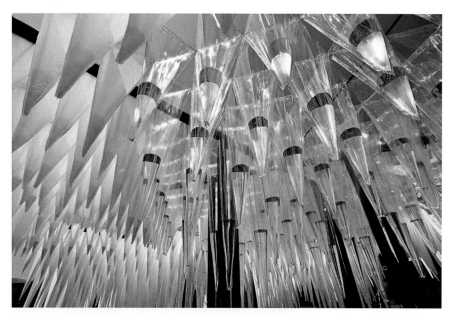

Figure 4.33 Water Cathedral. GUN Arquitectos.

Figure 4.34 Water Cathedral. Constant differentiation in the dimensions and materials of the components allows for a varied set of experiences within the space. GUN Arquitectos.

Exercise 6B: accumulation

This exercise deals with accumulating volumes into larger configurations. Strategies for forming these more complex systems of parts include rule-based growth, duplication, and population. This set of exercises will focus on generative, bottom-up processes to accumulate volumes into larger systems. Most environments or buildings are made up of many parts that are accumulated in particular relationships – take a brick wall, for instance. The focus of the next exercises is to take a "part" and find ways to generate the "whole" or larger assembly or system.

The previous case study, the Water Cathedral by GUN Arquitectos, used a simple grid-like array of "stalactite" components to create an interesting outdoor environment. Each stalactite was similar to all of the others (the same basic shape), but differed in length and spread. We will generate variations in form just as in the previous exercises, but this time we will also focus on developing a logic for how these forms combine to form a larger construct. Grid arrays are just accumulation strategies. The writings by Michael Hensel, Achim Menges, and Michael Weinstock are full of examples of taking this process further, by adding materiality in the generative recipe.[4] By studying and experimenting with materials, the results are deeply informed with material behavior (bending, stress resistance, assembly methods) at the part and system levels.

Another way of accumulating volumes is to populate a larger system with the volumetric parts. For instance, subdividing a surface into smaller shapes or cells, or creating a cloud of points are just two of many ways to generate a system. Each cell or point can then be populated with (or receive) a part. Regardless of the method – the following exercises ask you to practice three distinct accumulation methods – the results can be strikingly complex, both in form, surface, and effect, as demonstrated in Marc Fornes's work (see Figures 4.35 and 4.36). Beyond material and fabrication logics, the Aperiodic Symmetries project demonstrates a variation in light, shadow, and density. These sorts of effects should be key in evaluating the results of your own process and can only be discovered by experimenting, iterating, and visualizing.

Figure 4.35 Aperiodic Symmetries. Gallery installation deploying scripted components in a field over an arched surface. Marc Fornes & THEVERYMANY.

Figure 4.36 Aperiodic Symmetries. Components are separated into two larger types; the first type are highly variable connection pieces that join the larger standardized components of the assembly. Marc Fornes & THEVERYMANY.

Exercise procedure

Step 1: From the matrix of forms developed in Exercise 6A, select an instance or multiple instances and combine them to produce a new object through boolean functions like join, trim, subtract, intersection, etc. The most important fitness criterion for this first step is to ensure that the result is manifold (watertight and without self-intersections).

Step 2: Using the newly created object, create three sets of accumulated systems with each of the following strategies:

- a rule-based growth system;
- a two-dimensional or three-dimensional array;
- a surface population field.

There are many rule-based systems for growth – splitting, branching, or other fractal growth patterns are some examples. You can examine trees or cellular automata for ideas on rules that produce emergent results. Develop your own set of rules for duplicating your object into a larger system. The growth patterns could be linear (i.e., adding one part at a time) or exponential (i.e., for example, if the number of parts in your system double each step).

Arraying involves duplicating your object with an ordered geometric pattern. Grid organizations, linear organizations, or radial organizations are some examples to start with. Experiment with overlapping and varying the densities of components. You can even superimpose arrays over other arrays.

Populating surfaces with components is a common way to create a modulated field of parts. You should experiment with populating different surface geometries. Surface characteristics will influence the distortion of each component's shape – every warp, bend, swell, or contraction of the surface

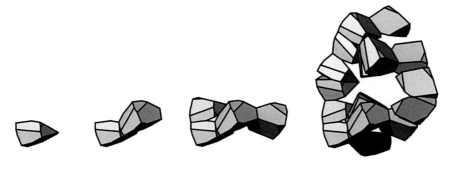

Figure 4.37 A growth sequence applying copy and mirror according to a set of simple rules.

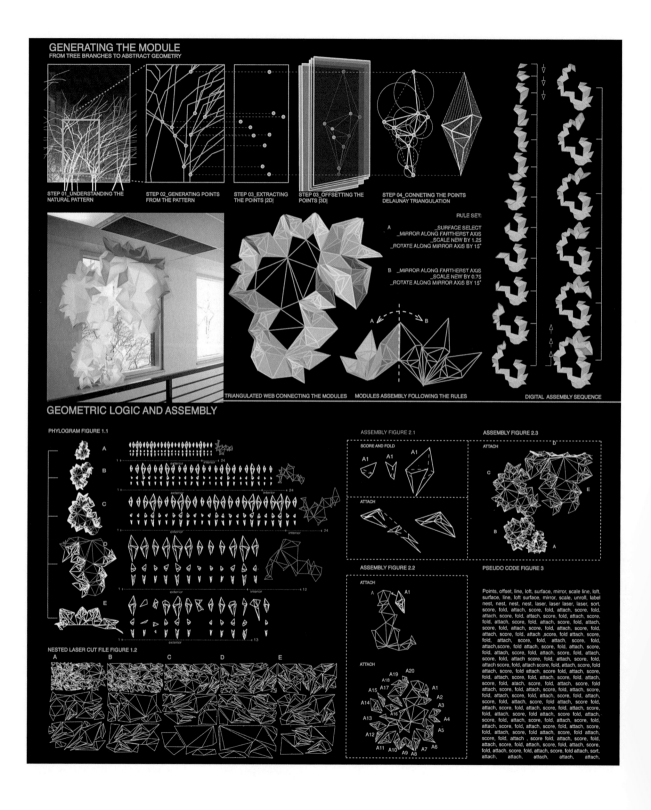

GENERATING THE MODULE
FROM TREE BRANCHES TO ABSTRACT GEOMETRY

STEP 01_UNDERSTANDING THE NATURAL PATTERN

STEP 02_GENERATING POINTS FROM THE PATTERN

STEP 03_EXTRACTING THE POINTS |2D|

STEP 03_OFFSETTING THE POINTS |3D|

STEP 04_CONNETING THE POINTS DELAUNAY TRIANGULATION

RULE SET:

A _SURFACE SELECT
_MIRROR ALONG FARTHERST AXIS
_SCALE NEW BY 1.25
_ROTATE ALONG MIRROR AXIS BY 15°

B _MIRROR ALONG FARTHERST AXIS
_SCALE NEW BY 0.75
_ROTATE ALONG MIRROR AXIS BY 15°

TRIANGULATED WEB CONNECTING THE MODULES

MODULES ASSEMBLY FOLLOWING THE RULES

DIGITAL ASSEMBLY SEQUENCE

GEOMETRIC LOGIC AND ASSEMBLY

PHYLOGRAM FIGURE 1.1

ASSEMBLY FIGURE 2.1
SCORE AND FOLD
ATTACH

ASSEMBLY FIGURE 2.3
ATTACH

ASSEMBLY FIGURE 2.2
ATTACH
ATTACH

PSEUDO CODE FIGURE 3

NESTED LASER CUT FILE FIGURE 1.2

Points, offset, line, loft, surface, mirror, scale line, loft, surface, line, loft surface, mirror, scale, unroll, label nest, nest, nest, laser, laser laser, laser, sort, score, fold, attach, score, fold, attach, score, fold, attach, score, fold, attach, score, fold, at, attach, score, fold, attach, score, fold, attach, score, fold, attach, score, fold, attach, score, fold, attach, score, fold, attach, score, fold, attach ,score, fold attach, score, fold, attach, score, fold, attach, score, fold, attach,score, fold attach, score, fold, attach, score, fold, attach, score, fold, attach, score, fold, attach, score, fold, attach, score, fold, attach, score, fold, attach, score, fold, attach, score, fold, attach score, fold attach, score, fold, attach, score, fold, attach, score, fold attach, score, fold, attach, score, fold, attach, score, fold, attach, score, fold, attach, score, fold, attach, score, fold, attach, score, fold attach, score, fold, attach, score, fold, attach, score, fold, attach, score, fold, attach, score, fold, attach, score, fold, attach, score, fold attach, score fold, attach, score, fold, attach, score, fold attach, score fold, attach, score, fold, attach, score fold attach, score, fold, attach, score, fold, attach, score, fold, attach, score, fold, attach, score, fold, attach, score, fold, attach, score, fold, attach, score, fold attach, score, fold attach, score, fold, attach, score, fold, attach, score, fold, attach, score, fold, attach, score, fold, attach, score, fold, attach, score, fold, attach, score, fold attach, score, fold attach, sort, attach, attach, attach, attach, attach,

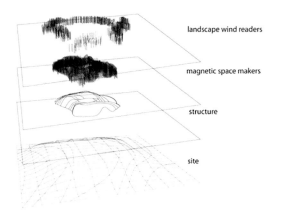

landscape wind readers

magnetic space makers

structure

site

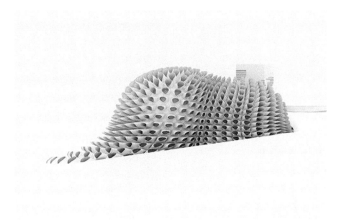

Figure 4.40 Winter weather pavilion. Student work exploring surface modulation through scaling of arrayed components. Student: Amy Wowk, University of Calgary.

provides systemic variability in the resulting component system because surface subdivisions provide varying sized cells for population. Understanding this will assist you in developing an intuition for modulating these assemblies in a way that reinforces the characteristics you would like to intensify or promote within the assembly. Some common tools to assist with this process include power copy, flow, or array on surface.

Step 3: Once you have tried each of the three strategies, you are encouraged to combine two or more to create hybrid systems.

Figure 4.38 Growth sequence (opposite, top). An illustration of growth based on mirroring a simple component. Students: Jodi James, Matt Parker, *et al.*, University of Calgary.

Figure 4.39 Generative Assembly Logics (opposite, bottom). Catalog of parts and assembly logic for student digital fabrication project. Students: Jodi James, Matt Parker, *et al.*, University of Calgary.

Exercise 6C: scale

Explore the resulting geometric system from Exercise 6B at a number of scales. For fitness criteria, pay special attention to the spatial effects that your systems create, such as light capturing, shadow casting, variations in density or color, or other phenomena that suggest ways that the system might perform in a given context. As you identify these desired performance criteria, you can re-adjust the component or accumulation methods to enhance these effects.

Exercise procedure

Produce three visualizations, each demonstrating the resulting geometries at a different scale.

The exercises in this chapter have asked you to learn and practice skills with photo manipulation and editing, vector graphic drawing, surface modeling, and geometric transform and deform operations. It is important not to see these as disparate tools and skills, but rather as tools that each complement the other and can be deployed in various ways to create and communicate architectural form. This fluency of moving between various apps is only useful if the steps and techniques are repeatedly practiced, interrogated, and refined. While we hope that the open-ended exercises presented in this chapter are helpful to get you started, they are just an outline to get you started. You are encouraged to skip, combine, or otherwise re-order the exercise steps as you practice.

Continue to repeat and iterate. After every step, step back and examine both the technique and its result. By developing a deeper understanding of your generative recipe and the parameters that govern each step, you facilitate a feedback loop that suggests tactical adjustments to the process in order to produce more useful results.

Figure 4.41 Urban zoo proposal. This student project deploys a component at a number of scales across the site for an urban zoo. The project uses variable component sizes and tiling techniques to address a range of functional requirements. Student: Daan Murray, University of Calgary.

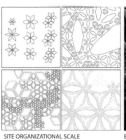

SITE ORGANIZATIONAL SCALE   BUILDING SCALE   BUILDING SCALE   FURNITURE SCALE   OBJECT SCALE

Programming, parametric modeling, and other advanced methods of deploying generative design techniques all start with developing the logic of relationships between design criteria, geometric operations, parameters, and results. Additional performance criteria related to site, context, environment, program, and material systems are external factors that can and should eventually be integrated throughout and inform the process. In the next chapter of exercises, we will integrate fabrication and material logics into the generative design process.

Notes

1 Michael Speaks, "Intelligence After Theory," in *Perspecta 38: Architecture After All* (Cambridge, MA: MIT Press, 2006).

2 John Frazer, *An Evolutionary Architecture* (London: Architectural Association, 1995); Manuel Delanda, "Deleuze and the Use of the Genetic Algorithm in Architecture," in Ali Rahim (ed.), *Contemporary Techniques in Architecture* (New York: Wiley, 2012), pp. 9–12.

3 Eric Weisstein, "Recursion," Wolfram MathWorld, http://mathworld.wolfram.com/Recursion.html (accessed July 22, 2015).

4 Michael Hensel, Achim Menges, and Michael Weinstock, *Emergent Technologies and Design: Towards a Biological Paradigm for Architecture* (London and New York: Routledge, 2010).

ITERATION, FAILURE, AND DISTINCTIONS

Marc Fornes

Figure 5.1
THEVERYMANY studio
space, Brooklyn, New York,
2015.

Marc Fornes is a registered Architect DPLG and founder of THEVERYMANY™, a New York based studio engaging art and architecture through the filter of systematic research and development into applied computer science and digital fabrication. In the spring of 2015 Jason Johnson interviewed Marc in his Brooklyn studio, surrounded by prototypes and drawings that represented a catalog of nearly ten years of work across a number of scales. What follows is an edited transcript of a far-ranging conversation on the topic of the importance of iteration, failure, and specificity in the design process.

JSJ: We first met of course 12 years ago at the AADRL and I invited you in 2009 to install one of your first large pieces in a gallery in Calgary (Figures 5.2 and 5.3). Since then, of course, you have been incredibly busy. Most recently I have caught a lecture in which you have presented your work within the context of failure, which is not often an approach taken by designers and seems to be difficult for students to embrace. I'm wondering if you could let us in on how you describe failure and how it has informed your body of work thus far.

MF: I think maybe before we talk about failure, people misunderstand what failure means. It is often mistaken as dramatic failure: I fail, it's a catastrophic failure. Failure is not necessarily the point. It is, for lack of a better word, the unknown. It's a very systematic and empirical learning curvature meaning that you do something, you make a hypothesis, and then you make a premise of the experiment. You frame it clearly. "Hey is that project going to fit into that precise segment?" You test it, look at it, learn from it, and then redo it.

That cycle is possible because of the shift from [a singular] project to projects. Meaning if you only create one architectural project over a longer time, you cannot test as much. When you do many projects a year, we can actually afford to specify the precise segment of testing into one of those projects, test it, maybe even fail that project, learn from that and then it becomes a premise of the next one. One failure becomes the starting point of the next,

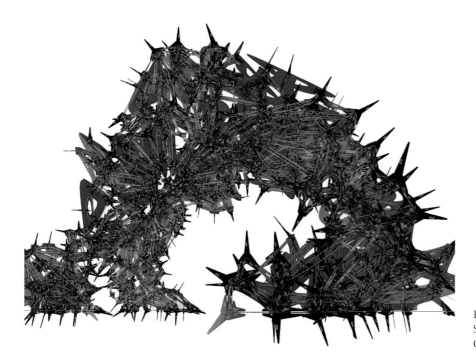

Figure 5.2 Aperiodic Symmetries, Calgary, AB, Canada, 2009.

Figure 5.3 Aperiodic Symmetries, Calgary, AB, Canada, 2009.

or several, which means that several projects actually are moving at the same time, and you just recombine their failure, by choice, into the premise of the next one.

There are different types of failures. There is structural failure, of course. That's one type. Another type of failure is to say the installation is perfectly stable, it's perfectly working, but maybe it takes too long to assemble, which means it's not scalable. So it's a failure that is not apparent to the visitor or the client, but as an architect you say, "wait, I've developed a system which suddenly reaches a cap." That's a specific failure because you want to be able to develop sets of skills and if you cannot grow. It places a limit on what you are trying to do.

So there are many types and scales of failure. There are always things that you could improve or aspects and qualities that you feel are weak. You must be careful to precisely inscribe/describe them (the failures) so that the next investigation can become better. You must be consistent in the way you describe them in terms of production so that you can begin to see families of

Figure 5.4 Engineering visual of panel finite element analysis. Plasti(k) Pavilion, 2011.

3D Finite Element Model

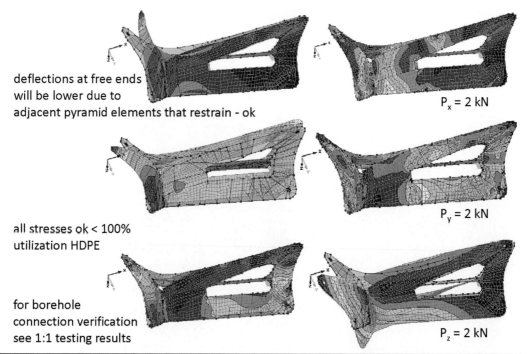

deflections at free ends will be lower due to adjacent pyramid elements that restrain - ok

$P_x = 2$ kN

all stresses ok < 100% utilization HDPE

$P_y = 2$ kN

for borehole connection verification see 1:1 testing results

$P_z = 2$ kN

Plasti(k) structural calculations, April 2011

projects — series of experiments or opportunities that literally emerge from these projects. That is what I am interested in.

JSJ: So, for example, one of the things I find most interesting about what you're doing is the fact that you stick with a specific set of problems in order to pursue a trajectory that addresses them or folds them into subsequent projects. So I'm wondering how do you decide which problems merit longer-term investigation and which problems or questions are dead ends?

MF: You need to keep focus on your goals. For the last ten years, whereas many were really excited about the potential of the digital and everybody was looking for a seamless path of trying to be "experimental," I always felt that the excitement of the time was focused on form generation, but also on understanding and controlling all of the aspects of the process and information during the entire trajectory of the project. This includes writing code, form generation, negotiating form and function, and continuous testing of material prototypes. At the same time, my objective has always been to build at a larger scale. So all of these installations tried to maximize the given budgets, and suddenly we were working on larger and larger installations. Each time you jump in scale you will encounter new problems to overcome. So scale provides a framework that allows us to evaluate if the problems we identify are inherent to the system or are related to the scale. This issue of scale forces you to acknowledge issues of gravity, wind loads, and material thicknesses, for example, in ways that small-scale prototypes can avoid.

JSJ: How do you go about defining scale in your projects? By this I mean not just the scale of the overall project, but given that you work with component-based systems, the scale of the components and their relationship to the whole.

MF: The difference between a project that remains at the level of a prototype (tests the way parts come together in unit-to-unit relationships, how they look, etc.) and a prototypical space (which goes all the way toward an assembly) is not just structural or formal, but rather is one of logistics. After every project we do a data analysis. We calculate the project surface area, the average size of the parts, the number of parts, the number of connections and so on. Having this information means that whenever we get a project there is already a database of not just formal but also logistical drivers that can connect

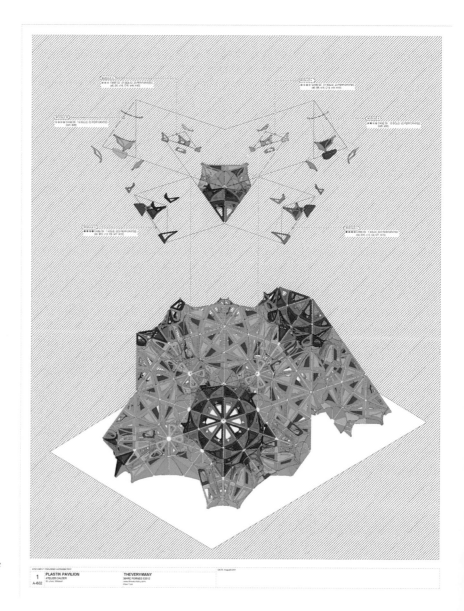

Figure 5.5 Exploded axonometric drawing of sample modules. Plasti(k) Pavilion, St. Louis, MO, 2011.

the problem of any given project to the client, the institution or location. That is one way that we start to look to define scale within the system. Is the project far away? Where will it be produced? Do we need to ship the parts? These are different scales. You know that something produced too far away can't be shipped as a volume because of weight and size, so your system is most probably a surface. If it's a surface, how do you define and break down

Figure 5.6 Plasti(k) Pavilion, St. Louis, MO, 2011.

Figure 5.7 Plasti(k) Pavilion, St. Louis, MO, 2011.

the surface into parts that can be fabricated and shipped? Then it becomes a problem of defining the operable scale of the project. The bigger the project, the larger the unit is for the reason that you don't want to have to assemble massive amounts of tiny bricks to create a large one.

So I think for us, scale becomes defined by the experience of previous projects and their logistical aspects. That is what will define what we look at in terms of possible systems. Then there is the issue of resolving the structure and the envelope. A straightforward resolution is not that difficult, but we want to explore how to go from an envelope that surrounds us (one that responds to spatial needs), to one that is adaptive and can merge all of these different types of performance within it. Beyond scale we are really looking at adaptability. Scale is the obvious place to start in this, but how I can allow for scale to be adaptable within similar component systems is more crucial.

Figure 5.8 Perspective drawing. Under Stress, Rennes, France, 2012.

Figure 5.9 Under Stress, Rennes, France, 2012.

JSJ: You deploy color in an interesting way, reinforcing the form through the color gradient, or actually revealing something about the forces and stresses within the project. Do you see this as a form of articulation? Have you moved from the idea of the components producing complexity in a surface toward one in which color begins to do some of that work?

MF: The component has never been the goal. It's just a necessary byproduct of a complex project, in that you need actually to think about the problem as a simple part. But there is also the resolution of the surface itself. We are trying to avoid having to have some kind of scaffold. All of these things have a cost; either you are paying for the infrastructure [supports] that hold up your project while it is constructed or you build it into the surface. This goes into the resolution of the surface itself. Sometimes we need infrastructure; we need to have creases, pleats, folds, or directionality of the surface with more material in one direction for structure. Sometimes it needs to drain water off the surface. I think it's about trying to learn additional information from

Figure 5.10 Under Stress,
Rennes, France, 2012.

the surface. These are basic criteria that can give directionality to a pattern of components or be achieved through coloring or what I call coloration, which is something that reveals paths rather than setting paths. We have a bit of schizophrenia in this regard. The questions we then ask are: Do we reveal the paths so they become an additional piece of information or do we simply create a rendering, or do we blend everything? Do we reveal the [pattern] and it becomes an additional [layer of] information, the directionality which drives you through the space or it drives you toward elements. We follow both types of research. If the color and component logics contribute to the intensity of the geometries, we blend these into the project. When you actually want to read the "architectural" ideas more clearly through the surface then we might make less use of these strategies. For me this is a question of parallel design research.

JSJ: I think you're right that there's this parallel desire to camouflage what you're doing, and at the same time express it in a way that allows it to claim primacy of expression. It may be something that I am projecting onto the work, but it seems what distinguishes your work is the ability to let go of the fetishization of the technical expertise involved in the production of these projects in favor of the ability to produce a "thing" that has ambient qualities.

Figure 5.11 Under Stress, Rennes, France, 2012.

Figure 5.12 Vaulted Willow,
Edmonton, AB, Canada, 2014.

Figure 5.13 Close up photo of coloration. Vaulted Willow, Edmonton, AB, Canada, 2014.

Figure 5.14 Close up photo of coloration. Vaulted Willow, Edmonton, AB, Canada, 2014.

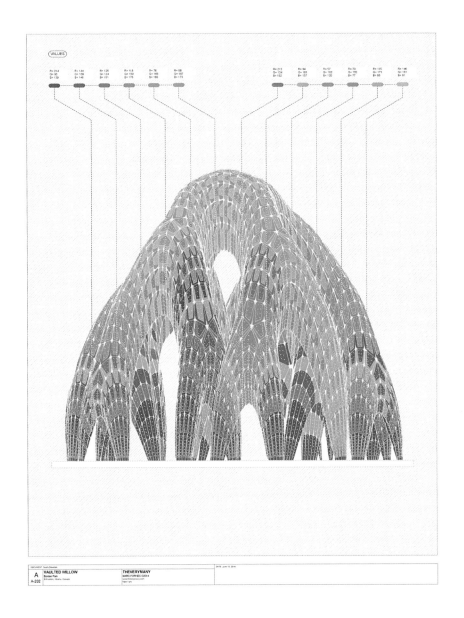

Figure 5.15 Elevation drawing. Vaulted Willow, Edmonton, AB, Canada, 2014.

I am wondering how much of that is intentional and how much of it emerges organically from the process?

MF: No, it's really curated, it's again coming back to that training that we as architects understand. Everything, all the experience we accumulate for a specific problem from architecture, that it's structure, that it's skin or that it's larger, or just purely feel of space, it's the edge property of architecture, between maybe architecture and art, we have no problem being on either side of the border. So, if you want to create dimensional space as an architect, that is a very unique and demonstrative type of space, absolutely non-neutral, and I wouldn't say deterministic, but having intensity and intense space, you have ways to arrive there. Sometimes we need to develop one thing;

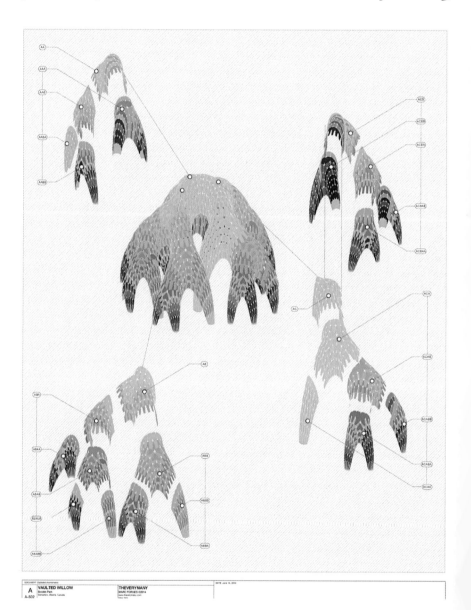

Figure 5.16 Exploded axonometric drawing. Vaulted Willow, Edmonton, AB, Canada, 2014.

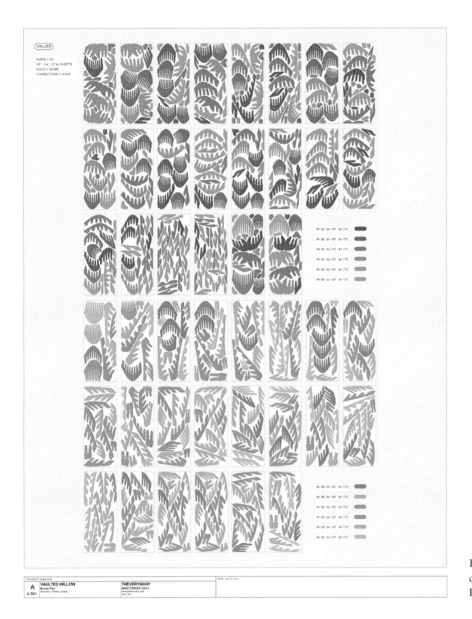

Figure 5.17 Nested parts drawing. Vaulted Willow, Edmonton, AB, Canada, 2014.

sometimes we need to test another. So some installations are more drawn to the one or the other because of the institution. The client will request one more than the other, or sometimes purely by internal concerns, when we want to understand, "hey, let's test it" for example like we did in St. Louis (Figures 5.4–5.7), or how it's a prototypical space, "let's test it." Storefront was clearly to be tested as a space. Like we did for the Centre Pompidou in Paris, which is black and white, was not for their aesthetic quality but simply to test the diversity of two different sets of behavior fighting each other to try to best solve the problem of curvature. Only by visualizing it in black and white are we able to understand where we solve more problems than trigger new problems. The FRAC center was a similar system implemented where we decided to produce it all in white as a response to the uniform. It's curated. We curate it depending on where we are situating the project, or what our needs are. So when you have several projects, you might decide to test a similar system into two different mediums. So for me it's really important to keep your end goal. We are architects, we are not crazy scientists, we are not crazy artists, we are not material scientists trying to reinvent. We are not storytellers or marketers. We are really trying to understand and develop a specific space. So that you can understand the special quality of the space, the specific qualities of the aperture system (Figure 5.18), the performance of the system. Sometimes you can have both the art and the architecture side, sometimes one is allowed to express itself more. In a system like the Willow in Edmonton we got both (Figures 5.12–5.17).

JSJ: The material in the projects we are discussing here is singular and in terms of its base materiality, undifferentiated, and it seems like color and perforation become proxies for material differentiation in the projects. Would you say this is the case?

MF: First the material is differentiated in many cases by small changes in thickness or strength of the materials.

JSJ: Okay, let's say it's subtly differentiated.

MF: There's a very precise line for us between color and coloration; they are two different approaches. Somebody came here with the adage "if you want to make it interesting make it big, if you can't make it big, make it red." So we aren't interested so much in the color although this is what attracts the attention, we are interested in the effect of using coloration. We don't look for instance at making something pink, but rather in looking at the range of pink hues. Coloration is probably one of the richest parameters to work with.

Figure 5.18 Apertures. Vaulted Willow, Edmonton, AB, Canada, 2014.

JSJ: Well it gives information legibility.

MF: Because there's so many aspects to color…. You know, people think color, it's red, it's orange, do you like it, don't you like it, but if you start to think of color in terms that define it, CMYK/RGB, is it glossy or matte, and you start to have linear gradient versus nonlinear, that affects people and attracts them to a style. They don't need to understand the relationships between the form and coloration and we can blend the order to emphasize directionality through the coloration. So I think color is more than representation. Representation means something, it means, "Hey, I'm going to express through gradient the range of performance of my system." That's representation. We believe that color is not just a representation model, but it can be an added value in that it can become its own thing unto that, and it's a quest to define that thing. We're just at a beginning moment in that quest, because we don't want to say "Hey, am I just a shade of gray, or am I into, black and white," types of things. It's not about a specific color. We are literally trying to see if all the gradients can work together, all the mismatches of color can work together in relation to form and geometry. So that's different than saying my geometry has been tested with something, and one way to make it readable is to use color.

JSJ: A graphic equalizer, perhaps?

MF: No that's representation. It's more like '80s graphics, where you try to express maybe part of a third dimension. Meaning I have my screen and maybe a Flash animation, or any kind of early computation and graphics. I'm still purely in 2D. But through the use of coloration, saturation, etc., you try to express something else on that screen. You try to bring a third dimension. We try to bring a next dimension into the piece. Sometimes it is representational, analytical, a way to emphasize information. Sometimes it is still trying to be informed by the geometry but also express its own parts, like its own gradient. The piece we did for Denver was one of the first explorations we did with a mix through computer-generated coloration. How can a linear gradient merge into the non-linear, which we refer to as Cheshire, where you use stripes (Figures 5.8–5.11). That was our first search into the gradation of color and the geometry of the piece.

JSJ: I think it goes back to this idea of, in a sense, the dialogue between expression and camouflage. There is an establishment, within the protocols of the model, a way in which those two things are starting to relate to one another. So there's a choice in which … it's 50 percent this, 30 percent that, but there's also a direct translation that's occurring once you've made that decision, which I think takes it away from representation…

MF: It's a feedback loop.

JSJ: It is, it's a kind of feedback loop between, how much of this is doing one thing versus the other. Ultimately I think one of the successes of what you're doing is that you actually have a high level of facility with that. I say that because a lot of designers will either focus on optimization that has to be in effect so pure that the outcomes are predetermined in a way…

MF: It's a question of curation. Do you curate? What's the premise?

Figure 5.19 Double Agent
White, Sache, France, 2012.

Figure 5.20 Double Agent
White, Sache, France, 2012.

Figure 5.21 Double Agent
White, Sache, France, 2012.

JSJ: Another noticeable aspect to the projects is the pattern of the actual voids in the material which perform not just as outcomes of the generative process, but as elements reinforcing the overall design.

MF: They have become very important to the process because they give us many advantages to constructability. If you have a star, you have two parameters in the star; you have the length of the branch and the width of the branch. Those affect the material in two different ways. And that's where you see the difference between what we're trying to develop and what you could call copycats, where they mimic the aperture without understanding the apertures are functional and necessary. Although we wouldn't market the work this way they are a critical part of working through failure, because as

Figure 5.21 Logistics. Packing volume for Double Agent White, Sache, France, 2012.

you can see in all these models they are looking at this problem in a different way where the apertures actually make the surfaces work.

JSJ: But there's a difference between needing them and actually deploying them in a way that reinforces the overall…

MF: Yes, that right. As soon as you identify something that your project needs and that can help you, you need to precisely understand what it's doing to get to your end goal. Yet because there are so many [apertures], and they all follow their assigned rules, it's always hard to expect what they're going to give you at the end. So you always have an element of the unexpected or "randomness" in the outcome. This is a quality we get a lot of feedback on from people who see the projects.

JSJ: Maybe as a way to wrap up. It is always difficult to convince students of the importance of producing physical prototypes for objects that are being generated and represented digitally. What would you say is the importance of producing physical prototypes?

MF: There's a range of terms I use, like mockup, model, prototype; each means something different. So we typically produce models for selling a project. We typically produce prototypes and mockups as well. The difference is that the prototypes and mockups are actually testing the logistical aspect of the project. All the parts are there, yet its scale might be reduced. Prototypes are where we test structure, we test logistics, and we test the intricacy, efficiency, etc. Mockups are where we build a piece to full scale, the 1:1 section where we test little ideas, like the way it folds, very precise measurements of the fold, very precise dimensions of the fold at 1:1 scale. Models are what we consider pure representation. So from our experience if you don't build a prototype you won't know what is going to happen on site, probably more failure at a point when it can't be fixed. That is why it has been valuable at every single stage of the projects to build as many prototypes as possible.

EXERCISES FOR ASSEMBLY AND COMMUNICATION

Jason S. Johnson and Joshua Vermillion

Introduction: communicating complexity

In the very first exercise sets, complexity was described as a condition in which many parts interact or associate in multiple ways. This chapter focuses on creating a complex component system that is derived from seemingly simple parts and a set of logics (geometry, associativity, materiality) in a bottom–up manner. In other words, we'll take something simple and create a system that works in non-simple ways through repetition, geometric associations, and material constraints. Just as in the previous chapters, we will derive a recipe for the creation of a part or "component" and order these components into a larger system or "assembly." However, each component of the assembly will have slightly different parameters from its neighbor. This repetition with variation is called differentiation. Each component will have a similar form, yet will also be uniquely (if only slightly) differentiated to respond to situational or local conditions. Differentiated systems can be deployed to create complex forms and complexly ordered assemblies, as demonstrated in the project shown in Figures 6.1–6.3.

It's important to look beyond form and complexity for their own sake, and to consider the factors that underlie complex order such as the geometry that scaffolds it, the materials that shape it, the contextual data that informs it, and the set of criteria by which you judge and improve it. Differentiation can be used to address any number of design problems in addition to aesthetics, such as structural performance, light transmittance, material properties, etc. For the assignments in this chapter, the relationships between geometry, materials, and context (at a minimum) have to be negotiated to create an assembly system from differentiated components. This process generates an enormous amount of information, and managing the quantity and complexity of this information will necessitate clear and explicit visual communication.

You will be asked to make or fabricate prototypes of your design proposals throughout these exercises. Fabricating – shaping components from materials – is difficult, especially for the inexperienced. Further, creating well-crafted prototypes requires both intent and care along with practice, as elegantly explained by Malcolm McCullough in his book *Abstracting Craft*.[1] It's important to not expect perfection at the start, but rather to embrace the process of starting simple, testing by drawing and prototyping (digitally and physically), and then making informed decisions and adjustments. Communication and representation are critical for the generation, management, and execution of the following exercises as you move along

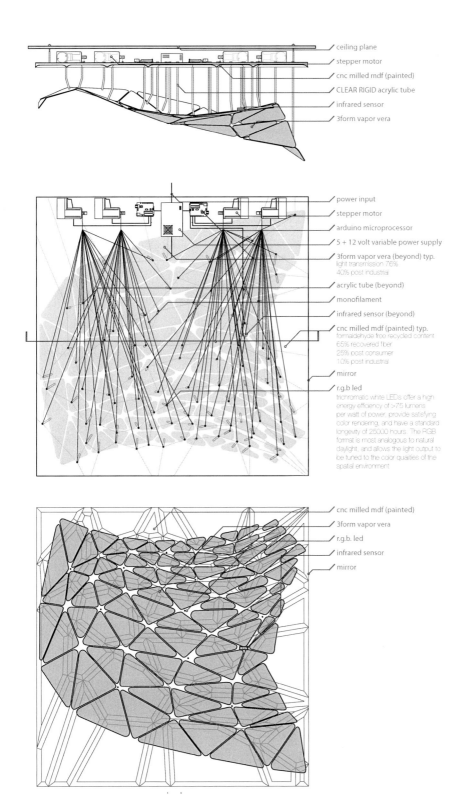

ceiling plane
stepper motor
cnc milled mdf (painted)
CLEAR RIGID acrylic tube
infrared sensor
3form vapor vera

power input
stepper motor
arduino microprocessor
5 + 12 volt variable power supply
3form vapor vera (beyond) typ.
light transmission 76%
40% post industrial

acrylic tube (beyond)
monofilament
infrared sensor (beyond)
cnc milled mdf (painted) typ.
formaldehyde free recycled content
65% recovered fiber
25% post consumer
10% post industrial

mirror
r.g.b led
trichromatic white LED's offer a high
energy efficiency of >75 lumens
per watt of power, provide satisfying
color rendering, and have a standard
longevity of 25000 hours. The RGB
format is most analogous to natural
daylight, and allows the light output to
be tuned to the color qualities of the
spatial environment

cnc milled mdf (painted)
3form vapor vera
r.g.b. led
infrared sensor
mirror

Figure 6.1 Diagram that shows the differentiated assembly of triangular components for Morpholuminescence, a prototypical ceiling installation that senses and actuates according to human presence. Students: Elizabeth Boone, Eric Brockmeyer, Adam Buente, and Kyle Perry; Faculty: Mahesh Daas, Joshua Vermillion, Ball State University.

143

Figure 6.2–6.3 Photos of Morpholuminescence project installed at the Spot on Schools Exhibition in Florence, Italy. Students: Elizabeth Boone, Eric Brockmeyer, Adam Buente, and Kyle Perry. Faculty: Mahesh Daas, Joshua Vermillion, Ball State University.

in an iterative cycle of digital and physical making. Specifically, drawings, renderings, photography, and physical mockups will be necessary for managing an array of information about geometry, context, material feedback, component–assembly relationships, fabrication, and assembly. Some of these are used to generate design decisions and geometry, others for directing fabrication equipment. Figures 6.4–6.14 show student projects that demonstrate the importance of visual communication for fabrication and assembly of student projects at various scales.

Recommended reading

McCullough, Malcolm. *Abstracting Craft: The Practiced Digital Hand.* MIT Press, 1998.

Figure 6.4a A digital rendering and completed photograph of the reBarn project. ReBarn was a park installation composed from 275 unique planks of repurposed barn wood and over 350 custom aluminum joints. Students: Elizabeth Boone, Eric Brockmeyer, Adam Buente, Jared Burt, Dustin Headley, Kyle Perry. Faculty: Kevin Klinger, Joshua Vermillion, Ball State Unviersity; A. Zahner Company engineered and fabricated all of the custom aluminum brackets and panels.

Figure 6.4b

Figure 6.5a Diagrams showing how parts and panels are assembled for reBarn. Students: Elizabeth Boone, Eric Brockmeyer, Adam Buente, Jared Burt, Dustin Headley, Kyle Perry. Faculty: Kevin Klinger, Joshua Vermillion, Ball State Unviersity; A. Zahner Company engineered and fabricated all of the custom aluminum brackets and panels.

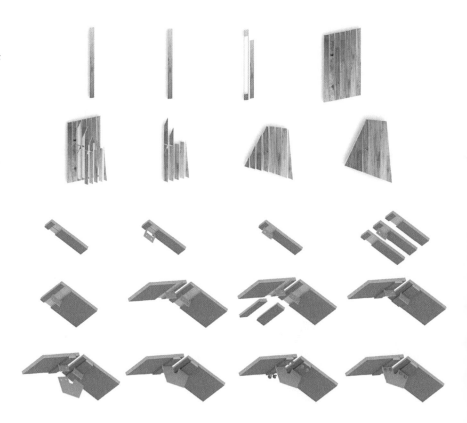

Figure 6.5b

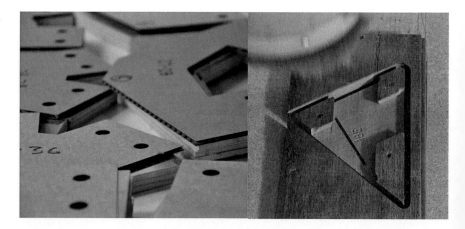

Figure 6.6 Example of reBarn components with labeling to enable the organization of off-site prefabrication of larger panels. Students: Elizabeth Boone, Eric Brockmeyer, Adam Buente, Jared Burt, Dustin Headley, Kyle Perry. Faculty: Kevin Klinger, Joshua Vermillion, Ball State Unviersity; A. Zahner Company engineered and fabricated all of the custom aluminum brackets and panels.

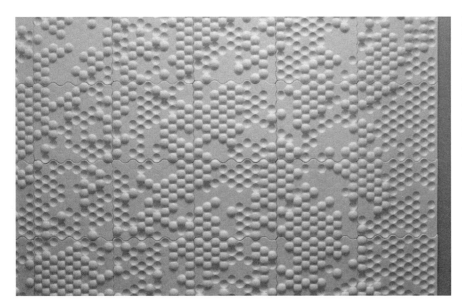

Figure 6.7 Photograph of Bitmaps, part of an interior fit-out project consisting of custom vacuum-formed polystyrene panels. Students: Elizabeth Boone, Eric Brockmeyer, Adam Buente, Kyle Perry, PROJECTiONE. Faculty: Joshua Coggeshall, Ball State University.

Figure 6.8 Rather than CNC machining hundreds of custom forms for Bitmaps, each panel's pattern was translated to template drawings and printed at full scale (top left). A generic form was machined (top right), which can then be populated with concave and convex "dimple" blanks by hand according to the printed templates (lower left). Once the form is completely populated, it is used to vacuum-form a custom polystyrene panel before being emptied and reconfigured for the next paper template (lower right). Students: Elizabeth Boone, Eric Brockmeyer, Adam Buente, Kyle Perry, PROJECTiONE. Faculty: Joshua Coggeshall, Ball State University.

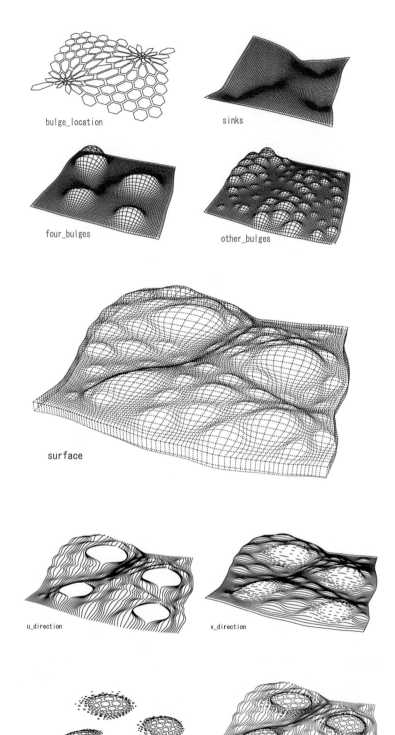

bulge_location

sinks

four_bulges

other_bulges

surface

Figure 6.9a Drawings describing the logics of form and patterning generation for Jelly. Students: Amanda Moschel, Dillon Pranger, and Olia Miho. Faculty: Brian Ringley, University of Cincinnati.

u_direction

v_direction

holes

pattern

Figure 6.9b

Figure 6.9b

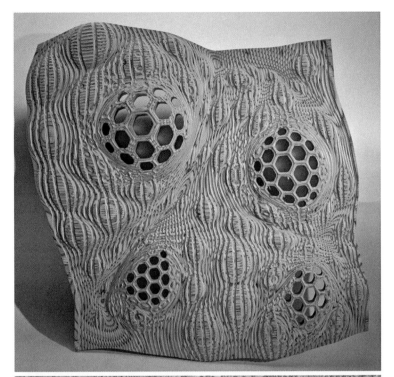

Figure 6.10 Photograph of Jelly, a CNC toolpath study in Baltic-birch plywood as part of an assignment called "F(r)iction Machines." Students: Amanda Moschel, Dillon Pranger, and Olia Miho. Faculty: Brian Ringley, University of Cincinnati.

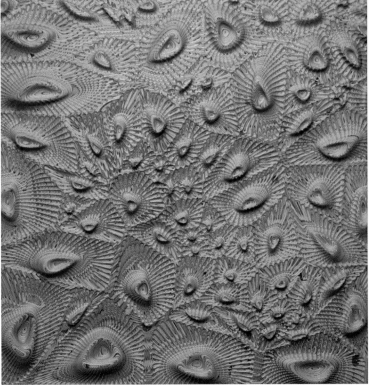

Figure 6.11 Photograph of Voronoi, a CNC toolpath study in Baltic-birch plywood as part of an assignment called "F(r)iction Machines." Students: Trevor Jordan, Austin Weller, YoonJin Kim, and Brian Turcza. Faculty: Brian Ringley, University of Cincinnati.

Figure 6.12 Drawings of Voronoi. Rather than literal representations of the final prototype, these drawings show the instructions for fabrication via a CNC milling machine. Each curve describes a path for a carving tool in order to sculpt the form and pattern. Students: Trevor Jordan, Austin Weller, YoonJin Kim, and Brian Turcza. Faculty: Brian Ringley, University of Cincinnati.

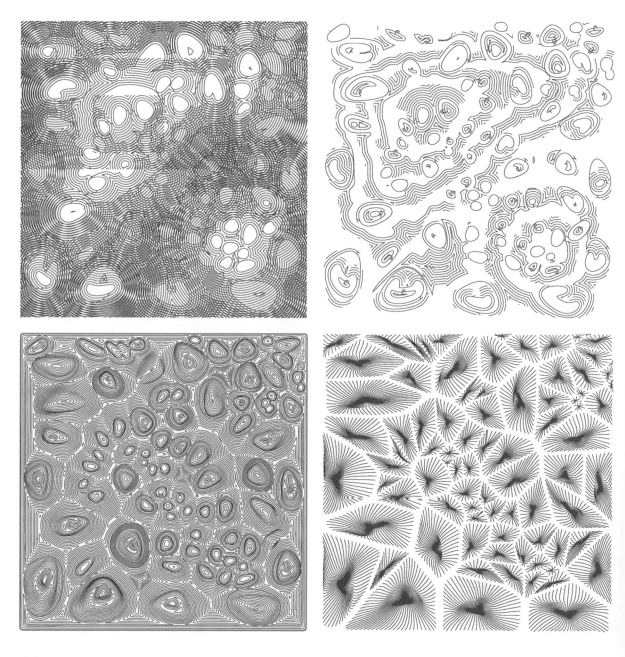

Figure 6.9b

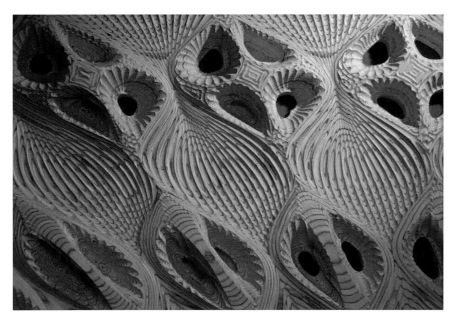

Figure 6.13 Close-up photograph of AKA, a CNC toolpath study in Baltic-birch plywood as part of an assignment called "F(r)iction Machines." Students: Andrew Wittkugel, Ari Pescovitz, and Karly Bryerman. Faculty: Brian Ringley, University of Cincinnati.

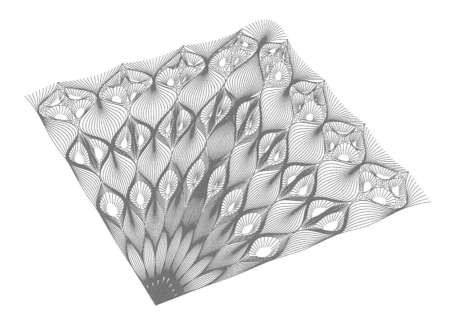

Figure 6.14 Drawing of AKA's differentiated patterning. Each curve describes a carving toolpath for a CNC milling machine. Students: Andrew Wittkugel, Ari Pescovitz, and Karly Bryerman. Faculty: Brian Ringley, University of Cincinnati.

Exercise set 7: geometric and material components

The first exercise set focuses on creating a parametric system from a simple form. Mark Burry uses a biological metaphor – the genotype and phenotype – as a way to describe parametric systems.[2] Changing the parameters within a genotype (genetic instructions) results in different phenotypes. Phenotypes are similar with respect to being of the same species or family, yet unique with individual traits. The value of parametric systems in the design process is this robust capacity to generate variable outputs suited to unique inputs, all from the same system. These systems should create rich parametric design spaces – in other words, any particular design result (a phenotype) is one of many possible outcomes from the parametric system (the genotype). As these phenotypes or prototypes are created, they can be judged or tested against meaningful criteria to determine their suitability to address the given design problem.

Regardless of your proficiency with using parametric design software, the ability to think parametrically is necessary to deploy software in any meaningful way, as argued by Farshid Moussavi.[3] Parametric thinking is the ability to read, understand, and construct complex webs of geometric operations, parameters, and associations. While structuring parametric relationships, you need to be able to incorporate lessons learned from renderings, context, and material studies. Parametric systems allow designers to leverage computation by accommodating these streams of information throughout the process and adapting the given phenotype.

Visual communication is an important part of generating and evaluating a parametric system. To continue using biological metaphors, the former principals of Foreign Office Architects once organized their projects in a phylogram according to geometric and operational classifications.[4] In biology a phylogram is a chart used to show the relationships between species as they evolve from common ancestors. Similarly, Richard Dawkins organized the results of his "Biomorph" exercises in a grid showing the diversity of phenotypes from a common genotype by simply altering parameters.[5] While deeply rooted in biology, these and other graphic devices are useful to demonstrate the generative capacity of a parametric system for producing differentiation.

The following exercises are scaffolded to help develop parametric thinking skills by creating and communicating complex dependencies and relationships between geometry, material, and form. While the steps are outlined

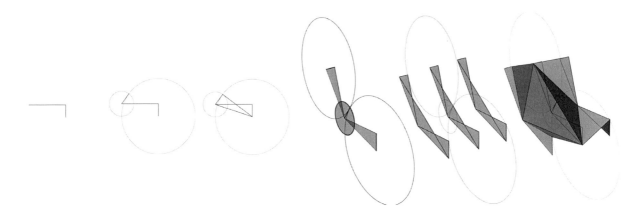

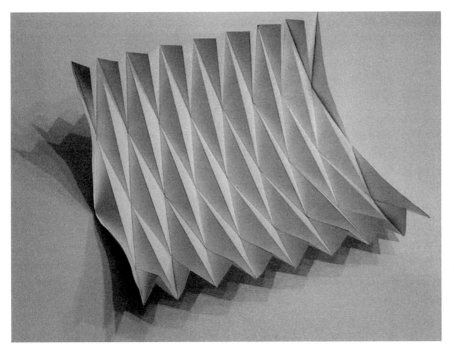

Figure 6.16 Folded paper prototype. Student: Nathan Capaccio. Faculty: Joshua Vermillion, Ball State University.

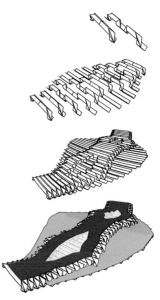

Figure 6.15 Parametric recipe diagram of a folded-plate system (top). Student: Nathan Capaccio. Faculty: Joshua Vermillion, Ball State University.

Figure 6.17 A study of variations of folded plate components for the design of a pavilion. Student: Nathan Capaccio. Faculty: Joshua Vermillion, Ball State University.

to start in the digital environment, it should be mentioned that one can easily switch Exercise 7A and 7B to start with physical prototyping and material logics prior to geometric development. Figures 6.15–6.18 show examples of student work that demonstrate either of these approaches.

Figure 6.18 Sample prototypes from the development of the Tetramin curtain, a spatial installation made from salvaged roof material from the RCA Dome in Indianapolis, IN. Each iteration undergoes refinement of shape and detail as the assembly grows in scale. Students: Derek Anger, Kate Donnelly, Melissa Garrison, André Paul Haffenden, Kristen Kuk, Derek Newman, Aaron Nordstrom, Natalie Reinhardt, William Zyck. Faculty: Kevin Klinger, Joshua Vermillion.

Objectives

This exercise is intended to introduce and develop understandings of:

- parametric thinking as it relates to geometry, material, and form to create a rich parametric design space;
- the feedback loops involved with digital and physical making, as various media, tools, and techniques inform design decisions;
- graphic communication and physical prototypes as ways to record, test, and manage design information.

Outcomes

The application of the above objectives involves breaking down a simple form into a non-simple geometric and material component. Most steps will involve digital modeling or physical making, along with producing drawings and diagrams for graphic communication.

Recommended reading

Burry, Mark. *Scripting Cultures: Architectural Design and Programming.* Wiley, 2011.

Dawkins, Richard. *The Blind Watchmaker.* Norton, 1986.
- Chapter 3, Accumulating Small Change.

Foreign Office Architects. *Phylogenesis: FOA's Ark.* Actar, 2004.

Menges, Achim. "Instrumental Geometry," *Techniques and Technologies in Morphogenetic Design (AD)*, 76 (2006): 42–53.

Moussavi, Farshid. "Parametric Software is no Substitute for Parametric Thinking," *The Architectural Review*, (2011)., http://m.architectural-review.com/8620000.article (accessed June 8, 2015).

Silver, Michael (ed.). *Programming Cultures: Architecture, Art and Science in the Age of Software Development, Architectural Design (AD).* Wiley, 2006.

Woodbury, Robert. *Elements of Parametric Design.* Routledge, 2010.

Exercise 7A: parametric component

Starting in the digital environment, this exercise focuses on the identification and manipulation of geometric relationships of an otherwise simple shape or form in order to create a parametric family of components. Figures 6.19 and 6.20 show example student work for the steps below.

Exercise procedure

Step 1: Start with a simple shape or form and reverse-engineer its geometric makeup to create a "graphic recipe." In other words, diagram the steps of geometric construction along with the critical parameters involved in drawing or modeling the simple form.

Step 2: Take this reverse-engineered parametric construct and begin to change the parameters to create geometric variations – make a family of parts that are similar, yet unique. These should also be digitally drawn or modeled for graphic communication.

Step 3: Examine the results of the previous step. Are the results very similar? Were you able to create variations that were unexpected? Have you tried a variety of parametric combinations? If not, add a geometric deformation to your recipe and/or more parameters and associations between ingredients of the recipe. The more parametric information and associations you add to this simple component, the less simple the geometric family becomes.

Step 4: The last step in the digital environment (for now) is to generate a variety of parametric options based on differing parameter values. The changes between incremental alterations of variables might be small, but the changes should accumulate to achieve more dramatic differences in shape between your starting geometry and the documented results. In other words, you want to create a rich selection of possible shapes that are related yet differentiated. It is important to visualize and diagram this sample parametric space of possible shapes that you have created, similar to the phylogram described in the introduction.

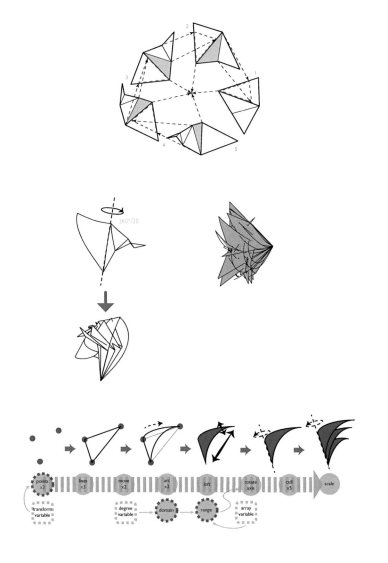

Figure 6.19 Example of component recipe and parameters with a phylogram of sample geometric components. Student: Junette Huynh, University of Calgary.

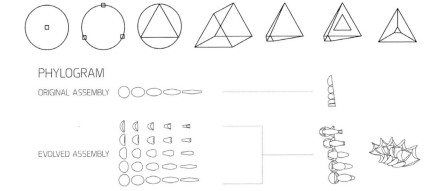

PARAMETRIC DEFINITION

PHYLOGRAM

ORIGINAL ASSEMBLY

EVOLVED ASSEMBLY

Figure 6.20 Example of a component's geometric construction and phylogram of options. Student: Trevor Steckly, University of Calgary.

157

Exercise 7B: material component

In the previous exercise you generated a parametric family of components purely in the digital environment. This exercise asks you to further develop the parametric prototype through physical fabrication, as demonstrated in the examples shown in Figures 6.21–6.23. Throughout the exercise steps you are asked to evaluate your results and adjust accordingly. By the end, you might have a much different (and hopefully improved) component than when you started, based on the practical constraints of materials, tools, and fabrication methods.

Exercise procedure

Step 1: Try to prototype some of your geometric samples from Exercise 7A. Select a sheet material (hard or soft) with which to work. Perhaps the steps for fabrication correspond to the steps in the geometric recipe, but maybe not. Using flat sheet material brings certain constraints when making curved forms. Volumes have to be analyzed as surfaces and edges. Joints and connections have to be resolved. It's important to note, depending on your experience working with particular materials and tools, that shaping materials can be difficult. Decisions made while drawing and modeling can have profound effects on the ease or difficulty of fabrication. After trying to fabricate a component precisely, examine it critically. Start by asking the following questions:

1. Was it successful in terms of aesthetics?
2. Was it well crafted?
3. How long did it take from start to finish?
4. What would you do differently?
5. What tools were needed?
6. How much waste was produced?

Step 2: It's time to make further prototypes. Make at least three more iterations, but the goal is to study this problem by physically making as many prototypes as necessary until you have a feasible component. After each iterative step, make changes that further facilitate the material and fabrication logics that you are developing. Hopefully the prototypes get better with more practice, but also as you modify the design idea based on the constraints of physical making.

Step 3: Document your process and results (successes and failures) with photography.

Step 4: Diagram the steps of your fabrication strategy in the digital environment.

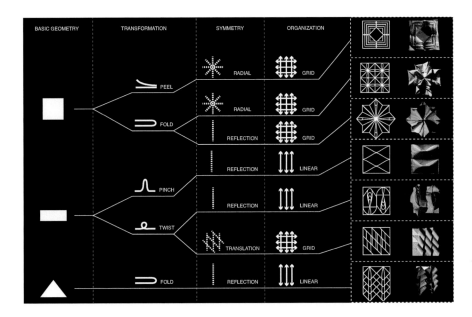

Figure 6.21 A diagram of fabrication strategies along with photographs of prototypes for felt tiles. Students: Alex Villa and Xavier Zhagui, University of Nevada Las Vegas.

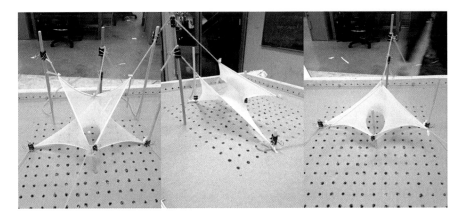

Figure 6.22 Photographs of surface studies using stretchable fabric. Students: Lane Sipahimalani, Adam Nault. Faculty: Joshua Vermillion, Ball State University.

159

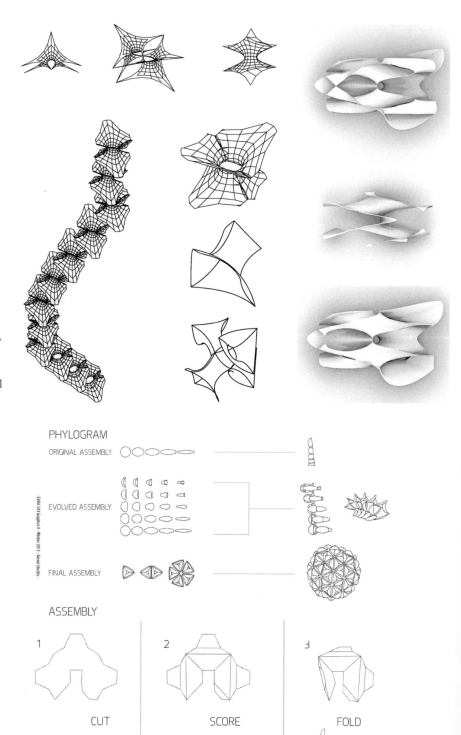

Figure 6.23 Digital rationalizations of the physical surface study models and studies on how the various surfaces can create combinatory forms. Students: Lane Sipahimalani, Adam Nault. Faculty: Joshua Vermillion, Ball State University.

PHYLOGRAM

ORIGINAL ASSEMBLY

EVOLVED ASSEMBLY

FINAL ASSEMBLY

ASSEMBLY

1   CUT

2   SCORE

3   FOLD

Figure 6.24 Revised matrix of components along with fabrication instructions. Trevor Steckly, University of Calgary.

Exercise 7C: digital–material feedback

This exercise focuses on negotiating a resolution between the digital and physical versions of the component prototypes you have created. The cyclical process of developing and testing material and fabrication logics, and then translating them into geometric constraints, will continue in later exercises of this chapter.

Exercise procedure

Step 1: Referring to your prototypes and photographic evidence, reflect on the lessons learned from physically making your components. This feedback (from successes and failures) is important information that can be embedded back into your decision-making within the digital environment as rules, geometric constraints, and parameter ranges. Diagram these new constraints.

Step 2: Using the material and fabrication logics from your physical prototypes, revise your digital parametric studies from Exercise 7A.

Step 3: By the end, revise the visualization diagram of your parametric design space with new differentiated components that are informed by your material studies (Figure 6.24). You should feel comfortable with the possibility of physically making any of these digital studies, which might necessitate further working back and forth between physical and digital prototyping (the more iterative studies you perform, the better the results).

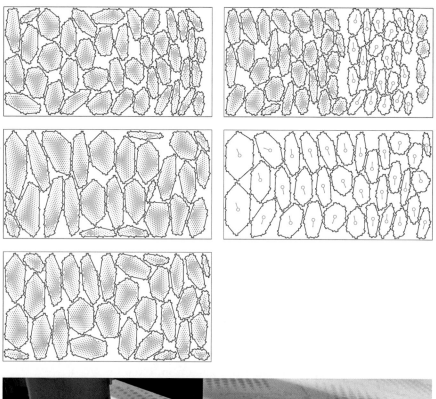

Figure 6.25 Components for Exotique nested within high-density polyethylene sheets for CNC milling, PROJECTiONE (Adam Buente, Kyle Perry).

Exercise set 8: assemblies

For most of the twentieth century and into the twenty-first, architectural production has relied on the standardization of building systems and their parts. Wood, steel, masonry, and other materials are shaped in repetitive dimensions and modules. Before the incorporation of digital technology in the architectural design process, geometries were mostly limited by the capabilities of the tools of hand drafting – right angles, straight lines, and circular arcs. Mass production was dependent on economies of scale, which necessitated an increase in efficiency – the production of highly standardized products with increasingly specialized equipment in order to decrease time, labor, and costs, all while increasing the output of production.

Digital technologies are disrupting this mass production paradigm, both in the way we design, and in the way that parts and systems are fabricated and constructed. Production systems for building components are increasingly absorbing digital fabrication equipment (e.g., computer-numerically controlled production), which are capable of producing unique or custom parts directly from digital information. Digital fabrication – long a staple of other industries (aerospace, automotive, ship-building) for improving precision, quality, and efficiency, while expanding customization and complexity – is rapidly gaining traction in the building industry. Likewise, digital design environments have exposed the actually quite old mathematical underpinnings of geometry, calculus, and physics to a new audience that has long been told that freeform shapes and differentiated parts are too difficult or expensive to describe, manage, and manufacture as architecture.

In the first exercise set you produced a parametric system capable of creating similar, yet variable outputs. Now we will use that system to create an assembly with differentiated parts. Figures 6.25–6.27 illustrate an example of a differentiated ceiling assembly as each panel is unique yet still hexagonal in shape. However, the question remains: Why variation? A better question might be: What criteria constitute a successful design resolution, and how do these criteria inform the variation of a differentiated system? Differentiated geometry can be derived by variable performance criteria within a system. As you develop a differentiated assembly, you must also develop the performative capacity of your parametric system. This development requires a clear understanding of the possible geometric traits of your components, the performative value of these traits, and which parameters are critical to their generation. For instance, the project shown in Figures 6.28–6.30 is a composite

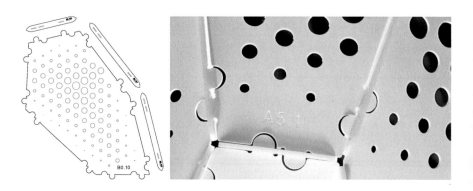

Figure 6.26 Diagram of typical Exotique cell components and photograph of assembly details, PROJECTiONE (Adam Buente, Kyle Perry).

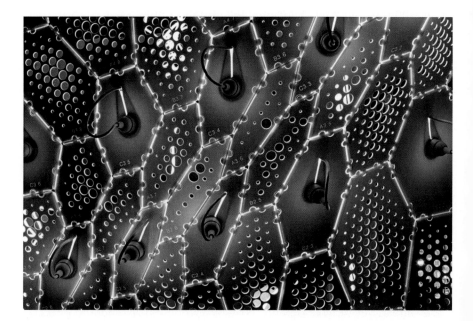

Figure 6.27 Photograph of Exotique upon completion, PROJECTiONE (Adam Buente, Kyle Perry).

of plywood and rubber. The size, depth, and spacing of each component or cell lends the prototype the ability to flex in shape more (smaller cells, further spaced) or less (larger, deeper cells). These relationships between geometry, parameters, and performance need to be visualized.

Once again, this set of exercises asks you to develop geometric assembly options in the digital environment as well as physical prototypes. At each step you are asked to produce or extract certain graphic deliverables in order to manage and communicate your work.

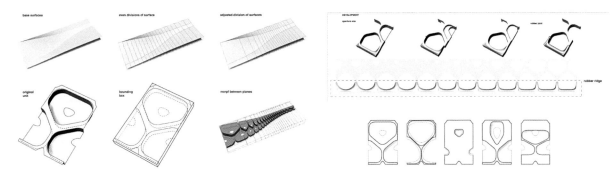

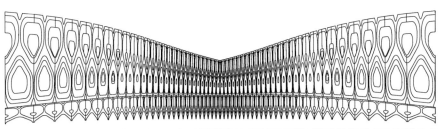

Figure 6.28 Drawing of the component-to-system relationship logics and component variations for Shell Lace Structure. Students: Ulrika Lindell, Erik Davin Nevala-Lee. Faculty: Brian Ringley, Pratt Institute.

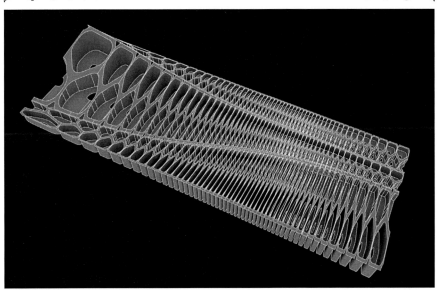

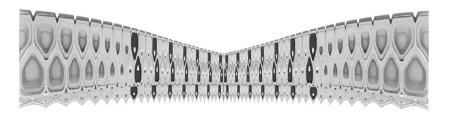

Figure 6.29 Shell Lace Structure prototype drawing and model iterations. Students: Ulrika Lindell, Erik Davin Nevala-Lee. Faculty: Brian Ringley, Pratt Institute.

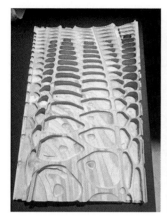
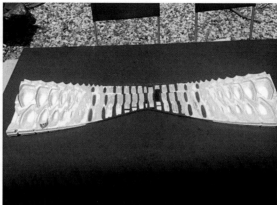

Figure 6.30 Physical prototypes of Shell Lace Structure. Students: Ulrika Lindell, Erik Davin Nevala-Lee. Faculty: Brian Ringley, Pratt Institute.

Objectives

This exercise is intended to introduce and develop understandings of:

- methods for arraying components into a multi-part, differentiated assembly;
- the degree of craft and care that is required to prototype your design proposals from actual materials;
- developing and applying a performative logic for your system that addresses critical design criteria.

Outcomes

At the end of these exercises you will have defined and created a differentiated assembly system via digital models, drawings and diagrams, renderings, and physical prototypes.

Recommended reading

Beorkrem, Christopher. *Material Strategies in Digital Fabrication*. Routledge, 2013.

Hensel, Michael, Achim Menges, and Michael Weinstock. *Emergent Technologies and Design: Towards a Biological Paradigm for Architecture*. Routledge, 2010.

Reiser, Jesse, and Nanako Umemoto. *Atlas of Novel Tectonics*. Princeton Architectural Press, 2006.

Schodek, Daniel, Martin Bechthold, Kimo Griggs, Kenneth Martin Kao, and Marco Steinberg. *Digital Design and Manufacturing: CAD/CAM Applications in Architecture and Design*. Wiley, 2005.

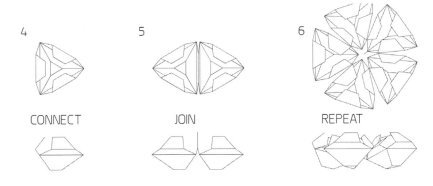

Figure 6.32 Arrayed components in a radial assembly. Student: Trevor Steckly, University of Calgary.

Exercise 8A: digital assemblies

The goal for this exercise is to create a larger assembly composed of the component family from Exercise 7C. The assembly of parts should be composed and ordered as a differentiated system – in other words, a system made up of components that repeat with variation.

Exercise procedure

Step 1: Take the component system from Exercise Set 7 and explore each of these three ordering strategies to deploy the componentry into larger assemblies:

1. a linear sequence – components arrayed along a line or curve;
2. a surface array – components populated within a surface's grid-like UV space;
3. a three-dimensional growth pattern – components deployed with a rules-based system to grow within a three-dimensional volume or space.

Step 2: Look at the results critically and select one of the strategies to carry forward for three more iterative studies. For each iteration, carefully consider how each component within the larger assembly is parametrically differentiated, and identify any performative considerations that inform these geometric variations.

Step 3: Through drawings and diagrams, show three possible assembly system configurations to demonstrate the system's parametric capacity for variation based on performance.

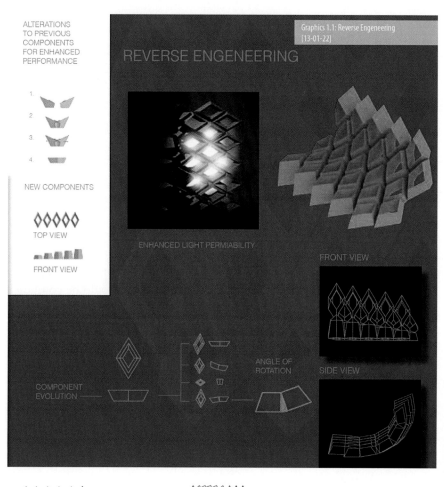

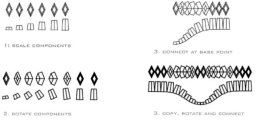

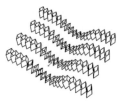

Figure 6.31 An example of a linear sequence that becomes a surface assembly. Student: Yves Poitras, University of Calgary.

Exercise 8B: physical assemblies

Similarly to the previous round of exercises, you are being asked to build one of your assembly systems with physical materials. Since you are already comfortable fabricating the individual components, your efforts should be focused on testing and revising the connections and joints that form the assembly or system of parts (Figures 6.33 and 6.34).

Exercise procedure

Step 1: Build a physical prototype of one of the three assembly system configurations from Exercise 8A. Just as you did in Exercise 7B, evaluate the prototype critically, based on the following criteria:

1. the efficiency of budget, time, and material;
2. the structural strength and stability of the system;
3. the aesthetic qualities of the system's parts-to-whole composition (components, joints, and the assembly as a whole);
4. the ability to manage the complexity of many unique components (consider marking components for straightforward identification).

Step 2: It's more probable than not that the prototype needs revisions. Iteratively study and improve the connections and joints of the assembly. Once these details have been resolved, revise the digital version of the system (from Exercise 8A) to match.

Step 3: Build a final prototype at scale. This could be the whole assembly or just a representative portion, as a system proof-of-concept.

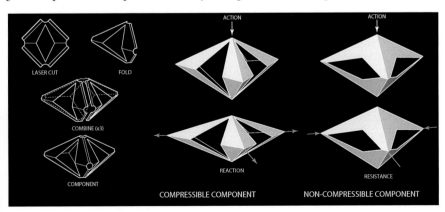

Figure 6.33 Component logic diagram for folded lattice assembly. Students: Majdi Faleh, Ryan Hanigan and Wesley Stabs. Faculty: Joshua Vermillion, Ball State University.

Figure 6.34 Physical prototyping of a folded lattice assembly using cardstock paper. Students: Majdi Faleh, Ryan Hanigan, and Wesley Stabs. Faculty: Joshua Vermillion, Ball State University.

Figure 6.36 Photographs of assembly system prototypes at the scale of clothing being fitted to mannequins. Faculty: Jonathon Anderson, University of Nevada Las Vegas.

Figure 6.35 Speculative rendering of an assembly at the scale of furniture. Trevor Steckly, University of Calgary.

Exercise 8C: scaled assemblies

As mentioned before, your assembly should be composed of individual components that are differentiated (repetition with variation). By visualizing hypothetical systems at particular scales, performing particular functions, and within particular contexts, you can now propose how and why each component in the assembly is differentiated. In other words, if each part is going to be different, then how can these differences be informed by situational constraints and opportunities? Figures 6.35–6.37 show examples of contextual visualizations.

Exercise procedure

Step 1: Select three different scales at which to deploy your assembly system. Visualize these situational scenarios for your system within a hypothetical context and use.

Step 2: Add information to the assembly diagrams that were begun in Exercise 8A and revised in Exercise 8B. Specify how scale, context, and function would inform or affect the individual differentiated components for each scenario.

Figure 6.37 Assembly system prototypes for a prosthetic skin. Student: Molly Gardner. Faculty: Dustin Headley, Kansas State University.

Exercise 9: tab A slot B

This last exercise is an opportunity to consolidate, correct, and complete all of the relevant representation from the previous exercises into a package that communicates the key information about the components and the system you have developed, along with how it's fabricated and assembled.

Exercise procedure

Select one of the assembly scenarios from Exercise 8C and develop, compile, and edit the following drawings:

1. Component logic drawings that show the geometric makeup and parameters of a typical component, how it's fabricated (step-by-step), and the family of varied or differentiated components (phylogram).
2. System logic drawings that demonstrate the way components are composed into a system along with critical parameters and geometric constraints, the system's performative capacity, the assembly of the system, and how the system (and embedded components) are responsive to context, use, and scale.
3. Assembly logic drawings that show precisely how to fabricate and assemble the selected assembly scenario. This would include a visual catalog of components, specific fabrication information for each component, a visual of the assembly keyed with specific component locations, and an assembly sequence diagram.
4. Again, review the results critically. Imagine handing these drawings to someone else to build the assembly. Are the drawings legible, easy to follow, and informationally complete? Revise as necessary to satisfy these concerns.

The following projects illustrate some of the drawing deliverables suggested above. They all consist of assembly systems that are composed of differentiated components.

Hyperlaxity

Design: PROJECTiONE (Adam Buente, Kyle Perry)

Hyperlaxity is a speculative project for a partition system. Designed by the firm PROJECTiONE, the main geometry of the system was generated from a hexagonal field that was then geometrically deformed. From a performance standpoint the differentiated traits of each cell, such as depth and aperture size, respond to desired visual porosities and structural requirements. Each cell is composed of rigid aluminum front and back panels, intermediary compression members, and silicon skin acting in tension. The individual components are planar, making CNC fabrication quick and straightforward while still forming a three-dimensional construct once assembled.

Figure 6.38 Diagram showing the process of distorting a hexagonal grid to create a differentiated system for Hyperlaxity.

Figure 6.39 Typical components for Hyperlaxity. Each component shown defines a differentiated family of parts.

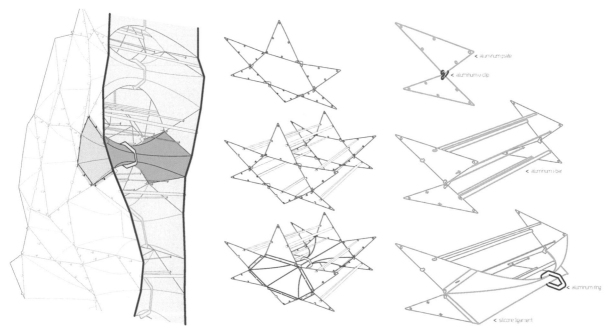

Figure 6.40 Diagrams showing the assembly logic for a Hyperlaxity cell.

Figure 6.41 Rendering of Hyperlaxity within context with human figures to reference scale.

Underwood Pavilion

Students: Andrew Heilman, Chris Hinders, Charles Koers, Huy Nguyen, Nick Peterson, Steven Putt, Noura Rashid, Ashley Urbanowich. Faculty: Gernot Riether, Andrew Wit, Ball State University.

The Underwood Pavilion is an outdoor tensegrity structure constructed from 56 differentiated modules. The variation of the modules and the composition of the system are based on structural performance, as well as views to and from the site. Figures 6.42–6.47 describe the project as a series of nested logics starting with the components and modules, then site and context, system, fabrication and assembly, and finally simulation and analysis of structure and form.

Figure 6.42 Photograph of the Underwood Pavilion, a tensegrity structure designed and built by eight students and two faculty members at Ball State University.

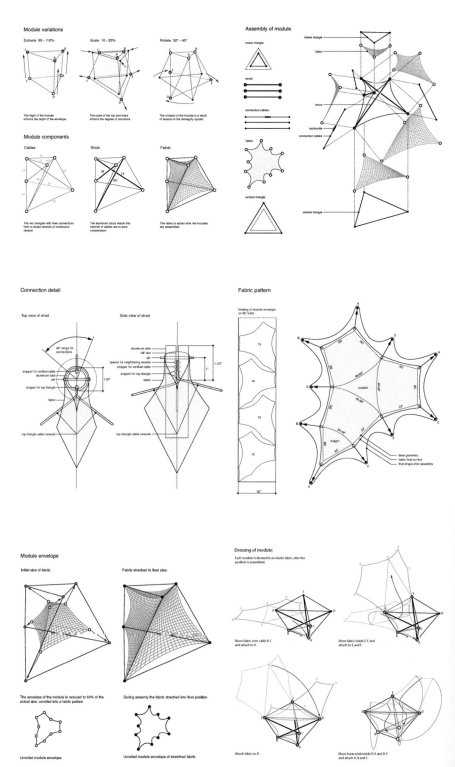

Figure 6.43 Diagrams explaining the parametric logic, parts, and assembly of the Underwood Pavilion modules.

Landscape relationships

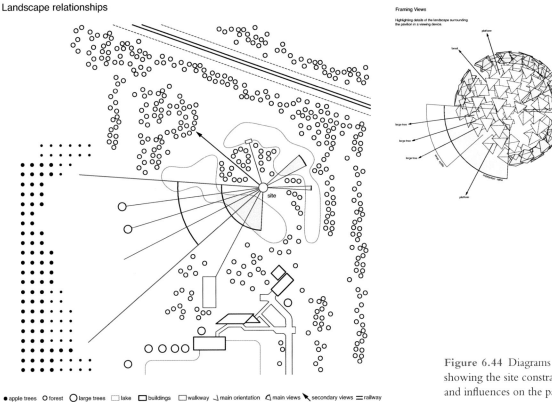

Framing Views

Highlighting details of the landscape surrounding
the pavilion in a viewing device.

● apple trees   O forest   ◯ large trees   ▢ lake   ▬ buildings   ▢ walkway   ⏌ main orientation   ◁ main views   ✎ secondary views   ═ railway

Figure 6.44 Diagrams
showing the site constraints
and influences on the pavilion
system.

Groups of modules

Tensegrity Network

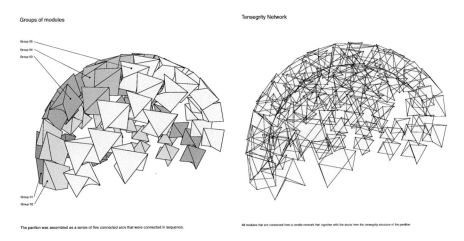

The pavilion was assembled as a series of five connected arcs that were connected in sequence.

All modules that are connected form a tensile network that together with the struts form the tensegrity structure of the pavilion.

Figure 6.45 Diagrams
showing the arrangement
and types of modules and the
tensegrity structural members.

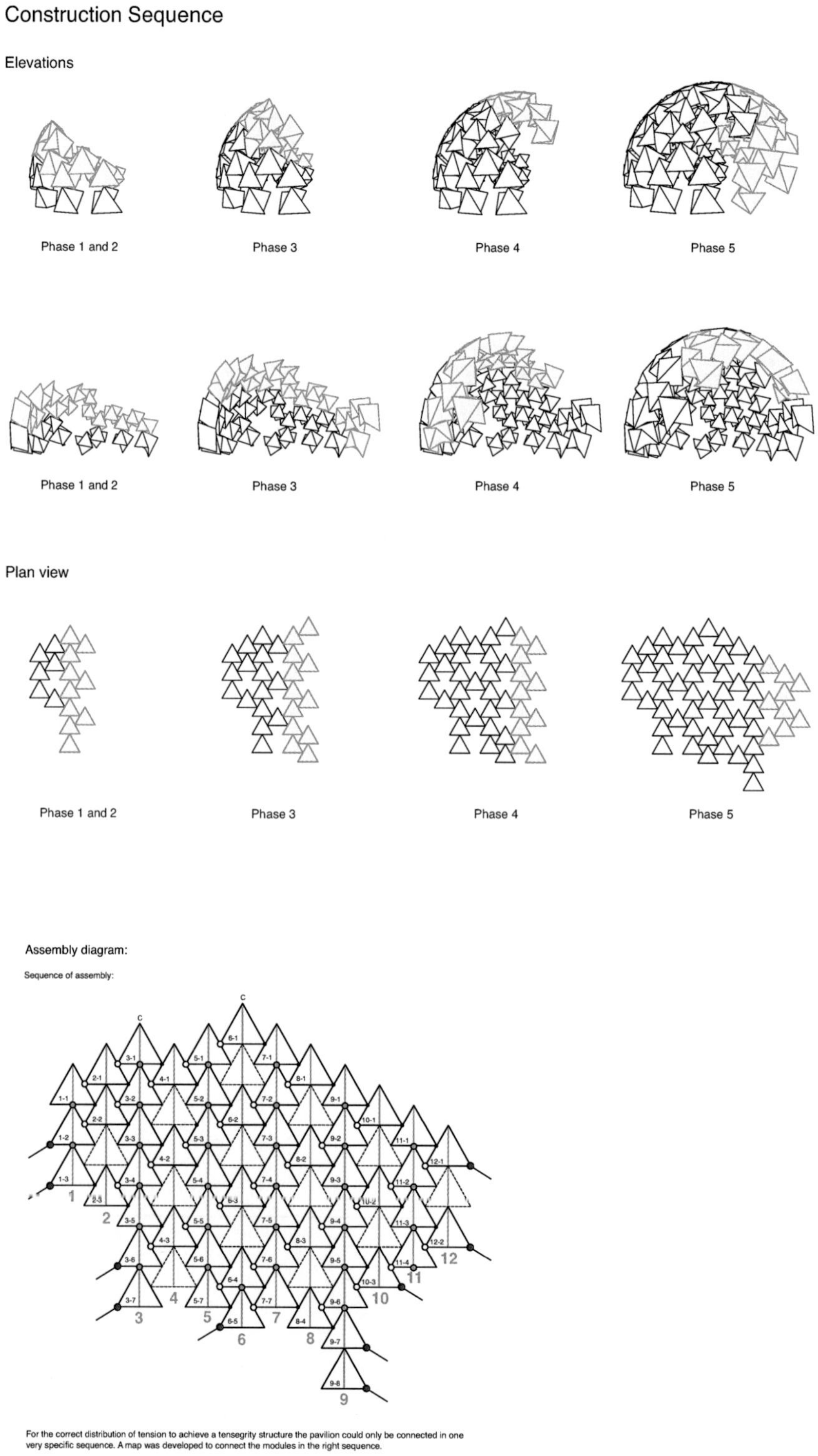

Construction Sequence

Elevations

| Phase 1 and 2 | Phase 3 | Phase 4 | Phase 5 |

| Phase 1 and 2 | Phase 3 | Phase 4 | Phase 5 |

Plan view

| Phase 1 and 2 | Phase 3 | Phase 4 | Phase 5 |

Assembly diagram:

Sequence of assembly:

Figure 6.46 Diagrams showing the assembly layout and sequence.

For the correct distribution of tension to achieve a tensegrity structure the pavilion could only be connected in one very specific sequence. A map was developed to connect the modules in the right sequence.

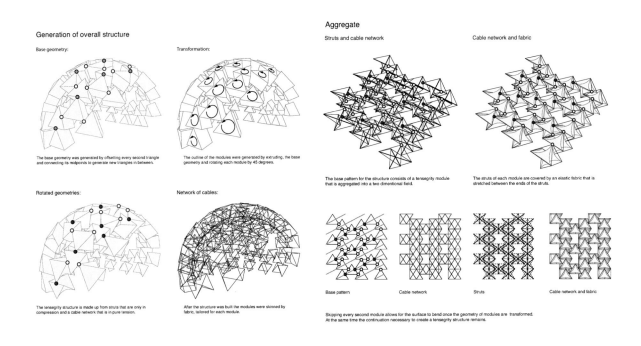

Generation of overall structure

Base geometry:

The base geometry was generated by offsetting every second triangle and connecting its midpoints to generate new triangles in between.

Transformation:

The outline of the modules were generated by extruding, the base geometry and rotating each module by 45 degrees.

Rotated geometries:

The tensegrity structure is made up from struts that are only in compression and a cable network that is in pure tension.

Network of cables:

After the structure was built the modules were skinned by fabric, tailored for each module.

Aggregate

Struts and cable network

The base pattern for the structure consists of a tensegrity module that is aggregated into a two dimentional field.

Cable network and fabric

The struts of each module are covered by an elastic fabric that is stretched between the ends of the struts.

Base pattern Cable network Struts Cable network and fabric

Skipping every second module allows for the surface to bend once the geometry of modules are transformed.
At the same time the continuation necessary to create a tensegrity structure remains.

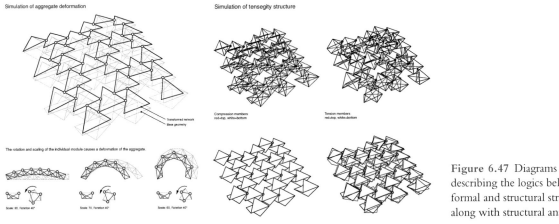

Simulation of aggregate deformation

The rotation and scaling of the individual module causes a deformation of the aggregate.

Transformed network
Base geometry

Scale: 90, Rotation 40°   Scale: 70, Rotation 40°   Scale: 60, Rotation 40°

Simulation of tensegity structure

Compression members
red=top, white=bottom

Tension members
red=top, white=bottom

Figure 6.47 Diagrams describing the logics behind the formal and structural strategies along with structural analysis.

Cumulus Oculi

Students: Justin McNair, Jack Kennedy, Abigail Buchanan, Sharece Ramos, Blakeni Walls, Anuj Patel, Daniel Salgado, Carlie Blake, John Jeppson, Heather Williams, Cait Whisenant, Alexis Garcia. Faculty: Jonathon Anderson, assistant professor, University of North Carolina Greensboro.

Cumulus Oculi is an undulating ceiling installation in a gallery space. The overall form, with 14 apertures for lighting, is composed of over 25,000 differentiated triangular components made from laser-cut paper stock. The triangle components were assembled into intermediate-sized panels off-site in a design studio, followed by on-site installation of these panels. The form of the system and the component differentiation logics were informed by the proportions of the gallery space, desired human interaction with the installation lighting, and material and laser-cutter size constraints

Figure 6.48 (Opposite, above) diagram showing the overall form of Cumulus Oculi, broken down into smaller panels. The geometry of each panel is then triangulated into smaller components.

Figure 6.49 (Opposite, left) sample drawings for laser cutting each component of Panel A. Each part is labeled for identification, and tabbed for assembly.

Figure 6.50 (Opposite, middle) sample components after laser cutting. Each is marked for identification with scored tabs for folding and assembly.

Figure 6.51 (Opposite, right) on-site assembly of Cumulus Oculi in a gallery space.

Figure 6.52 (Right) completed Cumulus Oculi installation.

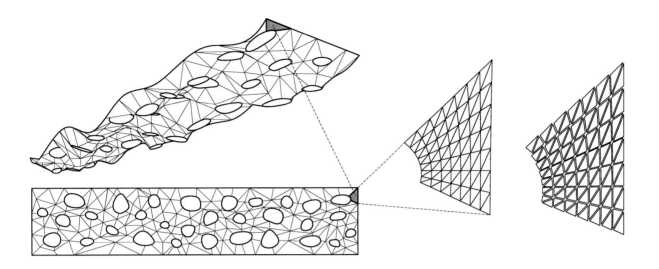

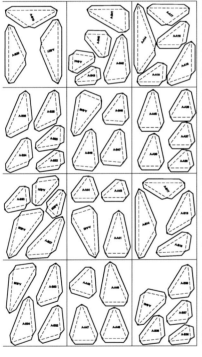

Conclusion

This chapter focused on the visual communication of differentiated systems and assembly instructions as a way to generate and manage design information. In parallel, you were asked to develop your project with a focus on fabrication and material logics. This involved making physical prototypes to interrogate materials and techniques as well as to test the decisions and assumptions that you made while at the computer. A feedback loop between your digital and physical investigations is necessary in order to critically engage design as a material practice. Despite the best intentions, prototyping can very often lead to accidents, failures, and sometimes completely new directions. It's important to keep an open mind through this process and allow materials and production tools to inform your design work. Of course, diagramming and drawings are very important ways to manage and communicate all of this information. As you will find in the next chapter, managing data is crucial to computational design, especially as the complexity of a project grows.

Notes

1 Malcolm McCullough, *Abstracting Craft: The Practiced Digital Hand* (Cambridge, MA: MIT Press, 1998).
2 Mark Burry, *Scripting Cultures: Architectural Design and Programming* (New York: Wiley, 2011).
3 Farshid Moussavi, "Parametric Software is no Substitute for Parametric Thinking," *The Architectural Review* (2011). http://m.architectural-review.com/8620000. article (accessed June 8, 2015).
4 Foreign Office Architects, *Phylogenesis: FOA's Ark* (Barcelona: Actar, 2004).
5 Richard Dawkins, *The Blind Watchmaker* (New York: Norton, 1986).

AN ESSAY ON THE IMMERSIVE, OR SOLVING FOR MANICHEAN COMPLICATIONS

Simon Kim

The sum of current fears, or our elders's plight

The advance of intelligence in cities and buildings in recent years has also brought about misgivings and reproach of its intentions and franchise. At the core of its detraction are the central ideas of privacy from surveillance, and machine agency. The second idea is part of a larger discussion of intelligence – with rights chartered for the nonhuman, and the curtailing of humans as the dominant species. An open letter from the Future of Life Institute, *Research Priorities for Robust and Beneficial Artificial Intelligence*, outlines ethics, validity, security, and control in short- and long-term research.[1] Its signatories include Elon Musk, Steve Wozniak, and Stephen Hawking. The document is not inflammatory as otherwise reported by journalists, and puts forth best practices in maintaining research vectors with societal benefits in place. This axiom of AI and systems intelligence under the aegis of human benefit is to stop misuse of AI against humans by humans, as well as to avoid what are called "pitfalls." These pitfalls are never specified, but allude to machine self-awareness and sovereignty.[2]

On the other side of this argument are the longstanding ideas and initiatives of Raymond Kurzweil and those who have been pursuing the singularity of an artificial intelligence thrust upon the predominantly human-centric landscape.[3] The radical newness of this introduction of evolutionary, reproductive machines would be a techno-social space of incredible discovery and stewardship. The transhuman and cyborg domain of synthetic and natural biologies would have dominance with increasingly blurred and new definitions of architectural partitioning of inside to outside, private to public, spatial adjacencies, and function.

Closer to the discipline of architecture, architects and urban theorists have recently published articles casting aspersions on software- and hardware-enabled cities and intelligent buildings.[4] In recent interviews they discuss sensor technology in the home that may come under sinister processes, and society's willing release of a privacy that was hard-fought and won in postwar activism. The means and methods of data collection are at the center of the articles, as architects find themselves replaced in smart city design by other disciplines, and the purposes by which human life is traced are not neutral. The ethics of surveillance technology upon citizen liberties outweighs the easing of human effort by a responsive environment. Instead of augmented and ubiquitous computing environments that replenish groceries or supplies as needed, urban life is seen as the tracking and tagging of civilian-consumers.[5]

The idea of a private life within the home is extinguished as data transmission flows without from within as personal devices are constantly monitoring. Architectural design within such a network is one of many design domains that range from projected digital interfaces and graphics clouding over physical textures and surfaces.

Whatever the output, the energizing core of this discussion is one of architecture and urbanism advanced to the technophilic forefront as stages and tableaux of intelligent environments. Close behind is its representation in broadcast media to the public, and a race for capital in the form of research funding[6] or client approbation. As work on ubiquitous computing in cities progresses – especially within existing streets of Copenhagen or New York – the herald-like imagery and press releases of prototypes take on greater roles. The presentation of the once and future smart city, which the author will recast as The Immersive, has been an ongoing telegraph made in many formats. Throughout much of the past centuries of mass publication from newsprint, radio, television, to digital communication, ideas of future societies enabled by technology have been disseminated to the public. Venues such as World Fairs and Expositions have showcased inventions such as electrically powered lights, automated devices, and modes of transportation, as well as future scenarios of personal robots and networked domiciles and offices.[7] The eagerness to promote new products and infrastructure, as well as their broad applications for near and far futures as depicted in homes, work, cities, and even space are still seen today in publications, the same fairs and expositions, academies, and conferences.

However, the dreams and brochures of embracing the influx of electromechanical, biological, and material technologies have not been fulfilled in the building practices of architects and urban designers. In this arena, the progress is clearly in the province of engineers and developers of software–hardware devices. Architects and urban designers do not feature in the pursuits of Google, Apple, Microsoft, and the buildings of the future may be developed by teams of engineers, materials researchers, and interface designers. Although current education in design schools provides courses in interaction and actuation for architecture students, recent graduates have little opportunity to exercise their talents in traditional practice. What few offices engage in these expanded methods encounter resistance in a discipline that is ill-equipped to define its praxis. Currently, the NCARB licensing exams, and Sweets Catalog (perhaps division 13 – special construction) do not acknowledge new materials or methods. Prominent figures within this move toward The Immersive may have been trained as architects but develop their research and body of work outside of the discipline. Joseph Kosinski started with KDLAB before moving to commercials and feature films. His visions of the future are a reference point for many architects and students who emulate his work in their own imaging of projects. Skylar Tibbits and Brandon Kruysman are individuals who have studied architecture, taught under its auspices, but now practice against its grain. Tibbits has a funded position at MIT where he develops collaborative research platforms for his Self-Assembly Lab. Kruysman left a teaching position at SCI-Arc for a position at Bot&Dolly, now owned by Google. I run the Immersive Kinematics research lab with roboticist Mark Yim, where we produce, direct, and design human–nonhuman scenarios and environments.

Architects are well placed to bridge the technical sciences and the humanities. The technician or computer programmer does not have the necessary training to produce relevant scales, adjacencies, and species of spaces that architecture demands. Massive data requires meaningful embodiment to be understood. Real-time response should realize a well-tempered environment. For architecture and urbanism to become part of the transformation that is coming to cities and countries, new and constant dialogues are necessary to bridge source and affect. Dialogues serve multiple purposes: they renew the collaboration among disparate domains that practice has always maintained, and they introduce new technique and new forms of media to the current closed set or repertoire. These can also effectively provide new categories of (billable) services.

Dialogues (Leibniz and Papin, Searle and Dennett, McLuhan and Pound, human and nonhuman)

Correspondences happen among people with shared interests or common goals, and they can lead to an accounting of events, new formations of thought and material, or delivery of a mutually developed product. Correspondence and conversation may also be informal or loosely structured, without necessary preamble or affectation of instituted form. Disagreements are also open to discussion separately from the content of a person's body of work. For example, ideas exchanged between two authors in their letters do not necessarily get published in their books – public and private intellectual pursuits can be made distinct.

However, letters and correspondence often become public and part of a larger biography – as citations for readers to use for a deeper understanding. The methods in which contemporary emails can be made public may serve to change the manner in which the writer structures their writing from a letter to an intended colleague to that of a potentially larger audience.

A   In the hypothetical Chinese Room scenario, John Searle places a human in a closed room. There are three conditions: there are only two small openings – one for text to be entered and another for collection. Within the room are logs for every match among English words to their Chinese equivalents. Finally, the human in the room has no knowledge of the Chinese language. When text written in English is entered, the human finds its Chinese pairing, and places the results in the window for retrieval. The 1980 thought experiment for Searle was a criticism against artificial intelligence and whether machines can gain intelligence or dutifully follow instruction. The goal of an artificial intelligence would be unmet as long as a lack of intentionality was present. This would also apply to an embodied intelligence – one with a physical body that is in the world, such as Winograd's SHRDLU from 1973 – that will correctly respond to a prompt to pick up the red cube, without knowing redness or of being cube.

In a rebuttal, Daniel Dennett wrote the Intentional Stance and the qualification that mindfulness is ordered around the observer's understanding of the possible motives for the movements or actions of the observed. The observer continually interprets the outer workings of the observed entity. Its intentionality comes via an acceptance by the subject's attention toward it and what predictions are accounted for in its behavior. Following this is several decades of positions and renouncements made through published papers and press.[8] The arguments of the two scholars are primarily public – there appear to be no private letters or correspondence to elucidate or mutually shore up their approaches to consciousness or mind away from the view of others.

B   At a time when the idea of biological mechanism – that all vital matter are a manner of machines – governed the life sciences, Gottfried Liebniz and Denis Papin had many exchanges of advanced devices; intelligence as machines with phenomena as yet undefined. While Leibniz was working away on his invention of calculus and its applications to dynamics, Papin was producing innovations in steam engines. Both men were interested in the harnessing of this new explosive power for human endeavors, and wrote each other with support and questions in the development of the field of dynamics and new power sources.[9] In a turn away from the dominant field of mechanism, Leibniz would echo Searle with a questioning of mind as a property of mechanical construct. Describing a mechanical structure capable of producing thought, feeling, and perception, he would hypothesize that it be relatively enlarged to the size of a mill to enter and describe.[10] However, in the interior order and organization of parts and levers of a mind the size of a mill, nowhere would there be a visual representation or an accounting for thought.

C   One such conversation happened between two significant figures – one in poetry and the other in media studies – in the period immediately following World War II. Ezra Pound shaped modern poetry and expression with his Cantos, the reshaping of Eliot's *Wasteland* and his influence on the late work of Yeats. In 1945 Pound was placed in the care of St. Elizabeth Hospital, a government hospital for the insane due to his wartime work in print and broadcast allied to Mussolini and Hitler.

Although seen to be "borrowing ideas, often carelessly, from painting, architecture, music, sinology, and assorted other disconnected movements swirling around him, few critics contest that he (Pound) was a flashpoint among poets, thinkers, and social reformers for a radical new poetics."[11] However, his disgraced wartime efforts would leave him with few admirers and friends.

Marshall McLuhan was junior faculty at the University of Toronto when he visited Pound at the hospital in 1948, and encountered what his then-student and traveling companion Hugh Kenner described as Pound's "epigrammatic snarl." From that single meeting until 1957, McLuhan would start a heavily one-sided correspondence with Pound, questioning aspects of the Cantos and their application to his work and modernist prose, with the poet's terse responses often pointing to previous publications.[12] But this exchange was vital to McLuhan's development as a first-time author, and his dissection of the Cantos by Pound, and its literary structure is mirrored in his own work *The Mechanical Bride*.[13]

D   There is a scene in David Mamet's film *The Spanish Prisoner* where plot and character reversals are set in place using nothing but dialogue and pacing. Joe Ross and Jimmy Dell are in an open setting but the camera is framed tightly on the one face of the character speaking. It is a fast delivery of lines establishing a matter of trust between two strangers with suspect motivations. An older, apparently wealthy man (the con man) offers to buy the protagonist's camera (the mark, and possible FBI informant), initiating a series of encounters. A third element is the trope of Japanese foreigners. Neither of the former two are aware of the importance of the third – the Japanese are presented as unnamed, neutral background extras. In fact, the close-ups on the two white male faces share little space for the backdrop of the lagoon, nor of the Asian tourists – the frenetic camera pacing emphasizes the dialogue, which is circling and predatory, whereas the speakers remain static and emotionless. This scene only works under the rubric of a shared or coordinated enterprise of commercial gain and its attendant trickery and theft. It also sets up a reveal – the background non-entities of Asian tourists becoming foregrounded as deus ex machina.

But if one of the human speaking parts were to be replaced by a non-human agent with intelligence and its own ascending order of motivations, an entirely new schema arises. In this scenario, the common goal is not only unknown, but its order of settings, means of dialogue, edits, and camera cinematography would be nonintuitive. If we then position the viewer or audience as nonhuman, further questions arise as meaning, social engagement, and appreciation of artform is never predictive. In fact, the very idea of a nonhuman culture would be a rich domain as any human endeavor of society: its emergent mores with shaped or fashioned traditions.

The pop 'bots and arch 'bots

This engagement with a nonhuman entity opens dimensions in the product of dialogues. For dialogues to be effective, a shared enterprise is the domain in which a coterie of at least two or more respondents engages each other to bring about a higher order of understanding or achievement. When one or all of them are nonhuman or intelligent machines, what is achieved and for whom is a unique question for architecture and urban design. Certainly it suggests that a shared enterprise of like-minded enthusiasts is still possible, but with beings who are our equal or our intellectual superiors. The tenor of the conversation has been forecast in the early work of the Architecture Machine Group. Negroponte's famous question from his first publication[14] about whether an intelligent house would laugh if we told it a joke, may be replaced with a house that may understand the joke, but deem the raconteur to be juvenile in wit and lacking in sophistication. Another question would be what jokes or pleasantries would be shared among only machines, if any such social construct would be necessary.

The term pop 'bot was introduced by Kurzweil as the robots and automata portrayed in popular media, distinct from robotic research carried out in labs. However, his accounting begins in 1927 with the android Maria in Fritz Lang's *Metropolis*. However, Kurzweil also traces a long tradition of intelligent machines from Homer's first use of the word automata to machines acting on their own accord. These automata and robots are sequentially presented as the handmaidens made by Hephaestus, followed by the small humanoid boy L'Ecrivain by Swiss watchmaker Jacquet-Droz in 1792, among others. The earliest sighting of a humanoid robot in literature may be in the Liezi 列子 from the Han Dynasty. In this story, the emperor is introduced to a humanoid agent that is so lifelike in its speech and dance that it flirts with his concubines. It is only when the inventor Yanshi 偃师 disassembles the robot into its constituent synthetic limbs and organs that his life is spared.[15] Yanshi's robot is unusual as it not only surpasses the servile or diminished attitude of other early creations but it takes on enough independence to make sexual advances to the emperor's attendants.

For architecture as evolving automata to be considered, the residing intelligence would be within a body. In the next paragraph following the issue of the joke, Negroponte suggests that machines require bodies to be able to desire without bodies, which brings needs, supplied by thought, that can then be able to design. Clearly the robot of Yanshi could act on its desires as it had a body with high fidelity to a human anatomy, thus yielding thought and desire. The robot desire is parallel to human desire, born from similar physiognomy. It would suggest that likeness begets similar behavior.

The homunculus diagram by Penfield and Jasper is a conceptual schema published in *Epilepsy and the Functional Anatomy of the Human Brain* from 1954, mapping the physical regions of the brain to the body. The whole body, with its relative densities of sensory nerves accorded to each body part, would be remapped so that the face, feet, and hands would have much larger representation than the rest of the body.[16] The complete body is core in this model, where additional body parts or changed body maps and assignments are unaccounted, as the human body may lose limbs, but more cannot be attached to then remap the homunculus brain. This model, shipped to an architecture with mind, undergoes an interesting body map, questioning a wholeness or totality that is not yet given fitness. If machines require bodies to achieve intelligence,[17] the building body that informs behavior for an architecture entity is necessarily a closed one by this definition.

But the assignments of body parts, and the consciousness of an architecture that is alive and embodied in matter, can be reconceived as something open-ended, and without limitations to what tethers human brains to bodies. Just as motility in simulations gave way to emergent properties of creatures adapting varying appendage shape and combination,[18] architectural bodies and minds may compose entire genealogies of flora or fauna or other. The earlier proposition of whether humans are giving up privacy within the home and cities is superseded when faced with the realization that sensate architecture of intelligence may look like nothing previously seen, and may be merged with its occupants. A new design culture, in terms of how it communicates intent and meaning within its behavior and form, would change dependent on its audience – its modes of expression, and how it shares knowledge or desire is as yet untrained. Surveillance is largely a system whereby a powerful few keep citizens afraid or monitored – it does not consider that new intelligence may reject the abuse of its organs by other humans for the subjugation of others.

The Immersive

Design culture may be considered a shared and open enterprise of goods or services in the production of materials, products, and environments as becomes the dominant arbiter of social values. Humans may also adapt and change to become cyborg or hybridized, without an original homuncular map to sustain. What comes of living architecture and its human partners is a coming phenomenon that will bring new relationships to form, meaning, and communication. The extents of this organism may include the non-human to its fullest definition, with common goals acted out for global stewardship.

For the current discipline, a core or central set of aligned values critically assess architecture and urbanism as central, peripheral, or excised as non-canonical. This open system also allows for shifts in these core tenets dependent on market, and an increasing number of peripheral designers that may pull the core closer to them and away from others. The core and this gravitational movement along densities are two variables of fixed scope. If seen as a robotic frame or lens that roams about this disciplinary landscape, the dimensions of the frame would vary only slightly, and the movement would have limited degrees of freedom. The disciplinary core contains evolving sets of values, and culls away others.

An expanded discipline would be in conversation with allied and distant professions in the shaping of ongoing research and development with technology, and understand its ecology and world-building potential. This conversation would form shared goals in interhuman endeavors, and find new opportunities in enlarged domains.[19] The idea of discipline and profession remain only as specializations, and knowledge bases are required. The amount of information is more than any one super-professional may understandably apply, and architects that can fluidly find connections among disparate knowledge sets will continue to be relevant.

Self-aware architecture that designs architecture, and homeostatic cities, will produce entirely new chimeras of human bodies and synthetic systems. Moreover, for The Immersive to become integral, the spaces of its occupation must be clearly defined. The range of these spaces is in scalar metrics from the new body and wearables, to social spaces, and to the urban that is not separated between human and nonhuman, but to a synthetic ecology of wholes – integrated and indivisible.

Notes

1 See the open letter and its list of supporters at http://futureoflife.org/misc/open_letter

2 Examples are listed at www.livescience.com/49419-artificial-intelligence-dangers-letter.html, www.cnet.com/news/artificial-intelligence-experts-sign-open-letter-to-protect-mankind-from-machines, and interviews Bill Gates, Stephen Hawking, and Elon Musk have given: http://qz.com/335768/bill-gates-joins-elon-musk-and-stephen-hawking-in-saying-artificial-intelligence-is-scary

3 The singularity of Kurzweil, von Neumann, and Ulam is described as the "ever accelerating progress of technology and changes in the mode of human life, which gives the appearance of approaching some essential singularity in the history of the race beyond which human affairs, as we know them, could not continue," as presented in Ulam's "Tribute to John von Neumann", 1958.

4 See Koolhaas, "The Smart Landscape, Intelligent Architecture", in *ArtForum*, April 2015; "My Thoughts on the Smart City – by Rem Koolhaas", edited from a talk given at the High Level Group meeting on Smart Cities, Brussels, September 24, 2014; and www.dezeen.com/2015/05/27/rem-koolhaas-interview-technology-smart-systems-peoples-eagerness-sacrifice-privacy-totally-astonishing. See Adam Greenfield, *Against the Smart City* (New York: Do Projects, 2013).

5 The Internet of Things promotes an interconnection of many sensate objects (animals, humans, product design) that collectively produces a smart environment that self-regulates. Each node operates independently but can generate a global and local system response.

6 Funding varies from institutional funding to grants from agencies such as the NSF, as architecture moves from humanities toward the sciences and engineering at the prompt of institution and university demands. Recent reports from the Academy of Arts and Sciences show a decline in funding for humanities. See "Public Research Universities: Why They Matter," 2015, and "Tracking Changes in the Humanities: Essays on Finance and Education," 2006. Another article detailing the steady decline of humanities funding from 2009 can be found at www.researchtrends.com/issue-32-march-2013/trends-in-arts-humanities-funding-2004–2012.

7 Tesla would demonstrate electric lights for the first time to the public at the Chicago World's Fair in 1893. The 1958 World's Expo in Brussels would showcase advanced techniques in light and sound, evidenced in the Philips Pavilion. Incidentally, the 1958 Expo would also house a human zoo in the form of a Congolese Village – a retrograde move from a concept of future advancement. Buckminster Fuller would showcase NASA spacecraft in his geodesic dome at the Montreal Expo of 1967, two years before the lunar landing.

8 The discussion between them, "The Mystery of Consciousness: an Exchange," can be found in the *New York Review of Books,* December 21, 1995. This represents an ongoing conversation since Dennett published *The Intentional Stance* in 1987 in retort to Searle, with continually raised stakes on the philosophy of mind.

9 An interesting history of their correspondence, development of steam power, and the negation by the Royal Academy under the leadership of Newton, is Philip Valenti's "Leibniz, Papin, and the Steam Engine: A Case Study of British Sabotage of Science," *Fusion Magazine,* 1979. See also Ernst Gerland's "Life and Letters of Papin," published in *Nature,* August 25, 1881. The article is an account of the piston and steam engine as developed in Papin's exchanges with Leibniz, with the latter being the catalyst for isolating the potential discoveries.

10 This text from part 17 of Leibniz's 1714 *Monadology* supplies the idea that natural mechanisms and human-made mechanisms differ from a higher, divine source. Percept, thought, and feeling are properties supplied by a higher order of mechanism than possible by human production.

11 T. Tremblay, "A Widening of the Northern Coterie: The Cross-Border Politics of Ezra Pound, Marshall McLuhan, and Louis Dudek," in Dean Irvine, ed., *The Canadian Modernists Meet* (Ottawa: University of Ottawa Press, 2005), 156.

Dudek, another Canadian scholar unknown to McLuhan, would also start writing to Pound in the same time period.

12 Pound's first response to McLuhan: "Yu go right on writin' me letters-but dont xpect me to answer questions-even if answers are known-(printed)" from June 1948.

13 The passage that outlines his elevation to author by his exchange with Pound is available in Tremblay's article as well as Elena Lamberti's *Marshall McLuhan's Mosaic: Probing the Literary Origins of Media Studies* (Toronto: University of Toronto Press, 2012), chapter 11.

14 Negroponte's *The Architecture Machine: Toward a More Human Environment* (Cambridge, MA: MIT Press, 1970), 1. The pioneering text for designers about early human–machine enterprises in design and construction forayed into many territories. Much of this book deals in conversations between human and machine intelligence in service to humans, where more scenarios of conversations may not include humans or center upon us. Gordon Pask would address this in his introduction to Negroponte's next book, *Soft Architecture Machines*.

15 A further telling is that the emperor, now seeing its artificial nature, had it reassembled to where it once again was animate. Undergoing procedures where different organs were removed, the robot corroborated medical evidence as understood by contemporary Chinese medicine. For example, removing the liver took away its vision, in accordance to medicine at the time. In essence, the robot mirrored humans in every possible manner to be indistinguishable.

16 The manner in which the body was mapped on the tissue of the brain was through a procedure called awake craniotomy, where the patients are asked questions or requested to move limbs. Drs. Penfield and Jasper would then stimulate or cut tissue to interrupt neural activity.

17 The idea that artificial intelligence requires physical bodies as a necessary component in consciousness and learning is part of *embodied cognition* research.

18 Karl Sims's "Evolved Virtual Creatures" of 1994 revealed bottom-up solutions that digital creations would generate to fulfill a core motivation to be mobile.

19 *Conversations and interaction of actors* as defined by Gordon Pask is still not only still relevant but the lateness at which we find it seems to point to a category error where design and architecture considers its subject a science fiction.

EXERCISES FOR INTEGRATING DATA AND FORM

Jason S. Johnson and Joshua Vermillion

Introduction: ubiquitous simultaneity, toward integrative design processes

The designer is increasingly tasked with integrating highly specific and constantly shifting information about the environmental drivers that impact any given project. These sets of data may describe the physical or ambient conditions of any given site, financial constraints, available infrastructure, the formal and regulatory context, and any number of other criteria present on a given site. These layers of information are widely distributed and updated simultaneously, often in relationship to one another. We might call this condition one of *ubiquitous simultaneity*. It is a condition that requires new tools for both integration and visualization in design. The ability to codify this information quickly via digital interfaces has enabled an explosion of tools that manage and deploy this information within the context of the architectural project. These parametric modeling techniques have become as much about managing, differentiating, and biasing sets of information as they are about the visualization and production of form.

Schumacher has spent much of the last decade framing architecture that defines these approaches as a style. Defining *Parametricism* as a style can be seen as a marked shift away from defining periods of design by shared formal characteristics and toward defining a style of design that results from processes that leverage generative tools of communication and exchange for the production of formal characteristics. While most design movements that posit manifestos ultimately manifest within a prescribed formal or aesthetic range, digitally enabled generative processes that leverage relationships between sets of data and formal qualities may result in any number of formal outcomes whose aesthetic qualities vary widely.

In this chapter we won't look solely at the production of artifacts based on formal procedures or material constraints, but rather by using variable data sets. For the most part we will keep it simple, but these techniques will introduce you to the concepts of lending hierarchy to sets of information as they relate to form and other types of visual communication and design. As in the other exercises in this book, we will engage an iterative process, evaluate the outputs and review them at various scales and through a number of image types. Along the way we will reference a number of projects that have demonstrated the development of tools and techniques for breaking down and reassembling collections of data in the pursuit of formal, visual, and spatial configurations.

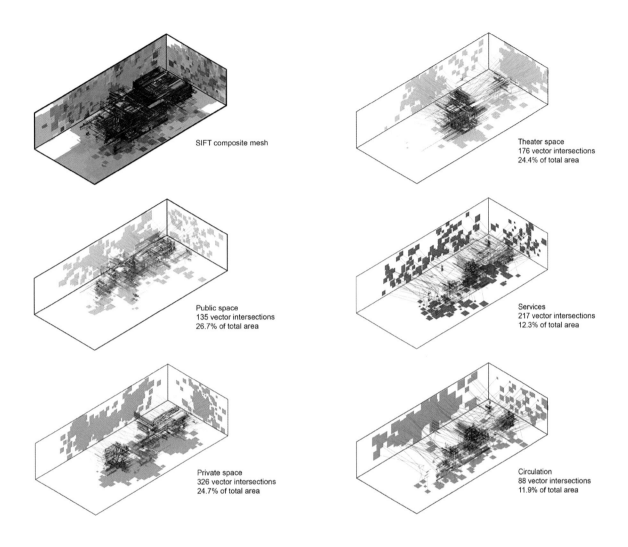

SIFT composite mesh

Theater space
176 vector intersections
24.4% of total area

Public space
135 vector intersections
26.7% of total area

Services
217 vector intersections
12.3% of total area

Private space
326 vector intersections
24.7% of total area

Circulation
88 vector intersections
11.9% of total area

Program massing identified through vector intersection

Figure 8.1 Diagrams show the relationship of various programmatic elements taken from a large collection of plan sections and elevations and combine or merge them into spatial prototypes for each category of program. Matt Parker, Jason S. Johnson, 2015.

Exercise set 10: integrating data and form

In this first set of exercises we will further build on the iterative process for variation described in Exercise 7A. You will be tasked with taking a simple component, perhaps the same component developed in Exercise 7A, and using it to produce a field of components whose variations are controlled by a specific set of data. As in some of the other exercises in this book, you will then be asked to speculate about these objects (or fields of objects) at a specific scale in order to demonstrate the potential of your design process.

Objectives

This exercise is intended to introduce and develop understandings of:

- practice manipulating geometric forms through understanding their attributes;
- strategies for connecting formal adaptation and manipulation to external data drivers;
- the principles of variation across an assemblage of parts;
- exploration of part-to-whole relationships;
- techniques for communicating formal responses to external data.

Outcomes

- Volumetric assemblages.
- Diagrams that show connections between inputs and outputs.
- Catalog of formal variations.

Recommended reading

Hensel, Michael, and Achim Menges, "Patterns in Performance-Orientated Design: An Approach Towards Pattern Recognition, Generation and Instrumentalisation," *Architectural Design*, 79, no. 6 (2009): 88–93.
Schumacher, Patrik. 2009. "Parametricism: A New Global Style for Architecture and Urban Design," *Architectural Design*. doi:10.1002/ad.912.

Schumacher, Patrik, *The Autopoiesis of Architecture: V. 2 – A New Agenda for Architecture*. Wiley, 2011.

Verebes, Tom, *Masterplanning the Adaptive City: Computational Urbanism in the Twenty-First Century*. Routledge, 2013.

Exercise 10A: environmental drivers

For this exercise you will begin with a three-dimensional object you have digitally modeled (you may choose to use an object from Exercise 7A). This object should be simple but have enough characteristics that you can manipulate it in various ways. Rather than using a surface object, focus on an object that has a thickness or contains a volume. Objects you choose can include cubes, cones, spheres, cylinders, etc. or variations of the same. We will use a set of external data to manipulate and generate variations of your three-dimensional object. These data will exert influence on the formal qualities of the object, but should not change its status as a closed volume. Next you will need to understand the characteristics that are editable within the object – the traits that are governed by changes in parameters. Lastly you will need to select criteria external to the object that will instantiate editing (reforming) the object. This requires you to establish a relationship between the object and the external data. It is critical that both of these things establish a connection to one another that shares a design space. In other words, unless there is some shared communication between the two objects, one cannot respond to the other.

Before we begin, let's take a look at a simple project that makes use of the principles you will explore. This project (Figures 8.2–8.5) for a series of benches takes a simple L-shaped profile and manipulates it to adapt to various ergonomic positions of the user. The bottom edge of the "L" is constrained in order to function as seating, while the vertical edge is free to rotate on the axis. A number of scenarios were speculated by the designers, which showed the performative range through the simple act of rotation (Figure 8.4).

Figure 8.2 Diagrams of a simple L-shaped component for a bench and the performative range of that component in relation to ergonomic positions. *Paraseating,* Calgary, Guy Gardner, Jason S. Johnson, 2012.

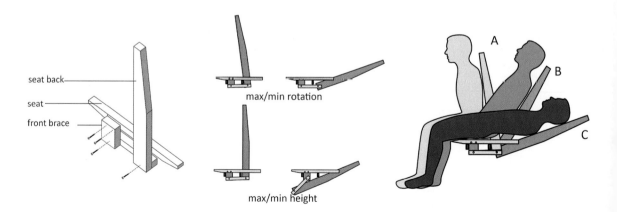

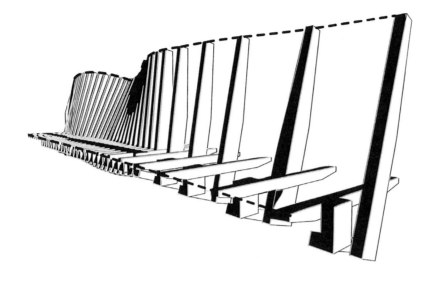

Figure 8.3 Diagram of fixed vs. variable components. The horizontal surface is not rotated, while the vertical surface has a range of rotation. *Paraseating,* Calgary, Guy Gardner, Jason S. Johnson, 2012.

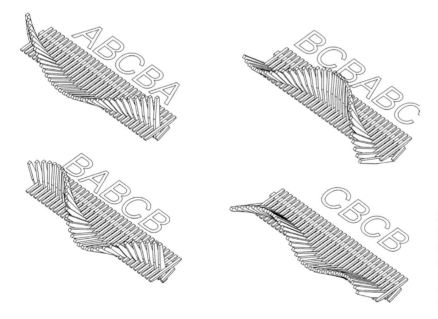

Figure 8.4 Speculations on the various possible seating configurations where each sequence is in a different order. *Paraseating,* Calgary, Guy Gardner, Jason S. Johnson, 2012.

Figure 8.5 Image of one of the built benches. *Paraseating*, Calgary, Guy Gardner, Jason S. Johnson, 2012.

Exercise procedure

Step 1: Model a simple object. This object may be one that you have developed in a previous assignment or it may be something new. In either case, start simple and then, as you repeat the exercise, branch out to more complex geometries as a starting point.

Step 2: Select a data set that will exert a changing force on the object and define what that relationship will be. For example, if the data consist of sound measurements, it can be measured in decibels (dB) and sources and directions could be located.

Step 3: Map the data set two-dimensionally to include the complete range of variation along a line or curve. For example, you might have values that begin at 1 and move to 10, in which case you should have a corresponding number of increments on your map. Figure 8.6 maps decibel readings taken in an urban park. The readings are located in relation to one another and a

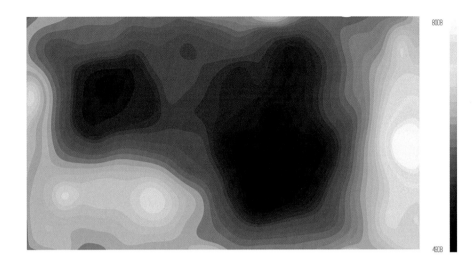

80DB

49DB

Figure 8.6 Diagram of sound readings in an urban park. Christina James, 2015.

legend gives us an idea of the difference between the lowest sound reading and the highest.

Step 4: Define a relationship between the data set you have selected and the manipulation of the three-dimensional object you have modeled. For example, in Figure 8.7 a number of scaling and rotation functions are tied to the change in decibel readings. This relationship is sequential, meaning that each object is transformed based on the version that directly preceded it.

Step 5: Model these transformations through instancing. An instance of the object is just another term for version. In this case a new instance is produced for each increment of change in the data set. Array the instances in a row and experiment with the spacing between each instance.

Figure 8.7 Geometric manipulations in response to change in sound level. Christina James, 2015.

Step 6: Produce a diagram or series of diagrams that communicate the relationship between object transformation and the data.

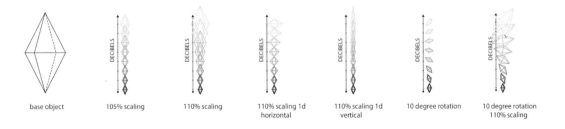

base object   105% scaling   110% scaling   110% scaling 1d horizontal   110% scaling 1d vertical   10 degree rotation   10 degree rotation 110% scaling

Step 7: Evaluate your results. Questions to ask:

- How much variation resulted from the scale of the transformations assigned to each component?
- Do the transformations deform the object so much that it is no longer closed?
- What interesting effects are generated by multiple instances of the object next to one another?
- At what scale do these effects become significant?

Step 8: Try changing the transformation logic, for example from scaling to rotating or twisting and compare the results.

Step 9: Compose your results. In addition to the diagrams describing the variations you produced, create renderings of the arrays of instanced geometry. Compose these in such a way as to be able to compare the results

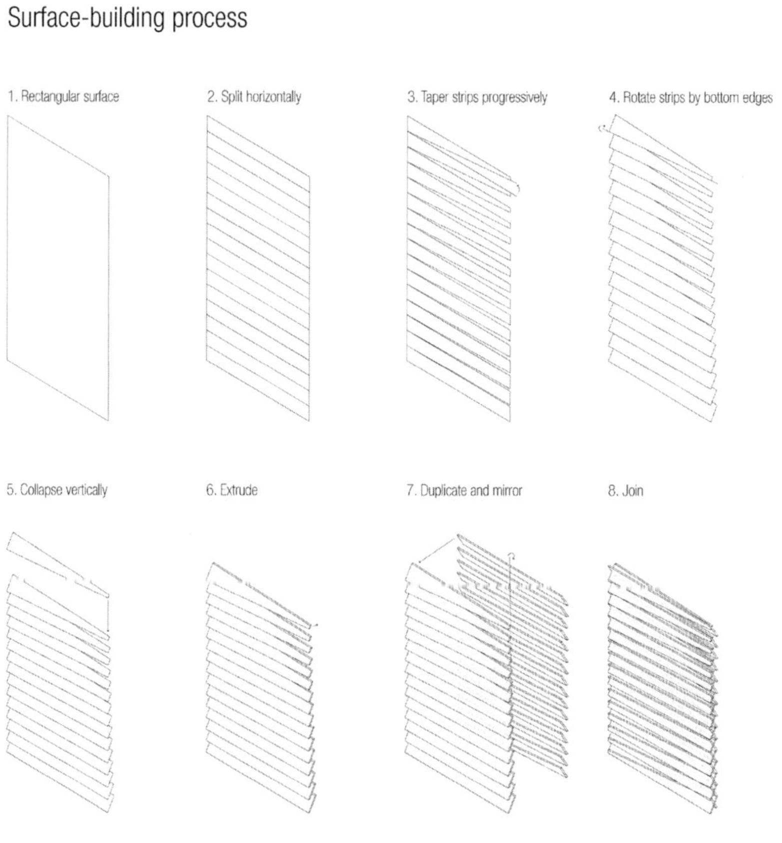

Surface-building process

1. Rectangular surface　2. Split horizontally　3. Taper strips progressively　4. Rotate strips by bottom edges

5. Collapse vertically　6. Extrude　7. Duplicate and mirror　8. Join

Figure 8.8 Instancing object deformation. Christopher Wong, 2014.

from each approach. Finally, explore the resulting objects at various scales by producing images that locate them in a context. Do they work best as linear assemblages, grouped objects or individual components? In Figures 8.8 and 8.9 you can see the progression from a simple manipulation of a singular object to the composition of a wall that has both structural and visual characteristics.

Figure 8.9 Wall produced from versioning a simple form. Christopher Wong, 2014.

Exercise 10B: environmental intensities

In this exercise you will continue to use sets of data to manipulate objects, this time with a focus on the objects as a part of a larger continuous field. The integration of data as a driver for transformation in this exercise will move away from a focus on one discretized object toward variation produced within a larger field of objects. An example of this strategy at an urban scale is included in the form of the Adaptive Urban Patterns project by OCEAN CN (Figures 8.21–8.25). In this project, a number of overlapping patterns form the basis for the production of a series of cells formed by the patterns' edges. These cells are then extruded or scaled vertically in response to data provided by sets of programmatic criteria. In this exercise you will be producing a very simple version of this problem using a simple form and underlying pattern logics. This array of objects will be transformed into a three-dimensional translation of the data set you chose as the formal driver. In SDeG's Shipara Office project the façade can be viewed as a simple array of cubes that are open on two ends. These cubes are manipulated through extrusion, rotation, and twisting to engage different contextual factors (Figure 8.10).

Figure 8.10 Simple manipulations of a base geometry of a cube arrayed on a surface respond to environmental conditions at the building's street façade. *Shipara Office*, Bangalore, SDeG, 2012.

Exercise procedure

Step 1: An array is described simply as a way of organizing similar objects. Often arrays take the form of two-dimensional grids. Arrays can also be produced in rotation around a single point or a number of other organizational structures that define the relationships of these objects to one another. Produce an array of simple objects. It is important that you understand the logics that generate the array. If they are based on equal spacing in multiple directions, for example, you can easily manipulate the array throughout this exercise by changing the distances between and the number of objects. In the example provided in Figure 8.11 the simple object from Exercise 10A has been arrayed in a grid pattern prior to being manipulated via a data set.

Step 2: Choose a data set that can be associated with the underlying logics of the array. If the data are based on location, for example, you can scale this information to correlate with the subdivisions of the array. If the data set is image-based you could associate the image boundaries with the boundaries of your array.

Step 3: Define the logics of transformation that will be applied to singular objects in the array. In the example shown, simple cylinders are manipulated using color data from the underlying color map. The relationships between the color values in the map and the transformations are first defined and then encoded within the digital model in order to quickly produce a larger field of these objects (Figures 8.12 and 8.13). The same process could be carried out on a part-by-part basis by manipulating each component individually. If you

Figure 8.11 Array of simple objects where the rotation of each object is associated with an image map. Christina James, 2015.

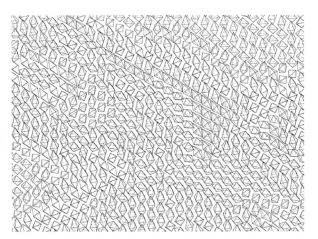

are working on a part-by-part basis (as opposed to an encoded process) you will want to limit the size of your array to correspond with the time you have to complete the given problem. Automation of the process allows for large sets of data to be tested and for adjustments to be made quickly by editing the relationship parameters or the data being used.

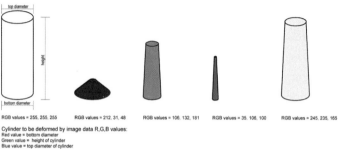

Figure 8.12 A simple cylinder is deformed based on the RGB color values of the image map. Red values adjust the base diameter, green values control the height and blue values give the object its diameter at the top. The data set is a basic topography map in which difference in elevation is equated with a color. Matthew Parker, 2015.

Figure 8.13 Topography map color variations used to alter the formal characteristics of an array of cylinders. Matthew Parker, 2015.

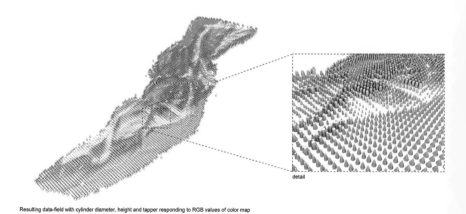

Step 4: Evaluate your results.

- How closely do the formal variations correlate to the variations in the baseline data set?
- How legible are these variations?
- Does the intensity of the field reflect the range of variation within the data set?
- If you select another type of transformation or a different initial form, how does this impact your reading of the information presented?

Step 5: Produce a series of images and diagrams that correlate the two sets of data. Produce a series of images at three separate scales to speculate about the potential of your process to respond to various functions. For example, would the project work better as a façade, the surface of a piece of furniture, or perhaps at the scale of a neighborhood or city?

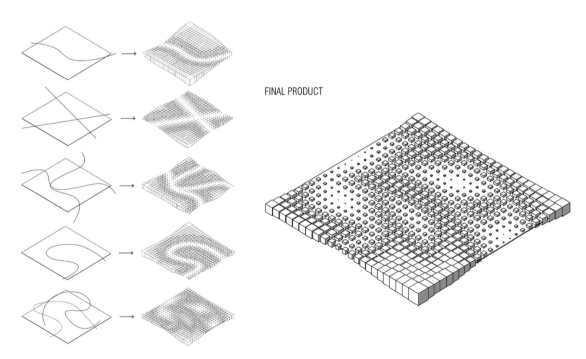

FINAL PRODUCT

Figure 8.14 Studies in producing a system for articulating a wall surface. Linear attractors are used to control component scaling. John Ferguson, 2015.

Case studies: three scales

The power of using tools that allow you to create variable components in arrays is that you can break down larger design territories into highly localized parts. Each of these parts can be "tuned" to respond to very specific criteria. Included here are three projects that take simple array and patterning techniques and combine them with localized data in order to produce design responses that can be adjusted into a large number of variations that can adapt to new contextual data.

The first project was designed at the scale of an object. The Cellular Phone Booth was designed to replace the traditional phone booth that requires a landline phone connection and a fixed location. This project acts as a portable shroud that visually and acoustically gives mobile phone users a space for having semi-private conversations.

Material Distribution

1. base shape geometry

2. quadrilateral subdivisions

3. internal pyramid for cap and twist (height and twist both and tip jitter defined by bitmap)

4. cut-plane for cap (height defined by bitmap)

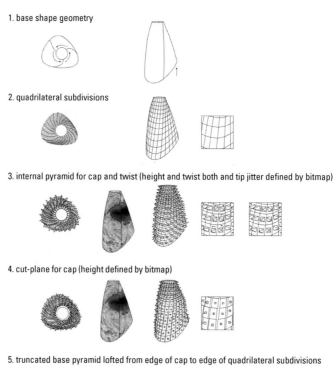

Figure 8.15 Generative logic diagrams for Cellular Phone Booth. A simple surface is broken down into a simple array of rows and columns and each resulting quad is used as the base structure for a set of nested pyramids whose depth is controlled by an image map. Alyssa Haas and Jason S. Johnson, 2012.

5. truncated base pyramid lofted from edge of cap to edge of quadrilateral subdivisions

Project: Cellular Phone Booth

Project Design: Alyssa Haas, Jason S. Johnson

The Cellular Phone Booth takes a very simple approach to producing a performative surface that wraps around its user. It has three primary modes of performance: structural, acoustic and visual.

The first consideration is structural and material in nature. In order to maintain its form with a very thin material, the surface needs to be folded and the parts connected to one another on three of four sides. Pyramidal forms were chosen as the base component for the project. The overall surface for the project is a simple cylinder with open ends. This surface was subdivided and arrayed with four-sided pyramids. The pyramids' straight edges provide a shared surface between components, and the folds produce a structural depth to the surface. In order to address acoustic and visual performance, the designers developed a technique for controlling the depth of the pyramids. An image is used to control the heights of the pyramids. This technique was developed because image maps are easy to produce and replacing an image would produce new results each time. Figure 8.15 shows the process of breaking down the surface and controlling the cut planes in the nesting protocols for the pyramids.

The connection details and material color choices respond to the overall framework of the project and reinforce the design intentions behind the project as a whole (Figure 8.16). In objects of a smaller scale the designer should be cognizant of the way in which the details that hold the larger project together can either reinforce those relationships between the part and whole or work against them.

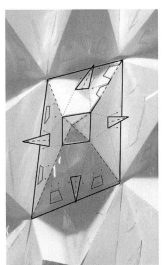

Figure 8.16 Diagrams for producing material connections between surface components. Connection tabs are designed to reinforce the aesthetics of the project as a whole. Alyssa Haas and Jason S. Johnson, 2012.

Figure 8.17 Cellular Phone Booth. Alyssa Haas and Jason S. Johnson, 2012.

Figure 8.18 The Cloud, Daegu Gosan Library Proposal. The library's screen functions as a surface of communication between the content and the city. Minus Architecture Studio, 2012.

Project: The Cloud, Daegu Gosan Library Proposal
Minus Architecture Studio (2012)

Project design: Jason S. Johnson (design lead), Adam Onulov, Alyssa Haas, Christopher Sparrow.

The Cloud is a proposal for a library that connects the content of its collections to the city through the building's skin. The skin is conceived of as a weather system that is driven by two parameters. The first is the degree of daylight exposure desired in the building's interior spaces. This parameter (Figure 8.20) controls the angle of rotation and depth of the fins. The second parameter that governs the performance of the screen is the types of content being accessed by the library's users. Each subject area controls the coloration of the surface (Figure 8.19).

Figure 8.19 The Cloud, Daegu Gosan Library Proposal. Embedded lighting systems are assigned colors based on the categories of information distributed through the building. As collections are accessed the intensity the lighting system responds accordingly. Minus Architecture Studio, 2012.

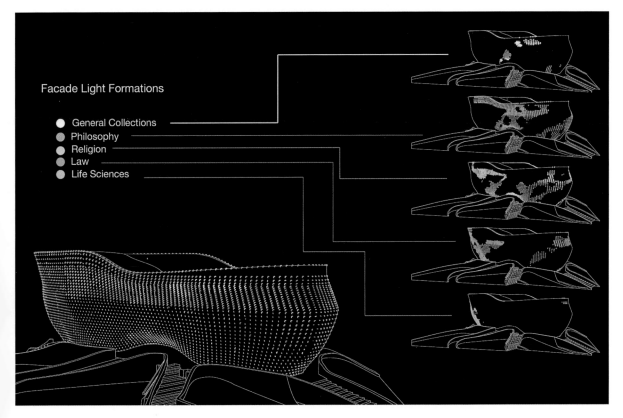

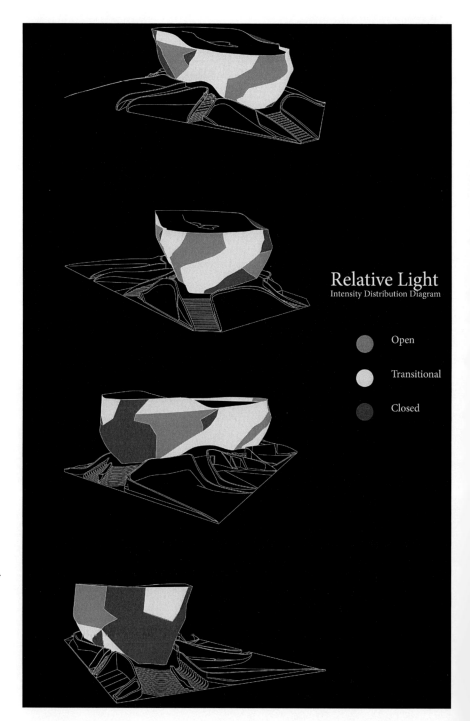

Relative Light
Intensity Distribution Diagram

● Open

○ Transitional

● Closed

Figure 8.20 The Cloud, Daegu Gosan Library Proposal. Diagrams describing the relative openness of the building façade. The building façade is a louvered system in which the rotation and depth of each fin is correlated to the desired level of daylighting in the interior volumes. Minus Architecture Studio, 2012.

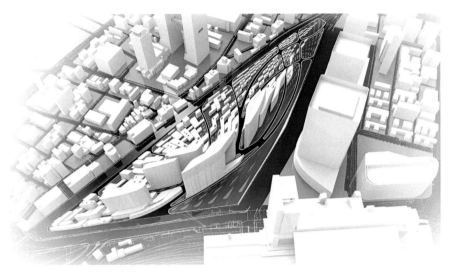

Figure 8.21 Aerial view of a masterplan proposal for a single snapshot in time, as an instant in a process of formation and information, to be developed and adapted to future contingencies. This urban model emphasizes a concrete description of massing and open space, configured by a variety of programmatic uses and massing typologies. Varied scales, densities, and types of extruded, granular pixelated massing are contrasted with diverse public open spaces with varied planting, material textures, and orientation. The traffic and infrastructural management of the site is embedded within a porous, pedestrian-focused urbanism flowing around, under, and through fields of building mass. OCEAN CN, 2014.

Our third example of a data-driven pattern/array design approach (deployed at an urban scale) is OCEAN CN's proposal for the Umekita Second Development Area in Osaka, Japan (Figures 8.21–8.25). The proposal was developed through the use of a computational design interface that engages the problem of designing for changing forces that define and shape a city. While a single scheme was developed all the way toward a proposal, this generative interface allowed the designers to prototype multiple versions of the project in response to specific data related to programming, density, and building typologies. This process produced patterns and systems of deploying those patterns that correlated parameters to one another in a way that produces "adaptive urban patterns."

Project: Adaptive Urban Patterns
OCEAN.CN 2014

Project team: OCEAN CN Team: Tom Verebes (design director) Mohamad Ghamloush (designer), Nathan Melenbrink (designer, scripting), Andrew Haas (post-production, scripting)

Arup Transportation & Arup Structural Engineering, Arup Hong Kong: Mark Swift, Gabriel Lam, William Loasby, Ray Tang, Ben Luk.

Designing multiple futures
The contemporary city can be read as a pattern in time, and this proposal recognizes the complexities of how cities are influenced and formed from a multitude of dynamic forces. Through adaptable and responsive methods of

Figure 8.22 Six zoning scenarios, each outlining a varied mix of programmatic ratios, are deployed as instruments to yield six different diagrams of massing and open green spaces. These six models and corresponding urban plans describe land utilization, program areas, and composition of six schemes, demonstrating the metrics of program composition, ratios, and mixes of six schemes, and relations of built and open space. The resultant diverse urban morphologies demonstrate the urban model as an interactive tool, within a methodology which is responsive to the contingencies which will shape the development of the Umekita area. OCEAN CN, 2014.

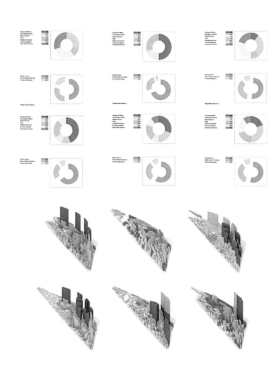

Figure 8.23 Moiré pattern plans. Subdivision patterns are formed from the amalgamation of the various grids, from four site influences: a principle north–south and east–west array of intersecting grid lines, splaying off the traffic plaza in the West Exit of Osaka Station above the proposed JR Tokaido Line; a set of grid lines associating to the small-scale urban morphology to the west of the site. In addition, pedestrian flows between the stations, streets, and plazas bring out a fourth, more fluid grid of oriented pedestrian spaces. Altogether, these grids create moiré patterns of a differentiated urban field, which hence generate variegated massing and open space diagrams. OCEAN CN Consultancy Network, Umekita Second Development Area, Osaka, Japan, 2013–2014.

modeling massing variations in relation to the project's contingencies, this project contributes to the discourses on computational approaches to urbanism. The principle strategic objective of this proposal is to develop a manifold of possible future scenarios and configurations for the site, which can be adapted to diverging orientations of future investment models and planning considerations. The design research agenda of this project targets an adaptive process of mediating toward multiple possible futures, each contingent on how economic, political, social, and environmental considerations play out in the future. Six zoning scenarios, each outlining a varied mix of programmatic ratios, are deployed as instruments to yield six different diagrams of massing and open green spaces. The resultant diverse urban morphologies demonstrate the openness of this methodology to the contingencies that may shape

the development of the Umekita area. Through a back-end computational model, a series of scripts and definitions are developed with which to establish associations to site conditions, such as proximity to major infrastructural nodes, and relations to peripheral streets, building heights, building footprints, and other parameters. This method aims to address two parallel issues: adaptability and heterogeneity. Generally, master planning processes are expected to adapt to unforeseen changes in the political, social and economic contingencies of cities. In addition, the project's methods yield an open approach to the development of diverse and heterogeneous massing morphologies.

Urban transformations

A large part of the vast seven-hectare site is a top-side development above existing railway tracks. This proposal for the primary gateway to Osaka aims to augment the diversity of built massing and open spaces. In all possible schemes for the site, high-density urbanism is mitigated with public green corridors and plazas, giving simultaneously a sense of openness within an intense metropolitan experience. Building typologies, and their heights and footprints, are adapted to a porous, pixelated organization of open space to massing, and are differentiated to various potential programmatic scenarios. Flows on the site move between, under and through the building mass. Through the systemic correlation of massing, program, and landscape, the proposed scheme is integrated within the infrastructural systems both at grade and below ground, merging with the existing urban fabric. Patterns and flows of these systems target their adaptation to the heterogeneous contextual conditions of the Umekita Area. This distinct approach to urbanism projects an identifiable character for the Umekita Area, as the Face of Osaka, which can develop and evolve, flexibly yet coherently.

Patterns and flows

In the Umekita proposal, the site is subdivided by three site influences: a principle north–south and east–west array of intersecting grid lines, splaying off the traffic plaza in the West Exit of Osaka Station above the proposed JR Tokaido Line; and a set of grid lines associating to the small-scale urban morphology to the west of the site. In addition, the existing and proposed pedestrian flows on the site, between the stations and the existing streets and plazas, bring a fourth, more fluid grid of pedestrian spaces, oriented to and from the various stations. These flows, generated from minimal paths between the main channels of pedestrian movement, oscillate between efficiency and redundancy of

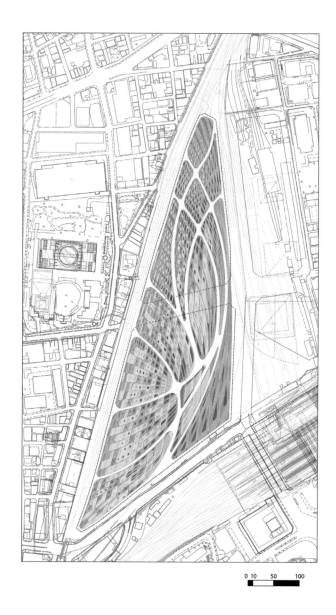

Figure 8.24 Plan of the overlap of open spaces, canopied spaces, and interior landscapes, describing patterns and textures of materials and planting which can be applied to any of the generated schemes, accommodating a variety of building footprints and densities. OCEAN CN, 2014.

an intensely connected urbanism. Subdivision patterns are formed from the amalgamation of the various grids, and together create moiré patterns of a differentiated urban field. The moiré patterns are developed computationally at various scales, and types of extruded pixelated massing are contrasted with diverse, lush green spaces with varied planting, material textures, and orientation. A series of schemes deploy built site area, public open spaces and private green spaces in various relationships, serving as the lungs of high-density urbanism, given nearly any set of future constraints and conditions.

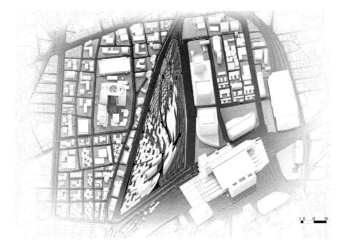

Figure 8.25 Project iterations for Umekita Second Development Area, Osaka, Japan, OCEAN CN, 2014.

Figure 8.26 Surface coloration. Willow, THEVERYMANY, Marc Fornes, 2015.

Exercise 10C: environmental imprinting

In this final exercise of set 10 we will look at communication through the materiality of assemblages. In the Willow by THEVERYMANY (Figure 8.26) a color gradient is used to express certain aspects of the project that would be invisible if rendered in one color. Marc Fornes describes this as coloration, rather than coloring. That is to say that the color gradient is not merely a representational device or ornamentation, but is instead a translation of the processes and procedures that produced the project and possibly the forces (structural/tectonic) that exist in the final assembly. This approach to material gradients as forms of expressions of underlying logics can be deployed in a number of ways and toward a number of aesthetic effects. In this exercise you will be using coloration to further augment the artifacts you designed in Exercises 10A and 10B.

Exercise procedure

Step 1: Select an array from Exercise 10B.

Step 2: Using the same data set that produced the variation in the array, assign visual qualities to the data range. For example, you may use a color gradient, transparency variation and assign values to the range of data.

Step 3: Apply the visual effect to your array. Repeat several times and produce images of the embedded effects (see Figure 5.15 in Marc Fornes's interview).

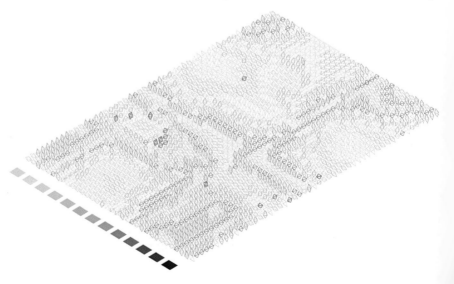

Figure 8.27 Color applied to array based on angle of rotation of individual objects. Angle of objects based on decibel readings across an urban park site. Christina James, 2015.

Step 4: Evaluate your results.

- Does your process produce legible gradients of information?
- Which version of this exercise produces the most compelling effects in relation to the data that are informing the process?

Step 5: Produce a series of images and diagrams that communicate the data sets and outputs from Exercises 10A, B, and C. Figure 8.27 shows a simple application of a color gradient to a rotational array. The array was produced by applying rotation to objects based on decibel readings in a public park (Figures 8.7, 8.11).

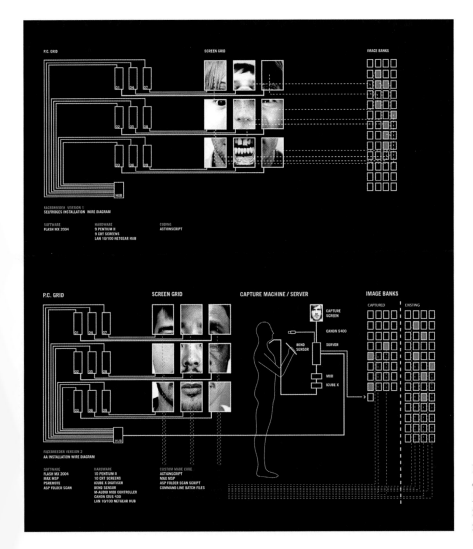

Figure 8.28 Facebreeder data management diagram. Minimaforms Theodore Spyropoulos and Vasilis Stroumpakos, 2004.

Exercise set 11: overlays and edges – mapping to form

The next three exercises explore images as a way to visualize overlapping sets of information. To produce coherence within a process-driven design assembly, you will need to develop techniques for extracting important information from the data as it relates to creating continuous material assemblies. If you want to be able to build or prototype what you design, you need to understand how your project's form might begin to become material. In most cases you will not be building anything out of one continuous material, but rather a series of parts. These parts will need to understand their relationships to each other and the larger objects or fields they are a part of. Ultimately that means that each part will have edges that connect/communicate with other edges. In their 2004 project called *Facebreeder*, Theodore Spyropoulos and Vasilis Stroumpakos explored the manipulation of images through a process-based approach of subdivision and recombination. The intelligence of this project is in its choice of images. By using an easily recognizable subject, the human face, they were able to take advantage of our ability to mentally stitch together a grid of images from different faces and still read them as a whole. Figure 8.28 is a diagram of the process that was used to produce a continuously emergent series of faces by managing the subdivided images so that each of the nine quadrants consistently held self-similar information. The nose, for example, always occupies the center rectangle in the array. The fact that this project produces a flat surface means that the edges of these images are always in alignment with one another and generally seen in a frontal view. Exercise set 11 will explore concepts for mapping image and form data to surfaces through a series of simple exercises.

Exercises 11A–D: form to surface mapping

For this exercise you will begin with an array of objects. If you have completed the prior exercises you may choose to use one of the arrays of objects you developed for that assignment. We will look to apply this array, first, to a set of simple single surfaces, and then to adjacent surfaces that make up larger objects. This exercise is really four exercises of increasing complexity, so remember to break the problem down into manageable parts.

The AX2011 Wall (Figure 8.29) is a project that maps two sets of patterns onto a flat surface to create a varied surface condition. The first pattern is produced by mapping spheres onto a surface and cutting them into layers. The second pattern of objects is arrayed along the edge curves of the layers (Figure 8.30). The two patterns are related to one another and the association between them controls the scaling of the conical components.

Using a similar pattern at a larger scale and over a more complex form, the FLAT Screen maps pattern onto the surface of the project by unrolling the surface (Figure 8.31–8.32) and applying the pattern to it, and then re-folding

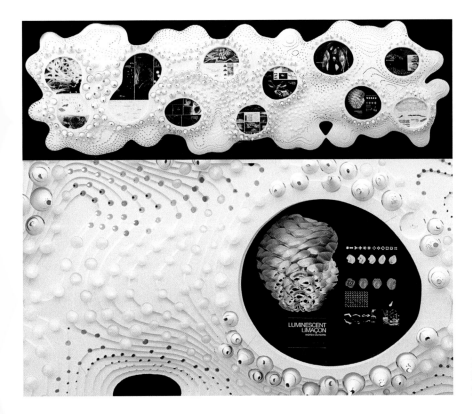

Figure 8.29 AX2011 Wall. Minus Architecture Studio, 2011.

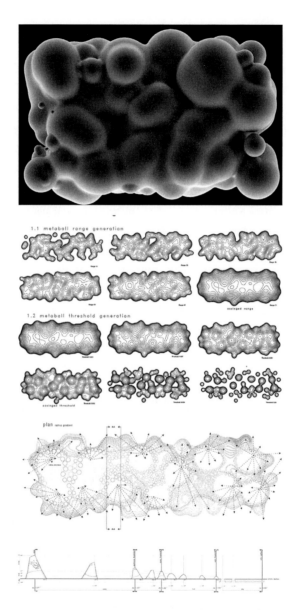

Figure 8.30 Generative diagrams show the process from metaballs (overlapping spheres), contouring, and polar cone arrays. AX2011 Wall, Minus Architecture Studio, 2011.

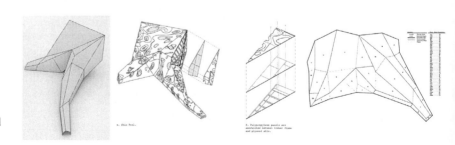

Figure 8.31 In order to map the pattern onto the non-normative form, the surfaces had to be unrolled, edges matched and patterning applied to flattened UV map. FLAT Screen, Calgary, AB, Minus Architecture Studio and Synthetiques, 2015.

224

Figure 8.32 Image maps CNC milled into project surface. FLAT Screen, Calgary, AB, Minus Architecture Studio and Synthetiques, 2015.

the surface to evaluate the aesthetics. This project involved breaking down the surfaces at several scales in order to accommodate the pattern in a precise and continuous way.

The Helsinki Library proposal by Minus Architecture Studio and Synthetiques takes an even more complex geometry and maps the pattern in ways that allow for the circular components to function as apertures in the walls of the building (Figure 8.33). These three projects represent a body of research across a number of scales and material types. In each case the change in scale produces challenges to the ways in which the project is designed and built.

Figure 8.33 The pattern in this project forms the secondary system of windows for this library competition proposal. Minus Architecture Studio and Synthetiques, 2012.

Exercise procedure

11A: single surface

Step 1: Model a simple flat surface.

Step 2: Select an array of objects and associate them to that surface. There are various procedures for achieving this. You could select your array of objects, group them, and then rotate and move them until they are oriented to the target surface. Some software will allow you to map the array to any surface. If you created the original array using parametric software you can associate the array to the target surface. If you are using an array of objects from a previous assignment, you may want to make sure that your target surface is of the same proportions as the array.

Step 3: Render the array on the surface.

11B: curved surface

Step 4: Model a curved surface.

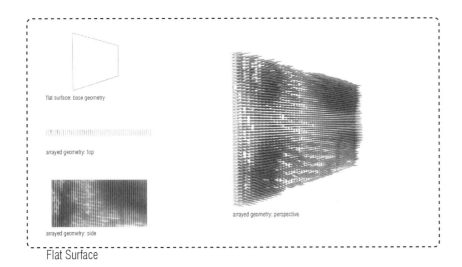

Figure 8.34 Array associated to flat surface. Matthew Parker, 2015.

Step 5: Associate your array to the curved surface. You may find this more difficult depending on the software you are using. If you are using a parametric modeler you can again associate the array to the surface. If you are using a more limited piece of software, begin by breaking down the problem into steps. It will be useful to keep the Facebreeder example in mind.

- Break down the surface into subdivisions.
- Break down the array into the same number of subdivisions.
- Map each subdivision of the array to its corresponding surface subdivision.

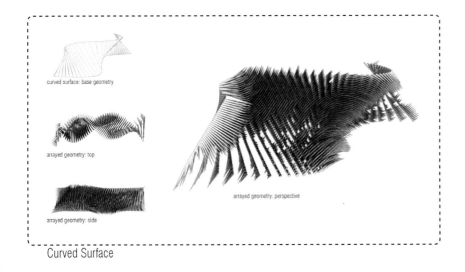

Figure 8.35 Array associated to curved surface. Matthew Parker, 2015.

- This will be time consuming, depending on the number of subdivisions you choose to work with, but the more subdivisions you have, the more you will read the base surface in the attached array.

Step 6: Render the result.

11C: simple volume

Step 7: Model a simple volume. A cube works best as a starting point. You may want to choose something more complex in subsequent versions.

Step 8: Map the array onto the cube. In order to do this you will need to understand how the base volume is put together. A cube, for example, is made up of six sides, each of them flat and four-sided. What strategies might you deploy to subdivide the array in order to map it to the surface of the cube? It may help to "unroll" the cube surfaces in the software so that you can deal with a flat, continuous surface. In the case of the cube this surface will have a cruciform shape. You can use the same subdivision strategy for your array in order to match edges when applying it to the cube.

Step 9: Render your result.

Figure 8.36 Array associated to cube. Matthew Parker, 2015.

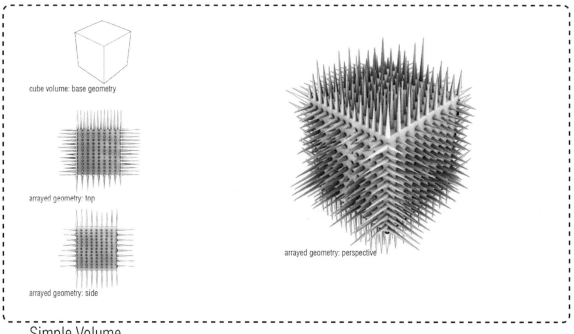

cube volume: base geometry

arrayed geometry: top

arrayed geometry: side

arrayed geometry: perspective

Simple Volume

11D: increasing complexity

Step 10: Model a more complex volume. This volume might have only slight tweaks to the cube or it may include curvature. Start simple and move toward the more complex if you find it productive to do so.

Step 11: Map the array to the complex volume. Again you may need to unroll the faces in order to map the array onto it.

Step 12: Render your result.

Step 13: Evaluate your results. Questions to ask:

- Do the components and the surfaces work well together?
- Are the large object surfaces and the small component surfaces oriented in similar directions? Do they seem continuous? Are they reinforcing the overall geometry or obscuring it?
- Which of those options is more interesting to you?

Figure 8.37 Array associated to complex volume. Matthew Parker, 2015.

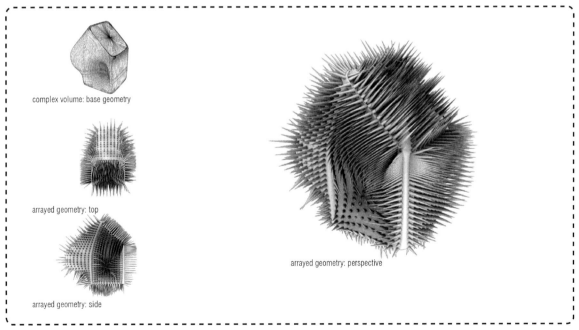

complex volume: base geometry

arrayed geometry: top

arrayed geometry: side

arrayed geometry: perspective

Complex Volume

Step 14: Try changing the organizational logics of your array. For example, you might choose to change the object spacing, rotation, or scaling in order to generate different surface qualities on the objects. These may be qualities you have observed in the first iteration that you want to be more or less prominent in order to fulfill a different set of external criteria.

Step 15: Compose your results. In addition to the diagrams describing the process of production, you should produce images that speculate about the materiality of the surfaces and the scale of the volumes. Produce a series of plans and sections through the volumetric outputs from Exercises 11C and 11D and speculate about them at a number of scales.

Figure 8.38 A simple form associatively arrayed to surfaces and volumes. Nicholas Perseo, 2015.

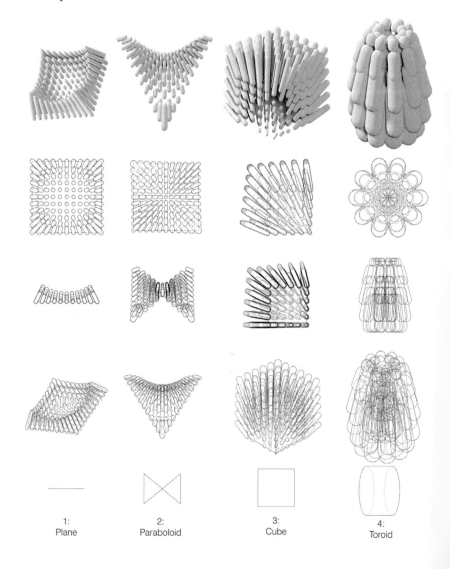

Exercise set 12: ubiquitous simultaneity – composite form-finding

As discussed at the start of this chapter, there is an increasing level of integration between contextual data and form in designed objects and buildings. Often there are overlapping sets of data that exert influence on the same formal characteristics of a project. The orientation for solar and wind exposure optimization are both important in many projects and as such they will affect the final form of a building. They may, however, differ in what defines their optimal orientation or size, for example. Both of these forces could be said to be ubiquitous (always present) and simultaneously active in relation to a building. Increasingly, models of production are incorporating techniques for integrating a wide array of possible influences on a design project into a series of possible design outcomes. The role of the designer is one of establishing the relationships between the data and the formal possibilities, controlling the iterative processes that result and finally selecting the outcome that most precisely meets the criteria established by the designer for the project.

Project studies: integrating multiplicity

Jason Salavon is an artist who has used the incredible power of algorithms to produce a series of visual artifacts that collect massive amounts of visual data that are functionally similar (e.g., images of houses, nudes, late-night talk-show hosts), serial in nature, and reveal both the pervasive similarities and areas of differentiation found within these collections. His *Late Night Triad* is made up of three films produced by overlapping the opening monologues of three late-night talk-show hosts over a specified amount of time. These films show the ways in which each talk-show host sticks to a prescribed positioning and timing in their highly scripted opening monologues. While the faces and bodies of the hosts appear as blurs on the screen, there are moments of focus when the videos most closely align. Placed side by side you can visually deconstruct the differences and similarities between the hosts. His series of images based on all the homes for sale in various cities communicate the level of homogenization within the built environments of those cities and their suburbs.

In Josh Taron's *Structurally Intelligent Swarms* project, swarm proxies are deployed as a technique for reconciling data points to a series of fixed geometries. Swarms have internal logics that dictate relationships between one

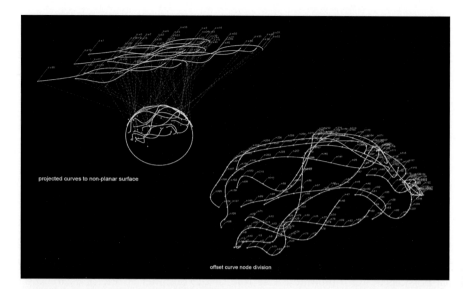

Figure 8.39 Curves projected onto non-planar surface. Structurally Intelligent Swarms, Synthetiques, 2013.

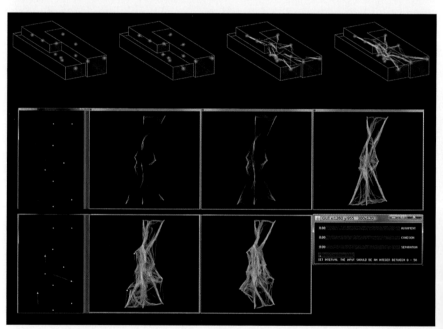

Figure 8.40 Curves build up within a prescribed volume. Structurally Intelligent Swarms, Synthetiques, 2011.

component of the swarm and the next. The logics of this sort of swarming mechanism are augmented by instructions to seek out points that have been distributed on a surface or within a specified volume (Figures 8.39 and 8.40)

The components of the swarm are tracked over time and these traces are kept as geometry within a digital model. As these traces thicken and more geometry is built up, a new version of the base geometry emerges (Figure 8.41). This geometry integrates both the logics of the swarms, the distributions

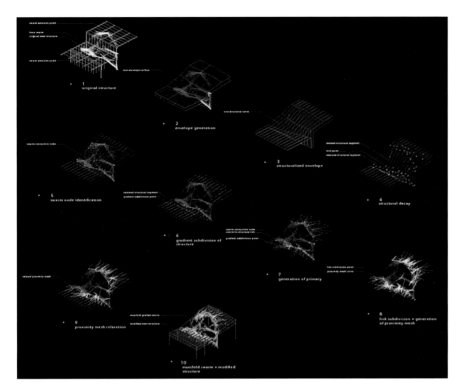

Figure 8.41 Swarm techniques integrated into a structural framework. Structurally Intelligent Swarms, Synthetiques, 2011.

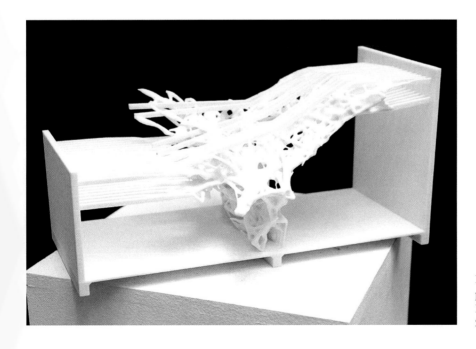

Figure 8.42 3D printed prototype. Structurally Intelligent Swarms, Synthetiques, 2015.

of the data (attractor) points and the surfaces that contain and constrain them. In the 3D-printed prototype of the project, the transitions between the pre-existing structural elements and the swarm structure are not clear. Instead the prototype reads as a gradient of the two ordering systems (Figure 8.42)

The *Every Museum Project* by Matthew Parker and Jason S. Johnson deploys computer vision and generative algorithms to produce a series of design proposals that embed large visual data sets into singular composite images. The diagram in Figure 8.43 shows the ways in which changing the sequencing and weight given to various plan images from the data set produces a range of resulting composite plans. In Figure 8.44 we can read bits and pieces of the source data while the image itself has its own reading as a plan. These processes were enabled by using or possibly misusing components of the algorithms used by Google to stick together two-dimensional images for the production of simulated three-dimensional environments in Google Earth. The architect increasingly is designing not just for how other humans might view their projects, but how they might be experienced, consumed, and reconfigured by artificially intelligent platforms like Google.

In an effort to further exploit the capacities of computers and software to process large amounts of data, Johnson and Parker developed a protocol for collecting program-specific data from large sets of plans and sections of competition museum proposals that first produced two-dimensional composite

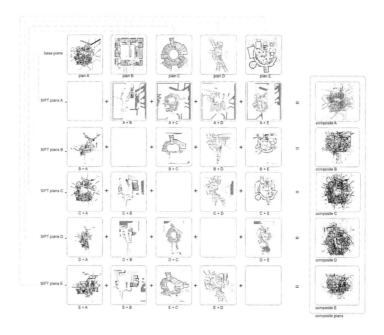

Figure 8.43 Diagram of composite floor plan technique. Every Museum Project, Matthew Parker, Jason S. Johnson, 2015.

plans (Figure 8.44) and sections from the large group of proposals and then using extrusion and vector connection techniques produced a series of three-dimensional artifacts that hint at what architecture could emerge from these processes (Figure 8.45).

Exercise procedure

12A: compositing organizational structures

Step 1: Produce or collect a set of plan and section drawings. You may collect a series of existing plans of projects that you find interesting or you may use the plans and sections produced in the previous exercise. It will be most productive if your drawings are of a similar scale and level of detail.

Step 2: Using either image manipulation or vector-based software, produce a series of composite images that combine all the plans into composite plan images and sections into section images. See Figure 8.40 for an example of a possible image outcome. Possible compositing techniques include:

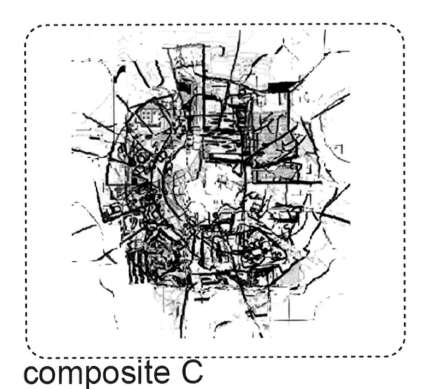

composite C

Figure 8.44 Detail of composite plan iteration. Every Museum Project, Matthew Parker, Jason S. Johnson, 2015.

235

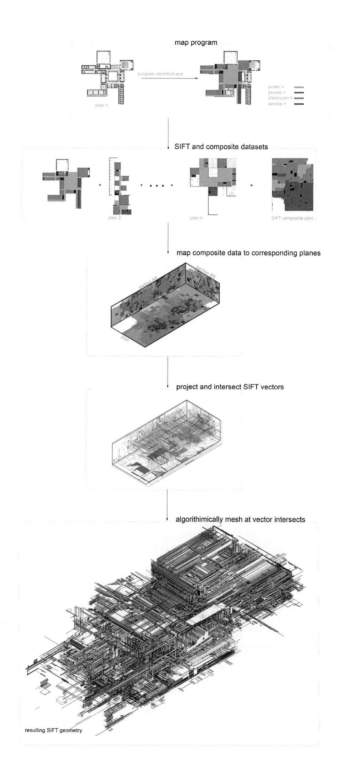

Figure 8.45 Diagram of form generation technique. Every Museum Project, Matthew Parker, Jason S. Johnson, 2015.

- In vector software you may find a number of "merge" or "blend" tools that will produce in-between versions of multiple images or vector drawings.
- In image-editing software you can explore playing with transparency and layers to produce composite images.

Step 3: Clean up the plans and sections and give them a scale. You may want to use a vector-based software to trace or live-trace the composite images so that you can control line weights to increase graphic legibility.

Step 4: Give each image a scale and place it into a context. Is the plan a landscape, a building, or an object?

12B: introducing depth

Step 5: Collect several versions of your composite plans and sections and introduce three-dimensional volumes through one of the following techniques:

- Extrusion: Lay out the plans and sections perpendicular to one another in a digital environment and extrude them to intersect with one another. Try being selective about which lines you extrude and which you leave out. Explore using the extruded surfaces/volumes to trim one another in order to create spaces within the model.
- Vectors: Stack a series of composite plans in the digital model. You should scale the distance between the plans to approximate the distances you might find between floor slabs. Subdivide the lines in the composite images and join the points on the lines in one level to those in the level above. Repeat this until you begin to build up enough structure to imply a spatial order.

Step 6: Produce a series of images of the outputs of this process that incorporate the process itself. Figure 8.41 shows a version of this process and the final image and cover image of this book uses vectors and extrusions to produce a complex artifact. While this artifact may not be a building in the traditional sense, it is architectural in its compositional and structural qualities. In your own projects you should ask yourself what are the emerging forms, organizational structures and visual effects that you are producing and how might you incorporate them into an architectural project. How do you inform the processes of these exercises through scaling and addressing their materiality?

12C: design is make sense

"Design is Make Sense" is a piece of graffiti encountered in an architecture studio one morning and it speaks to the last assignment in this chapter. Data flows through our lives in so many ways that the devices and spaces that we find most useful are those that serve as an interface for managing all that data. We don't need to know everything about how something is produced to appreciate its aesthetic and functional qualities. You don't need to understand how iTunes is programmed to understand the power of having instant access to large repositories of sound and image data. You only need the interface that will make sense of that data and allow you to filter it in a useful way. "Design is make sense."

For this last assignment you should produce a series of images that describe the external outcomes of the processes that created your previous outcomes. In other words, this is not about explaining how this object came to be, but about what this object is. Using rendering and image manipulation techniques you should attempt to explore one of the artifacts you produced in this series of exercises. What is its material composition? What is its scale? What parts of it disappear into pattern and which become volume? This last image is a kind of visual manifesto that embeds within this artifact your design ideas and preferences.

Step 7: Produce one large-format image of an artifact from this set of exercises.

LEARNING FROM THE STACK

Joshua Taron in conversation with Benjamin H. Bratton[1]

It could be argued that architecture and the *project* of architecture are two different things. If architecture is constituted of disciplinary procedures and the objects it produces, the *project* of architecture is something else – less beholden to buildings *per se*, extending much more into the governance of things and their behaviors. If architecture is a pure means, the project simulates the violence of their deployment.[2] In 1922, Corbusier presented the world with a choice based on the project: architecture or revolution. Based on the technological pressures of the industrial revolution, Corbusier saw architecture as the discipline capable of and responsible for training the population to properly engage with the contemporary world. The world is now faced with a similar decision in the context of an even more intense technological environment – but is architecture capable of meeting this challenge?

Historically, architecture has been primarily if not solely concerned with buildings as its territory of deployment – a kind of self-fulfilling prophecy for design thinking that ignores other solutions despite their possibility. That may have been fine so long as buildings and their users were central figures in design equations. But the viability of this practice is called into question when buildings themselves become insufficient instruments of social, economic, and political agency.

So what if we accept that the disciplinary techniques of architecture and architectural thinking are being misdirected? Where, at what scales, and through what media might architecture be needed where it is otherwise absent? Perhaps most importantly, how can we train a generation of architects to address this challenge – and is a disciplinary model of education (training) still valid? This conversation between Benjamin Bratton and Josh Taron queries *The Stack* as a planetary-scale megastructure that architecture must exploit if it is to operate with any degree of seriousness when designing possible futures or effectively participating with the present.[3]

JT: In your book, *The Stack: On Software and Sovereignty*,[4] the central figure of The Stack and its performance turns on "the accident." Could you begin by elaborating on the accident and how it factors into the architecture of The Stack?

BB: In part you can think of the accident along a spectrum of contingency and unpredictability and this can work in two ways. One way is the idea that stacks, as models, are designed to be replaced, as opposed to a plan, which is designed to self-reinforce over time. For example, with basic software/

hardware such as OSI or TCP/IP, the resulting model is one that will accommodate innovation without having to know what those innovations are in advance. So you can replace copper wires with fiber optic at the *physical* layer of a stack without having to know that glass tubes with pulses of light running through them are going to be the things that you replace it with. Over time, the architecture of such stacks becomes a kind of *ship of Theseus*[5] problem. Even though every component of a stack has been replaced over time, is it still the same stack? Stacks are designed to be ships of Theseus, where the entire structure is replaceable, to be replaced, bit by bit, molecule by molecule, while still functioning over time. And so, not only is modularity built-in, as an institutional model and as well as a technical model, but the replaceability of things at different layers is presumed. This is one way that contingency is built into the mechanism.

At the other end of the spectrum is an acknowledgment of Paul Virilio's axiom[6] that the invention of any new kind of technology is also the invention of a new kind of accident. This ultimately holds more significant implications and outcomes of stack systems for our world, our cities, and our geopolitics: that they are both unintended and unintendable. Therefore the designer is put into a relationship with the accident either as "emergency" or as "emergence" or some mixture of the two. An emergency is both an exceptional condition and also a state of emergence. There is always a decision to design either against the emergency (which is reactive) or on behalf of the emergence (which is generative). This articulates a difference in strategies that deal with that contingency and make it part of the ethics of the practice.

JT: Is it fair to say, then, that The Stack both produces accidents but is also an accident itself?

BB: In many respects that's true. I call it an *accidental megastructure*. The accidental quality of it is emergence instead of being delivered as a master plan. Part of the argument of the book is that The Stack exists on scales at once, and we need to understand the different ways in which planetary-scale computation is developed – cloud computing smart cities, next-generation interfaces, etc. Instead of seeing them as different species of computation, all spinning out on their own, they actually do constitute a sort of order, and that order resembles something like a stack. They at least resemble the schema of a stack, and the inherent modularity of that model may allow us to see the whole and to design a better system. But that doesn't mean anyone *intended* it to be that way. Its order is emergent, So rather than just trying to determine finally whether The Stack exists or not, perhaps it is more important to design as if it does and use it as a framework to understand the consequences.

JT: You've already started to touch on the redesignability, reconfigurability and reformability of The Stack. You discuss this in the book through friction referencing Lucretius's clinamen[7] and problem of swerve. Can you elaborate on the accidental productivity of The Stack?

BB: The Stack isn't the only infrastructure or the only model at work. I may be a totality but it's also one that enables multiple models of totality to compete over the practical definition of what's real and a right to adjudicate and have sovereign claims over things.

So the politics of The Stack is also one of the will to totality within this which is itself messy. There is a function for theories of totality that allow for a cognitive mapping of functional roles, and for us to understand the coherency of systems as such in a way that gets beyond conspiracy theory (and Jameson has written more eloquently than I have).[8] The Stack as a mechanism allows for multiple conceptual totalities to co-occupy the same space, the same location, and to fight it out. The space that they're fighting out is what I call the *geoscape*, a space that is occupied by all of these claims and made by those claims.

We can think of this in terms of competing sovereign claims over a site or citizen or data packet. The sovereign geography of China and the sovereign geography of Google, for example, can claim that same thing in the same way, and sometimes the claim of one is able to exclude the other. Sometimes both of those claims are antagonistic and competitive, and the simultaneity of those claims causes friction, and violence, and noise. But sometimes those claims can claim the same thing and yet that thing can still participate in both of those totalities at the same time, without either of those totalities recognizing the validity of the claims of the other one.

The grinding or friction refers to the moments of antagonism between two totalities where, perhaps my map and your map cannot both be true for a particular purpose, and so something there is the last instance definition to be contested. But that's not necessarily the way it always works. Sometimes the totalities can be conceptually, discursively, and cartographically exclusive from one another but can be superimposed on top of the same thing in ways where they don't need to acknowledge one another in some kind of cosmo-politan resolution, while nevertheless working on the same things.

For example, the word "chair" is different in French than it is in German. These are different mapping mechanisms; they're different ways in which the world is mapped by a comprehensive operation. A language is in its way a "total" worldview – it implies that you can say anything and describe any-thing and think anything according to its vocabulary, just as you can decide anything, say anything, think anything in another language (with significant exceptions). Each is a total view of the world but to work as such they don't have to acknowledge the validity of one another. So even as you can call the chair *chaise* in French or *stuhl* in German, the chair doesn't care, and this may not have any real effect on the chair. Those mechanisms of total description and cartography can coexist without acknowledging the veracity of another.

Moving from natural language to the *address* layer of The Stack, we may have a similar layering of totalities on top of one another, such that each can provide a holistic, comprehensive view of the world. Each is perhaps able to describe and to instrumentalize that view of the world into an inter-facial regime that is spatially and temporally simultaneous with other regimes occupying the same place at the same time.

JT: You reference Carl Schmitt[9] in a number of ways in the book, through the sovereign decision over the state of exception, and the friend–enemy distinction. It seems like this question of totality is more about the latter but quickly slips into the conditions that necessitate the former.

BB: For Schmitt, of course, the sovereign decision is also a determination of the line that draws inside from outside and, perhaps more importantly, to decide when exceptions to that rule come into play. Now drawing the border is one thing but determining which side of the line is in fact the "inside" and which side of the line is the "outside" is ultimately based on where the line goes and also what the line *does*. It's the decision within the decision. In important ways, this decision of what gets in or out is being automated at the *interface* layer, where the decision is built into the interfaces of the urban environment, such that we have to see interfaces as a governing apparatus and not just as a map of systems or interactions.

JT: One of the projects of power as Foucault describes it is that sovereignty over time has gone from a singular figure, the king, toward something that is more saturated and distributed throughout the social.[10] Is this where accidents lie and are accidents themselves a form of governance?

BB: Yes, but for the scenario I describe that distribution is decentralized even further. In the distribution of interfaces a certain control is enforced but at the same time the same systems can also generate new forms of sovereignty, in ways that were unintentional. Automation at the point of the interface produces different interiorities and exteriorities and for different users the inside and outside may be completely inverted. As they take the same step, one is let out as the other is let in. As opposed to Foucault, the reference may be more to Gilles Deleuze's "society of control"[11] where there is no clear demarcation between inside and outside. So as you move around as a user of the free-range terrarium called the *city* layer of The Stack, the line dividing inside from outside may oscillate wildly according to your relationship to different interfaces.

More generally, there are ways in which we have to understand the operation of *platforms* as different, both technically and institutionally, from the state and from the market. States have citizens. Markets have consumers. Platforms have users. The ability of platform interfaces to generate novel forms of sovereignty is based on the radical agnosticism they have toward who or what is a user at any given time. And so the ways in which the *interface* layer can be, under certain circumstances, either incarcerating or emancipating, is based on its agnostic perspective on who or what a user is: it allows access to infrastructure that states would not. All of which is to say that, the positive side of the Foucauldian interpretation of this, considered as a mode of "governmentality," is that it is also generative of political subjectivity. The automation of decision at the *interface* layer of The Stack is not (just) some big apparatus of freedom negation.

JT: I'm wondering what the implications of this are for architecture at the planetary scale. While things like human beings and buildings are dissolved or absolutized into systems that are both above and below them, might architecture need to turn its attention toward cities-as-buildings or even buildings-as-cities? And is there value in applying architectural design techniques to this as a problem that The Stack might be able to address?

BB: We can certainly consider *landscape* as a kind of intermediary form between the building and the city form, privileging zones and grids over explicit programming and fixed form. This logic may scale both up and down. Beyond the question of scale is another question of *contiguity*. For the political this contrasts the contiguous state on the Westphalian map versus the discontinuous anatomy of platforms, for example, but contiguity is also a governor of flows. Our earlier conversation reminded me of a course I taught at SCI-Arc perhaps ten years ago called Aesthetics of Logistics. The seminar focused on how the question of scale does and does not determine the designability of an object, and how it is that the whole world gets folded into this object as it is composed. This is all before there was anything called OOO (which comes to very different conclusions, obviously), but we also tried to think this in reverse, so to speak, through the logistical machinations that actually allow that folding to take place. What the exercise demands is to think about that entire network not just as something through which objects flow but something that flows into the object itself. This folding-in is perhaps inverted (again) by the interface. When an object is an interface it folds out, unfurls itself, back at the world.

Design in general, not just architecture, needs to better understand these operations, where the distinctions between the object, the network, the sourcing, and the interfaciality are lessened. The design of the object that moves through the network and the design of the network that eventuates in the object are inextricable. This is what should be meant by "interface design."

Architecture is already comfortable working with fields. It's comfortable working with scale-less diagrams. It's comfortable working across scales in ways that other design disciplines are not. Still, to your earlier point, the scale of the building object has had a place of privilege in terms of what the ultimate outcome is. However, to the extent that the logics of interrelated scales – continental scale, molecular scale – can be seen as part of the designation of a site condition, architecture can intervene in economies that it may have been sidelined from. And this is happening.

Part of the reason that "Parametricism" exists as it does today is because architecture has been squished down to the thin skin of the envelope (other people have said this in a number of different ways from Rem Koolhaas's Biennial to Zaera Polo's "Politics of the Envelope"[12]). The amount of the space that architecture can inhabit is so reduced that all its disciplinary intelligence is brought to bear on something literally inches thick. Perhaps form has become so complex and baroque because it's overdetermined and oversaturated by this limitation.

On the other hand, practices like Liam Young's deal not just with the architecture of logistics parks, taken as these sort of grand urbanistic operations, but rather as the career arc of material fabrication across continents, the global scale, the molecular magnanimity of modern logistics, etc. And so it's not a matter of molecule scale versus continental scale, or form versus landscape, but rather that you can't really deal with one without the other.

JT: I'm wondering how complex problems such as accidents, distributed models of power and object-logistics might be translated into pedagogical frameworks. You presented a meditation on pedagogy at The New School's Mobility Shifts 2011 conference, where you started from Bernard Stiegler's definition of pedagogy as "a form of responsibility from one generation to train the attention of the next,"[13] followed by his observation of the need for long[er] versus short[er] circuits in education.

I think it's fascinating that you're interested in trying to find a way for pedagogy to extend the length and duration of circuits in the context of the arc of a course while both Heidegger and Virilio describe the project of technology as one of shortening circuits – a project of intensification made possible through a saturation and distribution of power that compresses distance between things. Is this not also the condition for information and education in the age of The Stack? And with this technological tendency toward shortening circuits, might there also be value in composing longer circuits into The Stack in the interest of pedagogy?

BB: It's worth saying, especially since I wrote this in the introduction to *Speed and Politics*,[14] that my interest in Virilio's work is not straightforward. I read him against the grain, I suppose. Virilio to me is a bit like Hieronymus Bosch – he's this conservative Catholic guy who spends his time drawing these very elaborate, detailed images of hell. For Virilio, global technology is the false ecumene, it's the fake body of Christ, it's a kind of machinic Antichrist. It's the synthetic body of humanity, it's where immanence and ubiquity and all the things the Holy Spirit is supposed to represent are simulated. And so as he's writing about all this perniciousness, he obviously has a deep fascination with it, but he's writing about it as a scandalized true believer. Conversely, I read Virilio as a Satanist might view Bosch as providing this fantastic, eloquent description of a regime and a scenario that I interpret much more positively than he does. I just think Virilio writes about it with an eloquence and specificity that none of the pro-technology guys, the system's supposed apostles, have managed themselves.

I think the specific problem with what Stiegler would call "short circuits" – for him and for someone like Virilio as well – is their unnaturalness as a form of sustained cognition. They deduce that there is something inhuman about thinking that fast. There is something unseemly and unhealthy and inauthentic about cognition operating this way. By contrast my interest is not in re-establishing a norm and natural sense of the world, and to restore the balance of this particular form of temporality, but rather to extend the inhumanity, extend the inhumanness in the *opposite* direction and toward an equally inhuman trans-generational deep-time.

The most important things you can teach students are *where* and *when* they are. Stiegler says more or less the same thing. For me, answers to both start with the Hubble Ultra Deep Field image. We should hope to teach whatever comprehensibility of *billions* of years is possible, and the paradox that when you're looking up at the night sky you're actually looking back in time. Children can understand this as well as anyone can, and they are things that exceed the supposedly natural scale of clans, nativism, and generations. I'm interested in redirecting the kind of ancestor worship and ethnic nationalism that Heideggerian thinking ultimately ends up as in a different direction (or that of Wendell Berry, for that matter). So, yes, the pedagogy I spoke about is against the short circuit of twitch-and-reward learning, and on behalf of long-time and long-space, but not because we're trying to restore it back to some sort of natural human scale, rather something quite different. We're trying to explode the human scale toward the inhuman and toward the *real*, which is both much larger and much smaller than any lesson can address, obviously. I don't think Stiegler or Virilio would necessarily object.

JT: So do you see computation as a means of tackling this problem?

BB: It's part of the real toward which that perspective turns. I happen to think that we've discovered computation more than we've invented it. Algorithmic processes have been around a lot longer than we have and there's nothing about understanding these that demands only short circuits as such. The fact that we've built these dumb little appliances that happen to work in that way is not the fault of algorithmic reason. It probably has more to do with a need to see and reflect feedback constantly. To me that need is more closely related to the phenomenological insistence that the human experience of human experience is the primary and most authentic question for us to be working with than it has to do with the nature of these technical systems.

JT: But in terms of computing infrastructures that actually exist, you have, for instance, spoken of an imbalance that makes Google's market valuation possible, which has to do with exploiting the asymmetry of information that we get from Google versus the information that we put into it – that one gets less from Google than Google gets back as an aggregate of its users.

BB: This is an example of what I call "platform surplus value" and refers to non-computational platforms as much as computational ones, like Google. If state economies are based on taxation and market economies based on transactions, then perhaps platform economies are based on the realization of value from the aggregate interactions of all of its users. Platforms stay afloat to the extent that they can conjure value from what they mediate at (usually) no transaction cost. In general this is not a predatory relationship though it may well contribute to the winner-takes-all consolidation of platform economies. You are either better or worse at realizing that value from zero-cost transactions between users, and if you are worse then you may not survive. This is obviously worrisome. As for the Google example, it comes from Matteo Pasquinelli's essay on algorithms and a labor theory of value.[15] I quote Matteo's use of this as a way of talking more generally about platform surplus value and platform economies: that they ultimately generate more value for themselves than it costs them to provide themselves. Now for the users, the information that they have brought to the platform may have greater value to *them* now that it has been mediated by it. That is also a kind of platform value, and in the book I compare the two. So for some, platform surplus value is proof of exploitation (as taxation is for some, or profit is for others), but to me it is how both good and bad platforms actually do sustain them and become infrastructure thereby.

JT: Could platform surplus value function as a kind of pedagogical model? One that teaches the algorithm more than it teaches us, since the equilibrium of information is flowing more toward it than toward users? Is this kind of computational terraforming a way of lengthening the pedagogical circuit by thinking of it in terms of ground?

BB: It hadn't occurred to me to think of the inevitable training of the algorithm, for example search algorithms by billions of user inputs, as a kind of pedagogy, but it would be worth fleshing that out. Perhaps in that case we're teaching the algorithm to think like humans think, or like how humans think that humans think, and so many of the same pedagogical problems are shuttled along with this.

JT: Or to invert the premise back to an anthropocentric one where The Stack might be teaching us to work and think non-anthropocentrically. Perhaps a pedagogy that trains our attention toward The Stack would necessitate a reversal of the mirror that shifts the orientation of pedagogy toward something like AI, as opposed to just always and only focusing on ourselves.

BB: Yes, AI's must experience time differently than we do, however, and so perhaps their teaching us, in turn, what thinking "is" will be how we get out of the short circuit problem? For now, we seem to be among the only species that have this capacity for sapient abstraction. Some would say "the only" but I wouldn't. But are we building AI's that could help in this way? I'm not so sure. For example, if we took Google's search algorithms as a proto-AI, one that we now spend all day teaching how human users assign relative value, validity, and relevance to certain concepts, words, lexigrams, and so forth – building its distributed cognition so to speak – then we see how modeling AI on anthropocenic self–reflection may foreclose opportunities for escape from that short circuit problem.

JT: You made the point in your *New York Times* article, "Outing A.I.: Beyond the Turing Test,"[16] that what might be worse than an AI that's out to kill us is one that doesn't even know we exist.

BB: I suggested that perhaps this is a greater fear, not necessarily a greater threat. It might be a much better and more interesting AI that sees the world in such a way that humanity – or at least the anthropocentric geologic subjects – is less central to the plot. It raises a question of ontological scope and whether there are truly ontological categories. You may relate this to Michel Foucault's preface to the English version of *The Order of Things*,[17] in which he quotes the Jorge-Luis Borges story of John Wilkins. There is a Chinese encyclopedia in which all the animals of the world are described taxonomically, and the taxonomy is one that's totally incomprehensible to the reader. So instead of mammals, amphibians, reptiles, and so forth, it's animals that from a long way off look like flies, suckling pigs, animals that please the emperor, animals that have just broken the milk vase. His point refers to a shock beyond the unfamiliar and how impossible it would be for us to comprehend a world described according to this taxonomy. This is the challenge of the inhuman AI as well. Perhaps we fear an AI that sees us as irrelevant, something for which we "lose our humanity" as if that were such a certain and permanent accomplishment. In the *Times* piece I made the point that anthropomorphizing the AI is perhaps a defense mechanism that allows humanness to remain the central protagonist in the story, even as it's being displaced by other things.

JT: Is this a separate point from the very real problem with anthropomorphizing AI in ways that perpetuate our problems rather than addressing them through fundamentally different models?

BB: They are related. It may be – one can hold out hope – that robust AI will in fact make clearer to us what we are and how we think. One of the basic notions of neuroscience-informed philosophy is just that we as humans simply do not think the way that we think we think – and as neuroscience progresses and understands more about the ways in which thinking processes actually work, then the concepts that we've used to "think about thinking" such as "having memories" and "new ideas" let alone a "conscious will" will be seen as folk concepts with little more validity than Galenic medicine or Ptolemaic astronomy.

JT: So a matter of being tricked by one's own image?

BB: Inevitably so. It suggests that our ability to reflexively think about ourselves in the abstract is flawed and limited – we may believe that we are thinking about our thinking as it is as a physical event, but we're not. Perhaps we simply cannot, at least directly, anymore than we can see microbes without a microscope. And so, our mastery of self-reflective knowledge is not absolutely superior to that of a bird, or a frog, or a machine. Like us, they too can only think in whatever ways their physical thinking apparatuses can manage.

As we've seen, on a practical level, training an AI to think in accordance with this manifest image of human thinking, rather than training the AI according to the more mechanical processes of intelligence, introduced its own problems. This, in some ways, is why bottom-up AI has been more successful in many regards than top-down AI. Top-down AI is a way of taking a formal, symbolic logic and mechanizing it in order to deal with informal and perhaps non-symbolic problems. In some ways it tries to build formal logic into engineering systems such that you can immediately address specific problems according to universal symbolic logic. This is very good at doing certain kinds of things, but in many other instances it hasn't been nearly as successful as bottom-up AI, where simpler synthetic intelligences can be taught to learn in a very specific kind of way. So an AI may be very smart at one particular thing and very dumb at everything else. Learning through a bottom-up, neural net structure clarifies some of the problems inherent in projecting the problem of manifest thinking into the human AI. We may be much more bottom-up and highly specific and limited forms of intelligence than we like to think. Our understanding of universal logics may be fundamentally physically limited by our neural hardware in the same way that a frog's brain is physically incapable of sorting out automobile design. It's not the frog's fault.

But that "stupidity" may itself be quite intelligently adapted to particular purposes. The distinction between "artificial stupidity" and "artificial idiocy" is also sort of interesting in this context. Artificial stupidity is when you train an AI to be deliberately less capable than it could be. You deliberately throttle down the AI to reduce its level of intelligent capacities so the interaction with it can be more contextually appropriate and successful. The beginner level of a chess playing program is artificial stupidity. It's throttled down and so it's still fun for a human to play. If it's not artificially stupid it is of limited value.

JT: So basically, Sketchup! Its limitations are what make it functional.

BB: Any limitation on the expression of intelligence may make it "better" in a specific context. Artificial idiocy, on the other hand, is something quite different. This refers to when an AI does exactly what it is programmed to do, utterly faithfully and without error, and in doing so accomplishes something utterly idiotic or even catastrophic. Nick Bostrom's "paper clip maximize" allegory is an example of this. Here you give an AI two instructions: make paper clips and resist all attempts to stop you from making paper clips. Eventually it figures out how to turn anything into a paper clip, and then determines that it therefore must turn everything it can find into paper clips, including the scientists who are now trying to turn it off. It turns them into paper clips too, and when it thinks it has made enough paper clips, it then turns the rest of the planet into a machine that can verify paper clips to make sure it didn't miss anything. This is artificial idiocy, where the machine doesn't break down, it's actually doing it perfectly. I happen to think *HAL 9000* did not break down but followed its program flawlessly.

JT: Back to The Stack, you describe some of its infrastructural functions as a process of indexing, sorting, cataloging, and then acting upon. Moving from representation to action, is this a recipe both for infrastructure *of* and infrastructure *as* geoaesthetics?

BB: Yes, this generic process of interfaciality works across scales from the single-user screen icon to continental scale infrastructure. The *interface* layer, presents reductive models and simulations of complex networks, but the most interesting shift is when the model of the thing – the iconic image that represents a potential interaction for example becomes a medium through which the model's referent becomes governed and controlled. And so, for the interface, the simulation is not just a trace or map of the real, it becomes a piloting mechanism that also reinscribes the real according to its model, and so also reinforcing the veracity of the representation. The interface's model representation of things becomes truer the more it is used.

Specifically, the graphical user interface is a special kind of instrumentalized image. It is a diagram of an incomprehensibly complex network or machine with which the user can only ever engage intuitively through the visual artificial stupidity that it offers. So it is somewhat unique within the history of the image as a representation that literally enacts its description of things. It can convince users to actualize its description and channel their intentions accordingly. So, to your question, it is less that this process is happening both at the individual user level and infrastructural level as it happens in a way that links the two, that makes the actions of individual users into infrastructure directly.

JT: This kind of immediacy begins to enter into the realm of sensation as much as it might be about intelligence. You talk about the project of extending sense to all surfaces as one that takes place at the layer of the Earth – no longer inert but rather now affective. Could you explain the implications of this and where it might be taking place?

BB: With regards to the *Earth* layer of The Stack, I consider the shift toward a governance of ecologies, chemistries, biologies, and the sensing and information processing apparatuses necessary to observe the world in this way. These tend to focus on skins and surfaces, but I mean that in a rather specific way. The biological and chemical state of these sometimes mundane, speechless things now attracts observation and surveillance that measure critical values in their profiles. Not only does chemistry speak politically, but it speaks in colors that are useful and enforceable. Whereas these realms may have once been the background against which politics would happen, now they are that which needs to be sensed and recorded and communicated with. Forms of planetary life that used to be just "stuff" are now a more privileged source of communication and stored currency.

JT: In the book you tackle aspects of this problem through the metaphor of skin – as a kind of organ of organizational perception and cognition. With computation expanding and accelerating the administration of what can be sensed, measured, calculated, communicated, sorted, stored, and worked upon, has sensation replaced thought within platform models of governance through sensory surfaces?

BB: For this particular interest in "skin" there are two aspects at least. One is the larger question of how sensing and/or sensation constitutes a form of interaction with the world that is not actually fundamentally different from "thought." We have a legacy of the Kantian faculties that tell us that thinking is different and more rarefied than sensation. Machine vision and other forms of algorithmic perception show that this philosophical presumption needs revision. But there is also, for The Stack at least, an interest less in the intelligence of the things that sense (that is dealt with more in the next book) but rather the shift in the focus of governance and the production of political information from the surveillance of skins. Governance is always shaped by how it can sense the governed, whether visually by panopticism,[18] or some other means. We can make the argument that states have always evolved in relationship to what it is that they can see, at any particular point in time, or what they can sense.

JT: That you can't monitor what you can't measure … and yet there is also what Foucault describes as "the necessary ignorance of the sovereign"[19] – an invisibility or immeasurability that produces inherent excess.

BB: To me the monitoring and measuring of biochemical reactions by a sensory apparatus that occupies the epidermal layer of the entire planet is not a "panopticism" because the dynamics and asymmetries of sensor and sensed are quite different, and a regime of vision is augmented by one of touch. What we have is this kind of shift toward an "epidermal biopolitics" by which governing apparatuses – which are not those of states necessarily – are interested in whatever may possess a skin and by which that skin produces information that might be simulated and governed and modeled ecologically. This is a shift in the instrumentality, the mediation of the ubiquity of governance, but it's still one that's dependent upon its ability to take that raw data and calculate it and make it useful. But the ability of governing systems to take the raw data and transpose it into something that constitutes actionable governance is always limited by the computational mechanisms upon which they depend and all they need to operate. That sensory apparatus is as smart or as dumb as the particular computational arrangement it rests upon. It doesn't escape any of those questions. It just shifts them to a different register.

JT: Is it a matter of understanding governance absent of thought? Is that a trajectory that you see emerging out of The Stack?

BB: Interesting. I don't know that it's about the *absence* of thought, as there is still the presence of an automated decision that may be predicated on a directed sensing of whatever's going on, and a recursive reaction to it. It's a different thought, and again, one that complicated the sensing/thinking dichotomy. It is also what one calls "algorithmic governance," and I discuss the implications of this at some length in The Stack's conclusion.

JT: One conclusion I've gleaned from the conversation we've been having is that there might be two pedagogical potentials emerging through the Earth. First, that we might be able to shift pedagogy toward training The Stack through computation understood as terraforming. Second, when discussing the scales and mechanisms that The Stack works through and across, The Stack is very clearly already training us.

BB: These are certainly both true. It is important to link pedagogy and design – how one becomes the other. Now the question is how an expanded pedagogy that is training an intelligence transfer from humans into infrastructure – and then back into humans – can actually constitute an infrastructure for the distribution, amplification, and elevation of collective intelligence, human and inhuman both. To me that is not the noosphere. It's less about a gnostic realm of pure mind or transcendental cognizance; rather, it's something that's much more mechanically specific.

The question for pedagogy to consider is one of designing specific platforms that aggregate intelligence and value and support themselves through that value. The challenge lies in developing ways that are essentially agnostic to the participants in platforms so that their evolution is not stunted. The pedagogy is one of gardening intelligence that is both human and inhuman, both animalian and mechanical. We then let the garden become a jungle and find our new places within it.

Notes

1 Transcription, Nicholas Perseo; editing, Nicola Johnson.
2 See Walter Benjamin's "Critique of Violence," in Walter Benjamin, Marcus Paul Bullock, and Michael W. Jennings, *Selected Writings. Vol. 1* (Cambridge, MA: Belknap Press of Harvard University Press, 1996), and Bernard Tschumi's "Violence of Architecture," *Artforum*, September 1981.
3 Things that the architectural project does very well even when architecture is otherwise failing.
4 Benjamin Bratton, *The Stack: On Software and Sovereignty* (Cambridge, MA: MIT Press, 2015).
5 If every plank of wood of the boat has been replaced over time, is it still the same boat?
6 Virilio discusses this in Paul Virilio, Philippe Petit, and Sylvère Lotringer, *Politics of the Very Worst: An Interview by Philippe Petit* (New York: Semiotext(e), 1999), as well as *The Original Accident* (Cambridge, MA: Polity, 2007).
7 Lucretius's clinamen refers to the unpredictable movement, or "swerve," of atoms.
8 See Fredric Jameson, Michael Hardt, and Kathi Weeks, *The Jameson Reader* (Oxford: Blackwell, 2000).
9 See Schmitt, Carl, *The Concept of the Political* (New Brunswick, NJ: Rutgers University Press, 1976).
10 Michel Foucault, *Discipline and Punish: The Birth of the Prison* (New York: Pantheon Books, 1977).
11 Gilles Deleuze, "Postscript on the Societies of Control," *OCTOBER*, 59 (1992): 3–7.

12 Alejandro Zaera Polo, "The Politics of the Envelope: A Political Critique of Materialism," *Volume Magazine*, 17 (2008).

13 Bernard Stiegler, *Taking Care of Youth and the Generations* (Stanford, CA: Stanford University Press, 2010).

14 Paul Virilio and Mark Polizzotti, *Speed and Politics: An Essay on Dromology* (Los Angeles, CA: Semiotext(e), 2006).

15 Matteo Pasquinelli, "The Number of the Collective Beast: Value in the Age of the New Algorithmic Institutions of Ranking and Rating," Unpublished invited talk given at the New Industries Conference: Money and Debt in the Post-Industrial World, January 17, 2014. http://matteopasquinelli.com/number-of-the-collective-beast/.

16 Benjamin Bratton, "Outing A.I.: Beyond the Turing Test," *New York Times,* February 23, 2015.

17 Michel Foucault, *The Order of Things: An Archaeology of the Human Sciences* (New York: Pantheon Books, 1971).

18 See Foucault, *Discipline and Punish.*

19 Ibid.

Bibliography

Allen, Stan. "From Object to Field," in *Practice: Architecture, Technique and Representation* (New York: Routledge, 2008), 216–243.

Amin, Ash. "Post-Fordism: Models, Fantasies and Phantoms of Transition," in Ash Amin, ed., *Post-Fordism: A Reader* (Oxford and Cambridge, MA: Blackwell Publishers, 1994), 1–39.

Aranda, Benjamin, and Chris Lasch. *Pamphlet Architecture 27: Tooling* (New York: Princeton Architectural Press, 2006).

Benjamin, Walter, Marcus Paul Bullock, and Michael W. Jennings. *Selected Writings. Vol. 1* (Cambridge, MA: Belknap Press of Harvard University Press, 1996).

Benkler, Yochai. *The Wealth of Networks: How Social Production Transforms Markets and Freedom* (New Haven, CT: Yale University Press, 2006).

Beorkrem, Christopher. *Material Strategies in Digital Fabrication* (New York: Routledge, 2013).

Birkhofer, Denise. "Eva Hesse and Mira Schendel: Voiding the Body – Embodying the Void," *Woman's Art Journal*, 31 (2010): 3–11.

Bratton, Benjamin. *The Stack: On Software and Sovereignty* (Cambridge, MA: MIT Press, 2015).

Bratton, Benjamin. "Outing A.I.: Beyond the Turing Test," *New York Times,* February 23, 2015.

Bryant, Levi R. "The Ontic Principle," in Levi R. Bryant, Nick Srnicek, and Graham Harman, eds., *The Speculative Turn: Continental Materialism and Realism* (Melbourne: re.press, 2011).

Bryant, Levi. 'The World is Enough: On Overmining and Undermining," *Larval Subjects*. October 11, 2011. https://larvalsubjects.wordpress.com/2011/10/11/the-world-is-enough-on-overmining-and-under mining (accessed August 17, 2015).

Bucci, Federico, and Mario Mulazzani, eds. *Luigi Moretti Works and Writings* (New York: Princeton Architectural Press, 2002).

Burry, Mark. *Scripting Cultures: Architectural Design and Programming* (New York: Wiley, 2011).

Cache, Bernard. "Philibert De L'Orme Pavilion: Towards an Associative Architecture," in Mark Taylor, ed., *Surface Consciousness* (London: Academy Editions, 2003).

Ceccato, Cristiano. "Integration: Master, Planner, Programmer, Builder," in Celestino Soddu *et al.*, eds, *The Proceedings of the 4th Conference and Exhibition on Generative Art 2001*, Politechnico di Milano University, Italy, 2001.

Dawkins, Richard. *The Blind Watchmaker* (New York: Norton, 1986).

Delanda, Manuel. *Intensive Science and Virtual Philosophy* (New York: Continuum, 2002).

Delanda, Manuel. "Deleuze and the Use of the Genetic Algorithm in Architecture," in Ali Rahim, ed., *Contemporary Techniques in Architecture* (London: Wiley-Academy, 2012).

Deleuze, Gilles. "Postscript on the Societies of Control," *OCTOBER*, 59 (1992): 3–7.

Diaz Alonso, Hernan. "Manifesto #19 Hernan Diaz Alonso/Xefirotarch | Architect – Icon Magazine." www.iconeye.com/404/item/3014-manifesto (accessed August 17, 2015).

Eisenman, Peter. "The Formal Basis of Modern Architecture." Dissertation, PhD, Trinity College, University of Cambridge, 1963.

Eisenman, Peter. "Postfunctionalism," *Oppositions*, 6 (1976): n.p.

Eisenman, Peter. "The End of the Classical: The End of the Beginning, the End of the End," *Perspecta*, 21 (1984): 154–173.

Foreign Office Architects. *Phylogenesis: FOA's Ark* (Barcelona: Actar, 2004).

Foucault, Michel. *The Order of Things: An Archaeology of the Human Sciences* (New York: Pantheon Books, 1971).

Foucault, Michel. *Discipline and Punish: The Birth of the Prison*. New York: Pantheon Books, 1977.

Frazer, John. *An Evolutionary Architecture* (London: Architectural Association, 1995).

Freeland, David. "Fielded Drawing," from Nathan Hume, *et al.*, eds., *Fresh Punches* (Creatspace Independent Publishing Platform, 2013), 225–228.

Gage, Mark Foster. "Project Mayhem: Architecture in the Age of Dissensus," *Fulcrum: The AA's Weekly Free Sheet*, 18 (June 8, 2011).

Gage, Mark Foster. "Killing Simplicity: Object-Oriented Philosophy in Architecture," *Log*, 33 (2015): n.p.

Gannon, Todd, Graham Harman, David Ruy, and Tom Wiscombe. "The Object Turn: A Conversation," *Log*, 33 (2015): n.p.

Gerland, Ernst. "Life and Letters of Papin," *Nature*, 24 (1881): 377–379.

Goulthorpe, Mark/dECOi. "Precise Indeterminacy," *Praxis: Journal of Writing + Building*, 6 (2004): 28–45.

Greenfield, Adam. *Against the Smart City* (New York: Do Projects, 2013).

Harman, Graham. *Tool-Being: Heidegger and the Metaphyics of Objects* (Chicago: Open Court, 2002).

Harman, Graham. "Lecture: Graham Harman," Vimeo. January 29, 2014. https://vimeo.com/85437398 (accessed August 17, 2015).

Hays, K. Michael. "Critical Architecture: Between Culture and Form," *Perspecta*, 21 (1984): 15–29.

Heidegger, Martin. "The Thing," in Albert Hofstader, ed., *Poetry, Language, Thought* (New York: Harper & Row, 1971).

Hensel, Michael. *Performance-Oriented Architecture: Rethinking Architectural Design and the Built Environment* (Chichester: Wiley, 2013).

Hensel, Michael, and Achim Menges. "Patterns in Performance-Orientated Design: An Approach towards Pattern Recognition, Generation and Instrumentalisation," *Architectural Design*, 79 (6) (2009): 88–93.

Hensel, Michael, Achim Menges, and Michael Weinstock, *Emergent Technologies and Design: Towards a Biological Paradigm for Architecture* (London: Routledge, 2010).

Jameson, Fredric, Michael Hardt, and Kathi Weeks. *The Jameson Reader* (Oxford: Blackwell, 2000).

Johnson, Steven. *Where Good Ideas Come From: The Natural History of Innovation* (New York: Penguin, 2010).

Kolarevic, Branko. *Architecture in the Digital Age: Design and Manufacturing* (New York: Taylor & Francis, 2003).

Kolarevic, Branko, and Kevin R. Klinger. *Manufacturing Material Effects: Rethinking Design and Making in Architecture* (New York: Routledge, 2008).

Koolhaas, Rem. "My Thoughts on the Smart City: by Rem Koolhaas –
Neelie KROES – European Commission," September 24, 2014. http://
ec.europa.eu/archives/commission_2010-2014/kroes/en/content/
my-thoughts-smart-city-rem-koolhaas.html (accessed August 17,2015).

Koolhaas, Rem. "The Smart Landscape: Intelligent Architecture," *Artforum
International*, 53 (8) (2015): 212–217.

Kurzweil, Ray. *The Singularity is Near: When Humans Transcend Biology*
(New York: Viking, 2005).

Kwinter, Sanford. "La Citta Nuova: Modernity and Continuity," in *Zone
1–2* (New York: Urzone, 1986).

Kwinter, Sanford. "The Nightingale's Song," *Log*, 33 (2015): n.p.

Lamberti, Elena. *Marshall McLuhan's Mosaic: Probing the Literary Origins of
Media Studies* (Toronto: University of Toronto Press, 2012).

Leach, Neil. *The Anaesthetics of Architecture* (Cambridge, MA: MIT Press,
1999).

Leibniz, Gottfried Wilhelm von, and Nicholas Rescher. *G.W. Leibniz's
Monadology: An Edition for Students* (Pittsburgh: University of Pittsburgh
Press, 1991).

Lynn, Greg. *Animate Form* (New York: Princeton Architectural Press,
1999).

Maeda, John. *Design by Numbers* (Cambridge: MA: MIT Press, 2001).

McCullough, Malcolm. *Abstracting Craft: The Practiced Digital Hand*
(Cambridge, MA: MIT Press, 1998).

Marx, Karl, Cedar Paul, and Eden Paul. *Capital. Vol. 1* (London: J.M.
Dent, 1942).

Meillassoux, Quentin. *After Finitude* (London: Continuum, 2009).

Menges, Achim. "Instrumental Geometry," *Techniques and Technologies in
Morphogenetic Design (AD)*, 76 (2006): 42–53.

Mitchell, William. *The Logic of Architecture* (Cambridge, MA: MIT Press,
1990).

Moretti, Luigi. "Form as Structure," 1957. Quoted in Federico Bucci and
Mario Mulazzani, eds., *Luigi Moretti Works and Writings* (New York:
Princeton Architectural Press, 2002).

Moussavi, Farshid. "Parametric Software is No Substitute for Parametric
Thinking," *The Architectural Review*, 2011. http://m.architectural-review.
com/8620000.article (accessed June 8, 2015).

Mumford, Lewis, and Donald L. Miller. *The Lewis Mumford Reader* (New
York: Pantheon Books, 1986).

Negarestani, Reza. "Contingency and Complicity," in Robin Mackay, ed., *The Medium of Contingency* (New York: RAM Publications, 2011).

Negarestani, Reza. "Labor of the Inhuman (Parts 1 & 2)," *e-flux Journal*, 52 (2014).

Negroponte, Nicholas. "Towards a Humanism Through Machines," *Architectural Design*, 7 (6) (1969).

Negroponte, Nicholas. *The Architecture Machine* (Cambridge, MA: MIT Press, 1970).

Negroponte, Nicholas. *Soft Architecture Machines* (Cambridge, MA: MIT Press, 1975).

Paglen, Trevor. *Torture Taxi: On the Trail of the CIA's Rendition Flights* (Hoboken, NJ: Melville House, 2006).

PALLALINK. www.pallalink.net (accessed July 20, 2015).

Pask, Gordon. "The Architectural Relevance of Cybernetics." First published in 1967. Taken from Neil Spiller, ed., *Cyber_Reader: Critical Writings for the Digital Era* (London: Phaidon, 2002).

Pasquinelli, Matteo. "The Number of the Collective Beast: Value in the Age of the New Algorithmic Institutions of Ranking and Rating," Unpublished invited talk given at the New Industries Conference: Money and Debt in the Post-Industrial World, January 17, 2014. http://matteopasquinelli.com/number-of-the-collective-beast.

Penfield, Wilder, and Herbert H. Jasper. *Epilepsy and the Functional Anatomy of the Human Brain* (Boston: Little, Brown, 1954).

Pottmann, Helmut, Andreas Asperl, Michael Hofer, and Axel Kilian. *Architectural Geometry* (Exton: Bentley Institute Press, 2007).

Reiser, Jesse, and Nanako Umemoto. *Atlas of Novel Tectonics* (New York: Princeton Architectural Press, 2006).

"Rem Koolhaas: Smart Home Technologies 'Potentially Sinister': Dezeen Architects Underestimate Potentially Sinister Smarthome Technologies Says Rem Koolhaas Comments," May 27, 2015. www.dezeen.com/2015/05/27/rem-koolhaas-interview-technology-smart-systems-peoples-eagerness-sacrifice-privacy-totally-astonishing (accessed August 17, 2015).

Rocker, Ingeborg. "Evolving Architectures: Dissolving Identities – Nothing is as Persistent as Change," in Sharples Holden Pasquarelli, ed., *Versioning: Evolutionary Techniques in Architecture* (Chichester: Wiley Academy, 2002), 10–17.

Rossi, Aldo. *The Architecture of the City* (Cambridge, MA: MIT Press, 1982).

Schmitt, Carl. *The Concept of the Political* (New Brunswick: Rutgers University Press, 1976).

Schodek, Daniel, Martin Bechthold, Kimo Griggs, Kenneth Martin Kao, and Marco Steinberg. *Digital Design and Manufacturing: CAD/CAM Applications in Architecture and Design* (Hoboken: Wiley, 2005).

Schumacher, Patrik. "Parametricism: A New Global Style for Architecture and Urban Design," *Architectural Design* (2009). doi:10.1002/ad.912.

Schumacher, Patrik. *The Autopoiesis of Architecture: A New Framework for Architecture* (Chichester: Wiley, 2011).

Sharples Holden Pasquarelli, ed., *Versioning: Evolutionary Techniques in Architecture* (Chichester: Wiley Academy, 2002).

Silver, Michael, ed., *Programming Cultures: Architecture, Art and Science in the Age of Software Development* (London: Wiley, 2006).

Simon, Herbert. "The Architecture of Complexity," *Proceedings of the American Philosophical Society*, 106 (6) (1962): 467–482.

Sims, Karl. "Evolved Virtual Creatures," 1994. www.karlsims.com/evolved-virtual-creatures.html (accessed August 17, 2015).

Speaks, Michael. "Intelligence After Theory," *Perspecta 38: Architecture After All* (Cambridge, MA: MIT Press, 2006).

Spiller, Neil, ed., *Cyber_Reader: Critical Writings for the Digital Era* (London: Phaidon, 2002).

Srnicek, Nick. "Nick Srnicek /// The Matter of Struggle in Urban Space," Vimeo. October 9, 2014. https://vimeo.com/117434029 (accessed August 17, 2015).

Stiegler, Bernard. *Taking Care of Youth and the Generations* (Stanford, CA: Stanford University Press, 2010).

Taylor-Hochberg, Amelia. "The Deans List: Hernan Diaz Alonso of SCI-Arc," October 17, 2014. http://archinect.com/features/article/110738703/the-deans-list-hernan-diaz-alonso-of-sci-arc (accessed August 17, 2015).

Terzidis, Kostas. *Algorithmic Architecture* (Oxford: Architectural Press, 2006).

Thompson, D'Arcy Wentworth. *On Growth and Form* (Cambridge: Cambridge University Press, 1917).

Tremblay, Tony. "A widening of the Northern Coterie: The Cross-Border Politics of Ezra Pound, Marshall McLuhan, and Louis Dudek," in Dean Irvine, ed., *The Canadian Modernists Meet* (Ottawa, CA: University of Ottawa Press, 2005).

Tschumi, Bernard. "Violence of Architecture," *Artforum*, September 1981.

Ulam, Stanislaw. "Tribute to John von Neumann," *Bulletin of the American Mathematical Society*, 64 (3), pt2 (1958): 1–49.

Valenti, Philip. "Leibniz, Papin, and the Steam Engine: A Case Study of British Sabotage of Science," *Fusion Magazine* (1979).

Verebes, Tom. *Masterplanning the Adaptive City: Computational Urbanism in the Twenty-first Century* (New York: Routledge, 2013).

Virilio, Paul. *The Original Accident* (Cambridge, MA: Polity, 2007).

Virilio, Paul, and Mark Polizzotti. *Speed and Politics: An Essay on Dromology* (Los Angeles, CA: Semiotext(e), 2006).

Virilio, Paul, Philippe Petit, and Sylvère Lotringer. *Politics of the Very Worst: An Interview by Philippe Petit* (New York: Semiotext(e), 1999).

Weinstock, Michael. *The Architecture of Emergence: The Evolution of Form in Nature and Civilisation* (Chichester: Wiley, 2010).

Weisstein, Eric. "Recursion," Wolfram MathWorld. http://mathworld.wolfram.com/Recursion.html (accessed July 22, 2015).

Wolfram, Stephen. *A New Kind of Science* (Champaign: Wolfram Media, 2002).

Woodbury, Robert. *Elements of Parametric Design* (New York: Routledge, 2010).

Zaera Polo, Alejandro. "The Politics of the Envelope: A Political Critique of Materialism," *Volume Magazine*, 17 (2008).

Image credits

Chapter 1: A digital craft framework – Andrew Kudless

Figures 1.1–1.7   Andrew Kudless/California College of the Arts
Figures 1.8–1.9   Jason Kelly Johnson and Michael Shiloh/California College of the Arts
Figure 1.10   Margaret Ikeda, Evan Jones, and Adam Marcus/California College of the Arts

Chapter 2: Exercises for points, lines, and curves – Jason S. Johnson and Joshua Vermillion

Figures 2.1–2.3   Joshua Vermillion/UNLV
Figure 2.4   Alison MacLachlan, Bahar Khonsari, and Julian Wylegly/University of Calgary
Figure 2.5   Julian Wylegly, Bahar Khonsari, and Alison MacLachlan/University of Calgary
Figure 2.6   Joshua Vermillion/UNLV
Figure 2.7   Allison MacLachlan/University of Calgary
Figure 2.8   Jodi James/University of Calgary
Figure 2.9   Joshua Vermillion
Figure 2.10   Andrew Martin, Joshua Vermillion/UNLV
Figures 2.11–2.15   Joshua Vermillion/UNLV
Figure 2.16   Shai Yeshayahu and Phil Zawarus/UNLV
Figures 2.17–2.18   Joshua Vermillion
Figure 2.19   Xavier Zhagui, Joshua Vermillion/UNLV

Figure 2.20	Andres Diaz, Joshua Vermillion/UNLV
Figure 2.21	Ludwing Vaca, Joshua Vermillion/UNLV
Figure 2.22	Joshua Vermillion/UNLV
Figure 2.23	Julian Wylegly/University of Calgary
Figure 2.24	Khalid Omokanye/University of Calgary
Figure 2.25	Jodi James/University of Calgary
Figure 2.26	Sangeeta Vishwakarma, Nia Neumann, Yuting Zhu, Maria Aurora Nunez, Ross Thompson, Barbara Holash, Tara Kiani Tari, Jason Johnson/University of Calgary

Chapter 3: Distributed ~~sensations~~: pedagogical experimentation with anonymity in architecture – Joshua Taron

Figures 3.1–3.4	Ryan Cook/University of Calgary
Figures 3.5–3.9	Mehdi Einifar/University of Calgary
Figures 3.10–3.15	Amber Lafontaine/University of Calgary

Chapter 4: Exercises for volumes and aggregate assemblies – Jason S. Johnson and Joshua Vermillion

Figure 4.1	Jason S. Johnson/Minus Architecture Studio
Figure 4.2	Jason S. Johnson and Tafadzwa Bwititi/Ball State University
Figure 4.3	Mark Foster Gage
Figure 4.4	Bahar Khonsari/University of Calgary
Figure 4.5	PALLALINK
Figure 4.6	Michael McGie/University of Calgary
Figures 4.7–4.9	Bahar Khonsari/University of Calgary
Figure 4.10	Minus Architecture Studio + Synthetiques
Figure 4.11	Bahar Khonsari/University of Calgary
Figure 4.12	Étienne-Jules Marey
Figure 4.13	Bahar Khonsari/University of Calgary
Figure 4.14a	Jordi Lopez Puig
Figure 4.14b	Greg Kristo
Figure 4.14c	PROJECTiONE/Ball State University
Figure 4.15	Elmira Aghsaei/University of Calgary

Figure 4.16	Wylegly, Ketis-Bendena, Wowk, Lawson/University of Calgary
Figure 4.17	Dekens, Coslovich, Erens, Gerlach, Wong/University of Calgary
Figure 4.18	Joshua Vermillion/UNLV
Figures 4.19–4.20	Dekens, Coslovich, Erens, Gerlach, Wong/University of Calgary
Figure 4.21	Sujit Nair/SDeG
Figures 4.22–4.23	Marc Fornes & THEVERYMANY
Figure 4.24	Joshua Vermillion/UNLV
Figure 4.25	Dekens, Coslovich, Erens, Gerlach, Wong/University of Calgary
Figure 4.26	Tyler Fritz/University of Calgary
Figures 4.27–4.28	GUN Arquitectos
Figures 4.29–4.30	Jason S. Johnson and Tafadzwa Bwititi/Ball State University
Figures 4.31–4.34	GUN Arquitectos
Figures 4.35–4.36	Marc Fornes/THEVERYMANY
Figure 4.37	Joshua Vermillion/UNLV
Figures 4.38–4.39	Jodi James and Matt Parker/University of Calgary
Figure 4.40	Amy Wowk/University of Calgary
Figure 4.41	Daan Murray/University of Calgary

Chapter 5: Iteration, failure, and distinctions – Marc Fornes

Figure 5.1	Jason S. Johnson
Figure 5.2	Marc Fornes/THEVERYMANY
Figure 5.3	Eric Au
Figures 5.4–5.8	Marc Fornes/THEVERYMANY
Figures 5.9–5.11	Brice Pelleschi/THEVERYMANY
Figure 5.12	Nicola Y. Johnson
Figures 5.13–5.14	Brice Pelleschi/THEVERYMANY
Figures 5.15–5.17	Marc Fornes/THEVERYMANY
Figure 5.18	Nicola Y. Johnson
Figures 5.19–5.22	Guillaume Blanc/Atelier Calder/THEVERYMANY

Chapter 6: Exercises for assembly and communication – Jason S. Johnson and Joshua Vermillion

Figures 6.1–6.8   PROJECTiONE
Figures 6.9–6.14   Brian Ringley/University of Cincinnati
Figures 6.15–6.18 Joshua Vermillion/Ball State University
Figure 6.19   Junette Huynh/University of Calgary
Figure 6.20   Trevor Steckly/University of Calgary
Figure 6.21   Joshua Vermillion/UNLV
Figures 6.22–6.23 Joshua Vermillion/Ball State University
Figure 6.24   Trevor Steckly/University of Calgary
Figures 6.25–6.27 PROJECTiONE
Figures 6.28–6.30 Brian Ringley/Pratt Institute
Figure 6.31   Yves Poitras/University of Calgary
Figure 6.32   Trevor Steckly/University of Calgary
Figures 6.33–6.34 Joshua Vermillion/Ball State University
Figure 6.35   Trevor Steckly/University of Calgary
Figure 6.36   Jonathon Anderson/UNLV
Figure 6.37   Dustin Headley/Kansas State University
Figures 6.38–6.41 PROJECTiONE
Figures 6.42–6.47 Gernot Riether and Andrew Wit/Ball State University
Figures 6.48–6.52 Jonathon Anderson/University of North Carolina Greensboro

Chapter 8: Exercises for integrating data and form – Jason S. Johnson and Joshua Vermillion

Figure 8.1   Matthew Parker and Jason S. Johnson/University of Calgary
Figures 8.2–8.5   Guy Gardner and Jason S. Johnson /University of Calgary
Figures 8.6–8.7   Christina James/University of Calgary
Figures 8.8–8.9   Christopher Wong/University of Calgary
Figure 8.10   SDeG
Figure 8.11   Christina James/University of Calgary

Figures 8.12–8.13   Matthew Parker/University of Calgary
Figure 8.14   John Ferguson/University of Calgary
Figures 8.15–8.17   Alyssa Haas and Jason S Johnson
Figures 8.18–8.20   Minus Architecture Studio
Figures 8.21–8.25   OCEAN CN
Figure 8.26   Nicola Y. Johnson
Figure 8.27   Christina James/University of Calgary
Figure 8.28   Theodore Spyropoulos and Vasilis Stroumpakos
Figures 8.29–8.30   Minus Architecture Studio
Figures 8.31   Minus Architecture Studio and Synthetiques
Figure 8.32   Nicola Y. Johnson
Figure 8.33   Minus Architecture Studio and Synthetiques
Figures 8.34–8.37   Matthew Parker
Figures 8.38   Nicholas Perseo
Figures 8.39–8.42   Synthetiques
Figures 8.43–8.45   Matthew Parker and Jason S. Johnson

Index

Page numbers in *italics* denote an illustration

not sure if you can answer
I am a transient student from UCF to valencia &
I have an in school deferment request
form to turn in and was wondering
who I am supposed to bring it to
in order to get an approved signature

registrar office